Apple Motion 5 Cookbook

Over 110 recipes to build simple and complex motion graphics in the blink of an eye

Nick Harauz

[PACKT]
PUBLISHING

BIRMINGHAM - MUMBAI

Apple Motion 5 Cookbook

First published: May 2013

Production Reference: 1180513

Published by Packt Publishing Ltd.
Livery Place
35 Livery Street
Birmingham B3 2PB, UK.

ISBN 978-1-84969-380-6

www.packtpub.com

Cover Image by Prashant Timappa Shetty (sparkling.spectrum.123@gmail.com)

Credits

Author

Nick Harauz

Reviewers

Carlos A. Cañizares

Stefan Gampe

Acquisition Editor

Kartikey Pandey

Lead Technical Editor

Susmita Panda

Technical Editors

Dennis John

Dominic Pereira

Nitee Shetty

Project Coordinator

Abhishek Kori

Proofreaders

Stephen Copestake

Maria Gould

Indexer

Monica Ajmera Mehta

Graphics

Ronak Dhruv

Production Coordinator

Arvindkumar Gupta

Cover Work

Arvindkumar Gupta

About the Author

Nick Haurauz has directed and filmed a host of celebrities such as Nelly Furtado, Lady Gaga, and Richard Branson. He was responsible for crafting video magic for clients such as Diageo, Virgin Mobile, United Way, and Procter and Gamble.

He has an uncanny ability to engage his students and create a level of relatedness that keeps them coming back for more. As an FCP X, Motion 5, After Effects, Premiere Pro, and an Avid-certified trainer, he is able to put his BA in Film and Sociology from the University of Toronto to good use.

In 2005, Nick founded Inconscience Productions and continues to work with domestic and international brands to shoot, produce, and cut masterpieces. In 2010, he was handed the opportunity of a lifetime to co-edit a feature documentary entitled *My Father and the Man in Black*; the untold story of a bad boy Johnny Cash, his talented but troubled manager, Saul Holiff, and a son searching for his father in the shadow of a legend.

When he is not busy impressing his students at Witz Education and travelling to or from post-production conferences, this half Ukrainian, half Trinidadian can be found playing tennis.

This is his first book!

Acknowledgement

Writing my first book has been an incredible journey and it couldn't be possible without all the love and support from those around me. First, I would like to thank my family and friends for their patience and help during this time.

Thank you Digital Juice for allowing me to use some fabulous stock footage for the exercise files. They have an incredible collection of content for both Motion and Final Cut to enrich all types of projects. If you like the content used in the exercise files, please visit their website here at: http://www.digitaljuice.com.

Thank you Edward Gajdel for your pictures, Paul Kelly for your graphic files, and Marisa Seguin for your illustrations. Without content creators and collaborators like you, these lesson files would have never been accessible.

I would also like to thank Anne Renehan for giving me my first opportunity to learn Motion, Michael Cianflocca for your review, Jeff Greenberg from www.jgreenbergconsulting.com for your continued inspiration in the video community, feedback and advice, Greg Witz, Jared Kligerman, and Paul Macri at Witz Education who put up with me on a daily basis and who challenge me to produce rich educational content. The whole team at Witz Education truly rocks.

About the Reviewers

Carlos A. Cañizares is a Vancouver-based editor, digital compositor, and colorist.

With a background in film and design, Carlos is fluent in Final Cut Studio 3, Final Cut Pro X, Motion 5, DaVinci Resolve, and Adobe Production Premium CS6. He is also proficient in Photoshop, Illustrator, and InDesign, with a working knowledge of frontend web development through HTML, CSS, and basic jQuery.

His past collaborations include clients such as Elizabeth Carol Savenkoff of Vous Valet Vancouver, jazz singer Jaclyn Guillou, and Rugged Media Inc., to name a few. He has also taught Motion 4 and 5 as a substitute instructor for the Electronic Media Design program at Langara College, Continuing Studies.

He is currently the Editor of Earth Orbit Productions, the Audio Visual Producer of PS98 Music Ministry, and the Principal of his own freelance persona - CARLOS CANIZARES: POST PRODUCTION DESIGNER.

To the ones involved in getting me to where I am today, this book is a culmination of your unwavering love and support. You all know who you are. Thank you so much.

Stefan Gampe lives in Germany and works as a freelancer, video cutter, and a motion graphics designer too.

He has worked for many years with the programs in Final Cut Studio, Final Cut Pro X, Motion 3, 4, and 5, Color, Soundtrack-Pro, Aperture, and Photoshop.

His clients are from all areas of the media industry as well as companies, individuals, and artists.

A special thank you to all the people who have supported me, and a big thank you to the team at Packt Publishing. Also, a special thanks to Abhishek Kori and Joel Noronha.

www.PacktPub.com

Support files, eBooks, discount offers and more

You might want to visit www.PacktPub.com for support files and downloads related to your book.

Did you know that Packt offers eBook versions of every book published, with PDF and ePub files available? You can upgrade to the eBook version at www.PacktPub.com and as a print book customer, you are entitled to a discount on the eBook copy. Get in touch with us at service@packtpub.com for more details.

At www.PacktPub.com, you can also read a collection of free technical articles, sign up for a range of free newsletters and receive exclusive discounts and offers on Packt books and eBooks.

http://PacktLib.PacktPub.com

Do you need instant solutions to your IT questions? PacktLib is Packt's online digital book library. Here, you can access, read and search across Packt's entire library of books.

Why Subscribe?

- ▶ Fully searchable across every book published by Packt
- ▶ Copy and paste, print and bookmark content
- ▶ On demand and accessible via web browser

Free Access for Packt account holders

If you have an account with Packt at www.PacktPub.com, you can use this to access PacktLib today and view nine entirely free books. Simply use your login credentials for immediate access.

Table of Contents

Preface

Creating motion graphics and visual effects in the past used to be a daunting process. Performing tasks such as animating text, match moving, compositing, and connecting individual layers would involve extremely long workflows that would take days, even months to complete. That's where Motion comes in. It was designed to make these tasks simpler and easier so that the user can focus on the creation. The application works seamlessly with Final Cut and has the editor and motion graphics artist in mind every step of the way.

So, welcome to *Apple Motion 5 Cookbook*. Throughout this book, you'll learn to create sophisticated motion graphics using the incredible tools and content inside the application. Through a series of recipes, we will cover tips and tricks for easy navigation of the interface, animating layers with behaviors and keyframes, applying filters, using Motion's vast content library, creating replicator and particle systems, and working in both 2D and 3D environments. With exercise files accompanying this book as an additional download, you will walk away with real-world projects to apply your new skills to. Let's get cooking!

What this book covers

Chapter 1, Getting Around the Interface, explores becoming more comfortable inside Motion and navigating ourselves through the various windows.

Chapter 2, Looking at Motion's Library, explores working with and manipulating the vast content available to us right inside Motion.

Chapter 3, Making It Move with Behaviors, explores instant animation techniques by dragging and dropping various behaviors onto elements into our project.

Chapter 4, Making It Move with Keyframes, explores classic animation techniques in Motion and the options available to add, cut, copy, and manipulate keyframes on parameters.

Chapter 5, Let's Make Text, explores working with text in Motion by changing text style, saving presets, and animating text with behaviors.

Chapter 6, Paint and Masks, explores the Paint Stroke tool and the brush stroke presets available from the Library. We will also look at using masks to add effects to specific parts of our image, as a utility tool and to create animation.

Chapter 7, Let's Make Particles, explores the basics of Motion's extremely powerful particle systems and how we can manipulate its parameters to create dynamic motion graphics.

Chapter 8, Replicators – It's No Fun By Yourself, explores the basics of the replicator and how almost any element in Motion can be used to create seamless animation through patterns.

Chapter 9, Motion Tracking and Keying, explores VFX techniques including match moves, offset tracking, and green screen removal.

Chapter 10, Intro to 3D, explores adding cameras and lights to our projects to interact with our elements in 3D space.

Chapter 11, Publishing Your Work to FCP X, focuses on integrating Motion into FCP X by creating titles, transitions, effects, and generators for the Media Browser.

Chapter 12, Customization and Exporting, explores a few customization techniques for various workflows. We also look at exporting movies, stills, and image sequences from Motion and exporting through another application called Compressor.

What you need for this book

Users will need three applications to go through all the recipes in the book; Motion 5, Final Cut Pro X, and Compressor. These applications only run on Apple computers. All applications can be downloaded directly from the Mac App Store located on the dock of your computer. Please head to the Apple website in order to make sure you have the appropriate system requirements to run the applications. The Motion webpage can be found here: http://www.apple.com/finalcutpro/motion/. If you already have the application installed, make sure you are up to date with the latest software. All project files that you can download from the Packt Publishing website are compatible with Motion 5.0.7 and higher versions.

Who this book is for

This book is intended for Final Cut Pro users looking to incorporate more motion graphics in their workflows and Motion users who are looking to gain a comprehensive knowledge of the tools, tricks, methods, and options available in Motion to create great motion graphics and visual effects.

Conventions

In this book, you will find a number of styles of text that distinguish between different kinds of information. Here are some examples of these styles, and an explanation of their meaning.

Code words in text, database table names, folder names, filenames, file extensions, pathnames, dummy URLs, user input, and Twitter handles are shown as follows: "Navigate to the Photoshop .psd file on your system."

New terms and **important words** are shown in bold. Words that you see on the screen, in menus or dialog boxes for example, appear in the text like this: "Navigate to the **File Browser** by clicking it on the left-hand side of the interface."

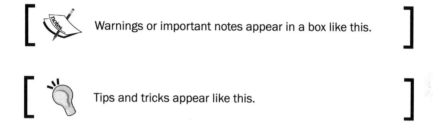

Warnings or important notes appear in a box like this.

Tips and tricks appear like this.

Reader feedback

Feedback from our readers is always welcome. Let us know what you think about this book—what you liked or may have disliked. Reader feedback is important for us to develop titles that you really get the most out of.

To send us general feedback, simply send an e-mail to feedback@packtpub.com, and mention the book title via the subject of your message.

If there is a topic that you have expertise in and you are interested in either writing or contributing to a book, see our author guide on www.packtpub.com/authors.

Customer support

Now that you are the proud owner of a Packt book, we have a number of things to help you to get the most from your purchase.

Downloading the example code

You can download the example code files for all Packt books you have purchased from your account at http://www.packtpub.com. If you purchased this book elsewhere, you can visit http://www.packtpub.com/support and register to have the files e-mailed directly to you.

Errata

Although we have taken every care to ensure the accuracy of our content, mistakes do happen. If you find a mistake in one of our books—maybe a mistake in the text or the code—we would be grateful if you would report this to us. By doing so, you can save other readers from frustration and help us improve subsequent versions of this book. If you find any errata, please report them by visiting `http://www.packtpub.com/submit-errata`, selecting your book, clicking on the **errata submission form** link, and entering the details of your errata. Once your errata are verified, your submission will be accepted and the errata will be uploaded on our website, or added to any list of existing errata, under the Errata section of that title. Any existing errata can be viewed by selecting your title from `http://www.packtpub.com/support`.

Piracy

Piracy of copyright material on the Internet is an ongoing problem across all media. At Packt, we take the protection of our copyright and licenses very seriously. If you come across any illegal copies of our works, in any form, on the Internet, please provide us with the location address or website name immediately so that we can pursue a remedy.

Please contact us at `copyright@packtpub.com` with a link to the suspected pirated material.

We appreciate your help in protecting our authors, and our ability to bring you valuable content.

Questions

You can contact us at `questions@packtpub.com` if you are having a problem with any aspect of the book, and we will do our best to address it.

1
Getting Around the Interface

In this chapter, we will cover:

- ► Choosing a Motion project
- ► Importing files to the Canvas, Layers tab, and Timeline
- ► Importing Photoshop and Illustrator files
- ► Making selections with Expose
- ► Changing the layer order
- ► Groups versus layers
- ► Making changes in the Properties tab, HUD, and Canvas
- ► Moving and trimming layers in the Timeline and the mini-Timeline
- ► Launching and customizing a template
- ► Keyboard customization
- ► Looking under the hood – key preferences for your workflows
- ► Sequencing stills in the Timeline
- ► Managing the Layers tab

Introduction

Welcome to *Apple Motion 5 Cookbook*! We've all got our reasons for being here. It could be the awesome $50.00 price tag that got us excited. Maybe it was a 30-second motion graphic intro we saw on television last night and want to duplicate, or the effects and transitions we love to work with in FCP X that we want to customize just a little more. Whatever the reason, one thing remains true; Motion 5 is a deep, powerful, and flexible application for a variety of creative workflows and the reason you're here is to learn how to better utilize it. Motion 5's interface can be a bit overwhelming the first time you open it, but with a little knowledge about how it works out of the gate, the better prepared we will be to focus on the good stuff; making our projects dance!

Choosing a Motion project

What do we want out of Motion 5? Where do we want our projects to live? How big should it be? The minute we launch Motion, we are presented with a lot of choices. Let's take an in-depth look at some of those options.

How to do it...

1. To launch Motion, click on the application icon on your Dock or double-click it from the **Applications** folder.

> **Downloading the example code**
>
> You can download the example code files for all Packt books you have purchased from your account at http://www.packtpub.com. If you purchased this book elsewhere, you can visit http://www.packtpub.com/support and register to have the files e-mailed directly to you.
>
> The high resolution colored images of the book can also be found in the code bundle.

2. Upon entering, we are presented with a welcome window called the **Project Browser**. It can be divided into three sections. On the left-hand side, we have the option of starting with a recent, blank, or pre-existing composition (this is where we can find our preinstalled Motion templates). Since this is our first time here, make sure **Blank** is selected from the list, as shown in the following screenshot:

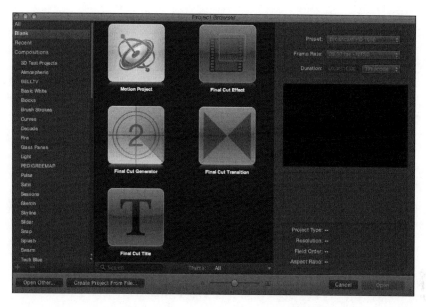

3. In the middle, we can choose between five projects. **Motion Project** is usually chosen when we want to start and finish our work solely in Motion. If we choose **Final Cut Effect**, **Generator**, **Transition**, or **Title**, we are telling Motion that when we save our project, we want to make it available in Final Cut. Depending on the type of project you select, it will save in the corresponding section in FCP X's **Media Browser**, as shown here. For now, make sure **Motion Project** is selected.

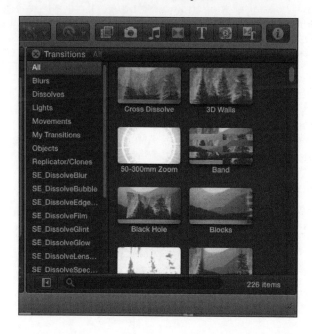

4. On the right, you can choose from a variety of different presets depending on the material you're working with or where you're exporting. Say your footage was shot in Europe with a DSLR camera. You could choose a **Broadcast HD 1080** setting with a **Frame Rate** value of **25**. The duration could match the length of the files you're bringing in and you could choose to display it as timecode, frames, or seconds. For this exercise, let's choose the **Broadcast HD 720** setting with a frame rate of **29.97** and a 6 second duration. Press **Open**.

5. The Motion interface launches and we're ready to bring in some media to work with.

There's more...

Here's a little more information on the different types of Motion projects and the attributes associated with them.

Motion templates

If you choose **Composition** from the left-hand side of the **Project Browser** window, you can choose from one of the pre-existing Motion templates available.

 Motion and Final Cut Pro X were meant to work together.

Turning Motion Projects to Final Cut Generators

If you open Motion by choosing **Motion Project**, you can still make it available in Final Cut by going to **File | Save As** and then clicking **Final Cut Generator** from the dialog box.

Most of the parameters we see in Motion can be brought into Final Cut. In fact, we can even create rigs where a slider, checkbox, or pop-up widget can change several parameters at once.

Rigging and publishing

While saving a Motion project for use in FCP X is already powerful, nothing beats being able to take specific parameter controls from Motion's architecture and make them available inside FCP X. You'll learn more about this extremely powerful workflow in *Chapter 11, Publishing Your Work to FCP X.*

 Project properties for Motion can be adjusted in the **Project Properties** menu.

Project Properties

If you choose the wrong project settings, don't worry; you can always go to **Edit | Project Properties** and change the preset, frame rate, and time display of your project.

▸ *Publishing a Motion 5 generator and its parameters to FCP X* in *Chapter 11, Publishing Your Work to FCP X*.

▸ *Creating an effect for FCP X* in *Chapter 11, Publishing Your Work to FCP X*.

▸ *Creating a transition for FCP X* in *Chapter 11, Publishing Your Work to FCP X*.

Importing files to the Canvas, Layers tab, and Timeline

Motion 5 gives us several options to bring in the material we want to work with. Some of this material can be from Motion's own library.

For these recipes, we're going to use the **File Browser** to load in our material. Think of it as a gateway to our system and its files displayed graphically.

Getting ready

If it's your first time to Motion, here's a brief breakdown of the interface:

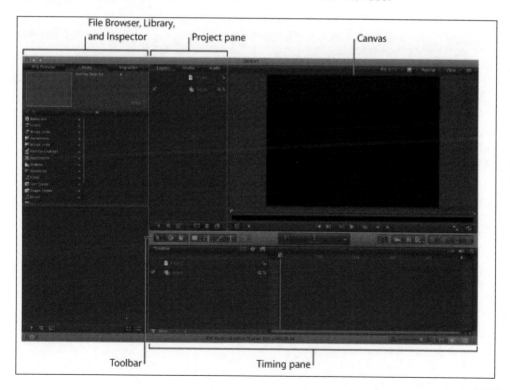

The Motion workspace can be broken down into the following sections:

► **File Browser, Library, and Inspector**: The left-hand side of the Motion interface contains three areas—**File Browser, Library**, and **Inspector**. You can click on the corresponding tab to see each area or use a keyboard shortcut. The **File Browser** is where you view the clips from your system and import them into your project. The **Library** allows us to see behaviors, effects, and tons of content directly within Motion that we can utilize for our projects. The **Inspector** is similar to the Inspector in FCP X. It allows us to change the parameters of a selected item.

► **Toolbar**: This contains tools for creating content and manipulating elements in your project. There are tools for creating shapes, manipulating cameras, and adding behaviors for automatic animation.

► **Canvas**: This allows you to view the current frame your playhead is on. You can also manipulate layers visible in the Canvas. The Canvas contains playback and view controls for both 2D, as well as 3D workflows.

► **The Project pane**: This pane contains the **Layers, Media**, and **Audio** tab, which display items in your project. You can view each tab by clicking on it or using a keyboard shortcut. The **Layers** list shows all elements (that is, still images, film clips, filters, behaviors) used in your composition; the **Media** list shows all external images, clips, and audio files you imported to your current project; and the **Audio** tab displays all the sound files you imported in your project.

► **The Timing pane**: This pane allows you to make changes to your elements over the span of your project. It contains three unique areas—the **Timeline, Audio Timeline**, and the **Keyframe Editor**.

> Make sure your playhead is on the first frame of your project throughout the exercises.

How to do it...

Before we begin, locate a clip on your system you would like to import into Motion or feel free to use a clip that comes with some of the later recipes. Launch Motion and choose a project based on the setting of your clip.

Follow these steps to import files to the Canvas:

1. With a blank Motion project open, navigate to the **File Browser** by clicking it on the left-hand side of the interface, or press *Command + 1*.

2. Locate the movie file on you system that matches your project's settings.

3. With the clip selected, drag it from the **File Browser** straight to the Canvas window but don't release your mouse.

4. By default, as you hold your clip you should see yellow lines appear. These are called **dynamic guides**. You can turn them on and off by going to **View | Overlays | Dynamic Guides**. These guides can help you align your video directly to the center of the Canvas.

5. Wait until you see both the vertical and horizontal guides. When you do, release your mouse as shown in the following screenshot:

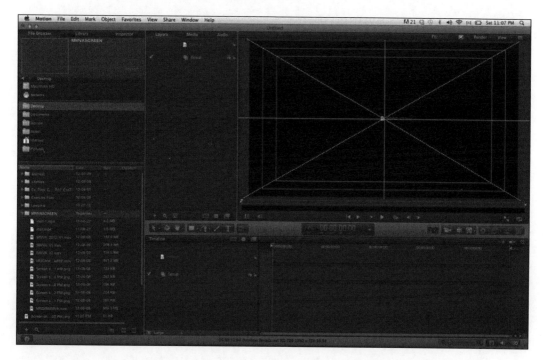

6. If your video seems too big, press *Shift + Z* to fit it into the Canvas window.

This is how we can import files to the **Layers** tab:

1. With a blank Motion project open, navigate to the **File Browser** by clicking it on the left-hand side of the interface, or press *Command + 1*.

2. Locate the movie file on your system that matches your project's settings.

3. With the clip selected, drag it from the **File Browser** straight on top of the empty group in the **Layers** tab.

4. Wait for the plus icon and release your mouse, as shown in the following screenshot:

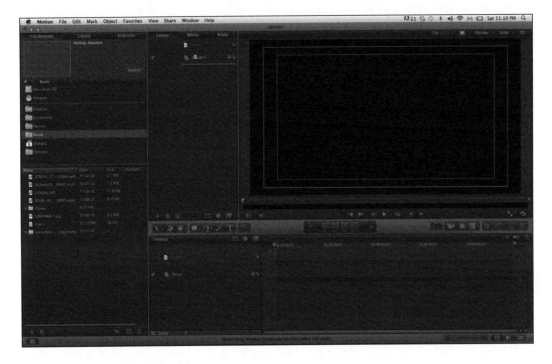

5. The video should appear directly centered in your Canvas window, If your video seems too big, press *Shift + Z* with the Canvas window selected to make it fit.

Follow these steps to import files into the Timeline:

1. With a blank Motion project open, navigate to the **File Browser** by clicking it on the left-hand side of the interface, or press *Command + 1*.

2. Locate the movie file on you system that matches your project's settings.

3. With the clip selected, drag it from the **File Browser** straight to the Timeline. Press the *Shift* key to help it snap to the playhead, but don't release the mouse.

4. Eventually a menu will appear asking us whether we want to composite or insert our images into the Timeline. Since there is nothing in our project, both options do the same thing. Choose **Composite**, as shown in the following screenshot:

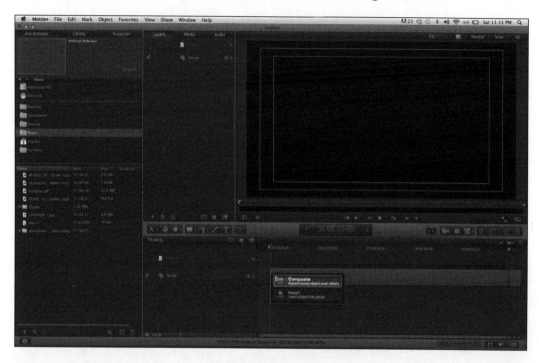

5. The video should appear directly centered in your Canvas window. If your video seems too big, press *Shift + Z* with the Canvas window selected to make it fit.

There's more...

Your playhead acts as where you position things in time. Keep track of where it is.

Know where your playhead is

The playhead is your friend. It shows you which frame you're currently viewing in the Canvas. It also acts as the location to which any file will go when you bring it into the project based on the default settings. Be aware of where your playhead is and know at what time your media starts. You can also change Motion's **Preferences** setting to always have layers created on the first frame of the project.

Viewing and previewing files in the File Browser

You can choose to change between icon and list view in the **File Browser** as you navigate your system. The following screenshot shows the view being currently set to icon. Simply click on the icon at the bottom of the window to switch between the views; you can also search and add folders in it too.

To preview a clip in the **File Browser**, simply single-click the file and a small preview will play in the upper-left hand corner. For a bigger preview, double-click the file to bring up a floating window, as shown in the following screenshot:

See also

▶ The *Importing Photoshop and Illustrator files* recipe.

Importing Photoshop and Illustrator files

We can import Adobe Photoshop (`.psd`) and Illustrator (`.ai`) files using any method from the previous recipe, but sometimes we may want more from these files. For instance, Motion can allow us to work with individual Photoshop layers but we need to import it in a specific way.

Getting ready

Locate a Photoshop file (PSD only) and Illustrator file (AI only) to use in the upcoming recipes.

From the **File Browser**, navigate to the Photoshop .psd file on your system, preferably one with multiple layers.

How to do it...

Follow these steps to import Photoshop files to Motion:

1. With a blank Motion project open, navigate to the **File Browser** by clicking it on the left side of the interface, or press *Command + 1*.

2. With the .psd file selected, drag it from the **File Browser** straight to the Canvas or the **Layers** tab without releasing your mouse.

3. By default, a pop-up menu appears allowing you to choose from merging the Photoshop file, selecting one of the individual layers, or importing all layers.

4. Choose **Import All Layers**, as shown in the following screenshot:

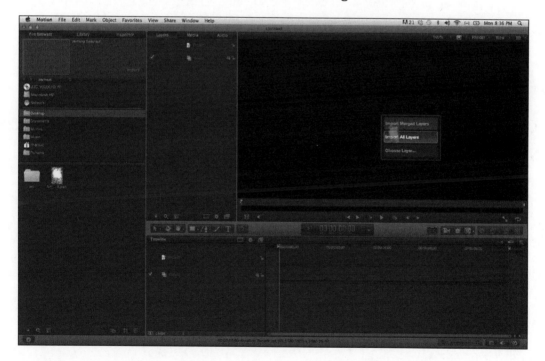

5. If your video seems too big, press *Shift + Z* to fit it into the Canvas window.

6. You may notice that the Photoshop file has all of its layers contained within a group (named after the Photoshop project) of a group (the default group for the Motion project). It's good practice to release the Photoshop layers from the Photoshop group and have them solely within the Motion group.

This is how we import Illustrator files:

1. With a blank Motion project open, navigate to the **File Browser** by clicking it on the left side of the interface, or press *Command + 1*.

2. With the .ai file selected, drag it from the **File Browser** straight to the Canvas or the **Layers** tab and release your mouse. You cannot see an Illustrator file's individual layers.

3. If your video seems too big, press *Shift + Z* to fit it into the Canvas window.

4. At first, everything looks fine, but as soon as we start scaling the file we'll notice some deterioration of the graphic. Press *F1* to navigate to the **Properties** tab of the **Inspector**. Locate the **Scale** property and scale up the image by double-clicking on it and entering a new value. Keep scaling till you notice pixelation.

5. Vector-based images from Illustrator are supposed to allow us to scale up the image to infinity and beyond. The problem is the minute we put the file in Motion, it places the file into a pixel-based world. To have this infinite scaling opportunity, we need to tell Motion to not give this file boundaries or take away its fixed resolution. To do this, navigate to the **Media** tab and select the AI file from the list; use the following screenshot for reference:

6. Press *F4* to go to the **Media** tab of the **Inspector**, and deselect the checkmark next to **Fixed Resolution**, as shown in the following screenshot:

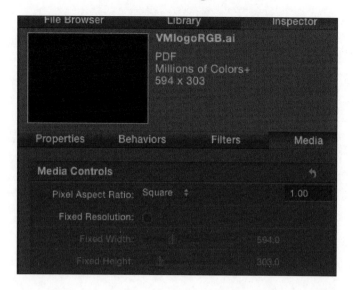

7. Try scaling up the object again from the **Properties** tab of the **Inspector** and notice how crisp it looks.

See also

▶   The *Importing files to the Canvas, Layers tab, and Timeline* recipe.

Making selections with Expose

Sometimes when you try to make a selection from the Canvas window, things can get frustrating. You'll want to select an item, but because images overlap quite often, Motion gets confused and will select the wrong image. Say hello to **Expose**. Expose will break apart all of your layers temporarily and allow you to easily select what you need. Let's see it in action.

How to do it...

1. Launch Motion and select the **Swarm** template category. Under the **Swarm** category, select the **Swarm-Menu** template and click **Open a copy**.

2. Move your playhead to 5 seconds.

3. What you really want to do is select the background, but because of all the foreground elements it's difficult to get to. Press *X* for expose.

4. Notice how all your layers have been separated in the Canvas, and can be easily selected as you hover over them with your mouse. Find and select the **Background Menu**, as shown in the following screenshot:

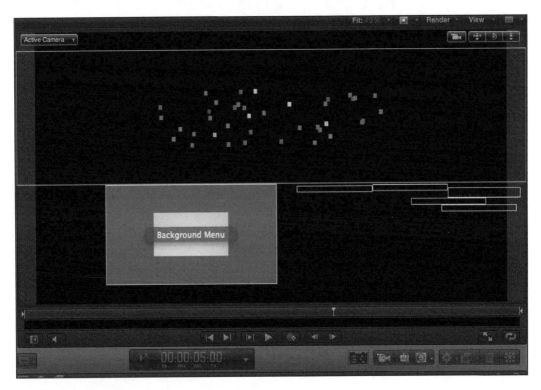

5. The **Canvas** view goes back and the background is selected.

Changing the layer order

In 2D projects, layer order matters. Let's say we had a project with three backgrounds. The background that would appear at the top of the layer stack is what we will see. The other two layers would be invisible.

How to do it...

1. From this chapter's exercise files, open the `01_05` project.

2. There are three gradient layers in this project but in the Canvas we only see the **You can see me** layer. Select this layer and drag it underneath the **I'm hidden too** layer without releasing the mouse. Make sure you see a blue line with an icon and *not* the plus symbol, as shown in the following screenshot. If you do, drag with your mouse slightly to the right and then release your mouse.

3. Notice that you can now see the **I'm hidden** layer being displayed. Select the **I'm hidden too** layer and drag it above the **I'm hidden** layer.

4. The **I'm hidden too** layer should now be seen.

There's more...

We can easily move layers in the **Layers** tab using shortcuts.

Moving layers with shortcuts

Sometimes when you drag elements in the **Layers** tab, you may accidently create a group instead of moving a layer. By using the keyboard shortcuts *Command + [* and *Command +]*, we can easily move a layer up and down in a group.

See also

► The *Groups versus layers* recipe

Groups versus layers

Whenever we add a layer to our Motion projects, it has to be contained in a group. But what exactly is the difference between layers and groups? Well, for one thing, a layer is an element—a picture, movie, text object you've brought in or created. A group is a container for those elements. It can be used to organize materials in your project or perform operations to several elements at once. For those of you who use Final Cut Pro X, you may be familiar with compound clips. Compound clips allow you to reverse render operations or make universal changes to several objects at once. Let's take a brief look at some of the fundamental differences between groups and layers in this following exercise.

How to do it...

1. From this chapter's exercise files, open the `01_06` project by double-clicking on it.

2. There is one group that contains a circle and a square. Click on the **Library** tab.

3. Select **Filters | Distortion | Bulge** and compare your results to the following screenshot:

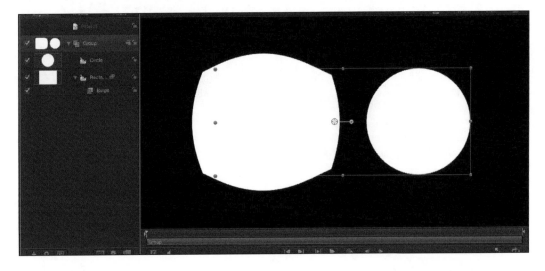

4. Notice how the bulge only affects the rectangle. Press *F3* to open up the **Filters** tab of the **Inspector**. Adjust some of the parameters to get a feel for what it does.

5. Select the **Bulge** filter and drag it from **Rectangle** to **Group**. Notice how the bulge now affects both the circle and the rectangle, as shown in the following screenshot:

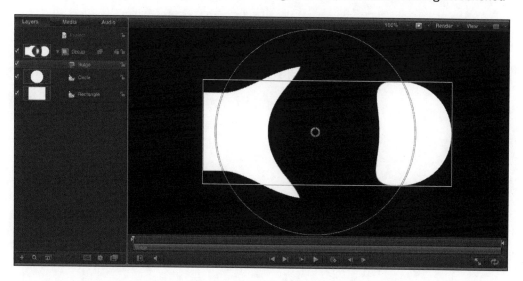

6. Delete **Bulge** by selecting it and pressing *Delete*.

7. Select the **Circle** layer and press *F1* to go to the **Properties** tab of the **Inspector**.

8. Drag the **Scale** slider to the right up to 150, or double-click on the scale number and manually type it in, as shown in the following screenshot:

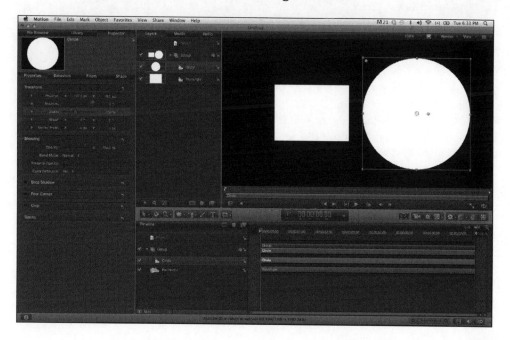

9. Go to the **Edit** menu and select **Undo** until you get back to 100.

10. Select the group and press *F1* to go to the **Properties** tab if needed. Drag the **Scale** slider up and notice how both the circle and rectangle increase in size, as shown here:

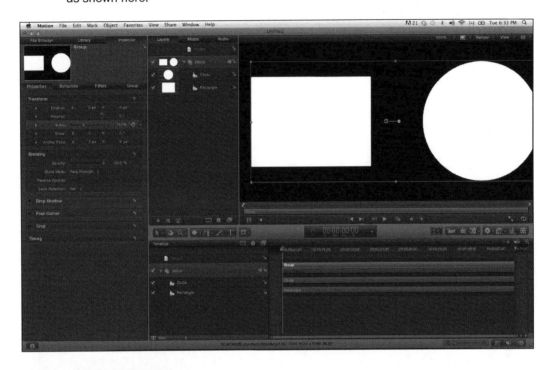

How it works

A default group was created with the Motion project. If you want to create a group in Motion from multiple layers, you can select them; just go to the **Object** menu and select **Group**. There is also a plus icon at the bottom of the **Layers** tab, as shown in the next screenshot. This creates an empty group above the selected group. If nothing is selected, the group goes to the top of the **Layers** tab.

There's more...

I cannot stress enough that it pays to learn your keyboard shortcuts. It will allow you to perform tasks more quickly and efficiently instead of going to menus.

In this recipe, you went to the **Edit** menu to undo your last action. If you look under that menu, you will see that the shortcut key is *Command + Z*. This is one of the shortcut keys that isn't only good in this application, but on the majority that run on your OS system.

Here is a brief list of some keyboard shortcuts that are great to start learning and are exactly the same in most Mac applications:

- ▸ **Command + A**: Select all
- ▸ **Shift + Command + A**: Deselect all
- ▸ **Shift + Command + G**: Create a new group
- ▸ **Command + O**: Open
- ▸ **Command +S**: Save
- ▸ **Shift + Command + S**: Save a copy
- ▸ **Command + X**: Cut
- ▸ **Command + C**: Copy
- ▸ **Command + V**: Paste

Making changes in the Properties tab, HUD, and Canvas

Motion is all about allowing you to make changes to the elements in your project. Some of these changes will be animation tweaks while others will be regular scaling and repositioning tasks. Let's take a look at a different way of changing the scale and position of a still image.

How to do it...

1. With a blank Motion project open, navigate to the **File Browser** by clicking it on the left-hand side of the interface, or press *Command + 1*.
2. Locate a still image file on your system that is large enough for your project's settings.
3. With the still selected, choose **Import** from the top of the **File Browser**.
4. Select the still image in the **Layers** tab and press *F1* to go to the **Properties** tab of the **Inspector**.
5. Adjust the **Position**, **Rotation**, and **Scale** settings of the still to your liking.

6. Click the reset arrow at the top of the **Transform** section to reset all of the properties, as shown in the following screenshot:

7. If your photo was larger than your project's properties, it may now be larger than your Canvas. Motion's default method when importing photos is to scale them down to fit the project. When you reset a still image, it goes to its original scale value. If this is the case, all you need to do is scale the photo down until it fits nicely in the Canvas window.

8. With the photo selected, go to the **Window** menu and select **Show HUD**:

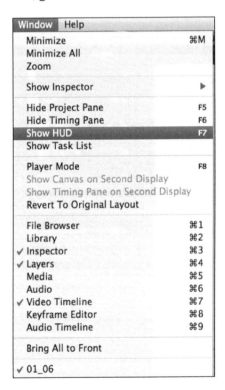

9. The **Head Up Display** (**HUD**) is a semi-transparent floating window that shows certain properties of a selected layer, filter, or behavior. In certain instances, it provides us with quick access to some of the most used parameters of the current selection. In the case of this still, it gives us **Opacity** and **Blend Mode**. Adjust the **Opacity** value to around 80. Go to the **Edit** menu and choose **Undo**.

10. With the still selected, notice the bounding box around your photo. If you can't see it because the photo is full-frame, press *Command + -* to zoom out on your Canvas. We can manipulate several **Transform** category properties directly in the Canvas, and this bounding box allows us to do just that.

11. Drag any side corner of the image and scale the image down. Notice how the image doesn't scale uniformly unlike how it did in the **Inspector**. Press *Command + Z* to undo.

12. Hold down the *Shift* key and grab the side corner again. Notice how the image scales uniformly. Press *Command + Z* to undo.

13. Press *F1* to open the **Properties** tab of the **Inspector**. Hold down the *Shift + Option* key and click the side corner again. Scale the image downwards while paying attention to the **Inspector**. Notice how the scale updates. Also notice that by pressing *Shift + Option* not only does the object scale uniformly, but it also scales from the center.

There's more...

Some of you may have noticed the **i** icon at the upper-right hand corner of the HUD, as shown in the following screenshot:

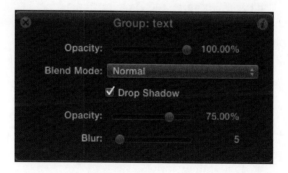

By clicking it, we got to the **Inspector**. Whenever you work in Motion and the HUD doesn't have what you're looking for, go to the **Inspector** for more options.

Also, when we held down the *Shift* and *Option* modifier keys, we were able to scale our photo uniformly from the center. The general rule is this: modifier keys can make our life easier when trying to manipulate properties in the Canvas and the HUD.

For example, if you try to rotate your image in the Canvas by dragging the circle to the right of the center and hold down *Shift*, we can force our still to move in 45 degree increments.

In the HUD, sometimes when you try to adjust properties, the slider moves too fast. If you *Option* + click the line, you can then move properties in smaller increments.

Moving and trimming layers in the Timeline and the mini-Timeline

So eventually as Motion graphic designers, we're going to have to animate stuff and part of that battle lies is our ability to move around and adjust layers efficiently in the application.

There are two ways by which we can adjust the timing as well as trim layers in Motion—by using the Timeline and mini-Timeline. The big question is why choose one over the other. As of Motion 5, both areas are displayed as soon as you enter a project. The Timeline will show all of your layers and the relationship those layers have with one another, spread over time.

The mini-Timeline only shows the selected element from the **Layers** tab (that is, filter, behavior, clip, and so on).

The Timeline is great for making timing adjustments when they revolve around the relation of one layer to another. On the other hand, the Timeline can become a very busy place, very quickly. The mini-Timeline is a great place to focus in on the selected item at hand. Let's have a look at adjusting layers in both the areas.

How to do it...

1. From this chapter's exercise files, open the 01_08 project.

2. There are two groups in this project; a text group and background. Press the Space bar to play the project.

3. This animation was done with behaviors, which we'll explore in *Chapter 3, Making It Move with Behaviors*. Simply, one text layer fades in after another. Before fixing the timing of the text, you may have noticed that the text appears off alignment. Click on the **Disclosure** tab for the **Text** group and click on the **THREE** layer and *Shift* + click the **ONE** layer. From the **Object** menu select **Alignment | Distribute Vertical Centers**. Your text is now distributed evenly.

4. In the following screenshot, you can see the order of our number layers in the Timeline. We want to change the order of the layers by fading in the first layer, followed by the second, and the third. We're going to make our first change in the mini-Timeline. To hide the Timeline temporally, go to **Window | Timeline**. Select the **THREE** layer, and from the **Mark** menu, choose **Go To | Selection In Point**. We want **ONE** to begin at 1 second. Select **ONE** and drag the layer's in-point value until it reads 00:00;01:00.

5. Move your playhead to the beginning of the Timeline by pressing the home key or *Fn +* ← on a laptop. Play the animation. While the **ONE** layer now fades in at the same time as the **THREE** layer, you'll notice that it cuts off at the end. Drag the **ONE** layer's out-point in the mini-Timeline so it lasts till the end of the project.

6. Let's finish the rest our work in our Timeline. Press *Command + 7* to toggle back to the Timeline.

7. Let's move the **THREE** layer to where the **TWO** layer ends. Drag the **THREE** layer while holding down the *Shift* key. Wait for its in-point to snap to the **TWO** layer's out-point and then release the mouse.

8. Make sure nothing is selected by pressing *Shift + Command + A*. Type 2, followed by the return to move to the two-second mark. Select the **TWO** layer and press *I* to trim its in-point to the playhead.

9. Press the home key and then the Space bar to check if the timing works. Use the following screenshot to guide you:

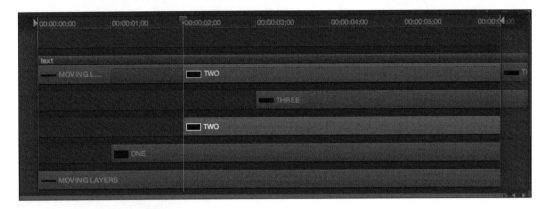

There's more...

You can move your playhead by entering in numeric values. It's a good habit to make sure no layer is selected before attempting this operation. Press *Shift + Command + A*. Now, press *Shift + = + 1 + .* followed by *Enter* to move the playhead one second forward. Press *– + 1 + .* and hit *Enter* to move the playhead one second back, and press *5 + .* and hit *Enter* to move the playhead to approximately five seconds.

You can move layers the same way you move your playhead. Select the layer you want to move in the Timeline and press *Shift + =*, or the minus symbol, followed by the number of frames or seconds you want to move it by.

Launching and customizing a template

One of my favorite things to do when I first started learning Motion was to open some of the templates the application shipped with and try to figure out how it was created. This gave me a real feel for the inner workings of Motion and the possibilities! Let's open one of Motion 5's templates and customize some of the features.

How to do it...

1. Launch Motion from the Dock or the **Applications** folder.

2. From the left-hand side of the **Project Browser**, choose the **Skyline** template folder.

3. Select the **Skyline Menu** project, and from the bottom-right hand side, choose **Open a copy**.

4. Press *Shift + Z* in the Canvas window to fit the project and press the Space bar to play it back.

5. The project starts off with a radial background where buildings and a ribbon grow from offscreen to onscreen followed by a few titles fading in over top of them. After reviewing, we've decided we'd like to change the color of our background, the color of the ribbon, and put in some text to suit the project better. Move your playhead to an area where you can see all of your elements onscreen, or double-click in the **Time** field and enter 3.25.

6. In the **Layers** tab, reveal the content of the **Background Group** by clicking the disclosure triangle. You will see a single layer that is a still image; it has a radial gradient, as shown in the following screenshot:

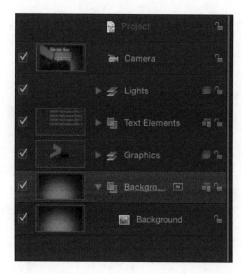

7. Since this is a still image from another application, we have to add a filter to change its color. Press *Command + 2* to go to the **Libraries** tab of the **Inspector**. Go to the **Filters** category, select the **Color Correction** folder and locate **Colorize** (use the following screenshot as your guide). Drag it to the **Background Elements** layer. Press *F3* to go to the **Filters** tab of the **Inspector**. Control-click the **Remap White** value and select a blue color of your liking.

8. Let's repeat this step for the ribbon. Click the disclosure triangle to close the **Background** group. Click the disclosure triangle to reveal the content of the **Graphics** group and the **Ribbon** group, as shown in the following screenshot:

9. The **Ribbon** group is composed of three rectangle objects that have behaviors animating them onscreen. While we can locate the original rectangle shapes and tweak their color, it's a lot easier if we add a filter to the group and change the color for all the elements within that group. Press *Command + 2* to go to the **Library** tab. Go to the **Filters** category, select the **Color Correction** folder, and locate **Colorize**. Drag it to the **Ribbon** group in the **Layers** tab, as shown in the following screenshot:

10. Press *F3* to go to the **Filters** tab of the **Inspector**. Right-click on the **Remap White** value and select a yellow color of your liking. Repeat this step for **Remap Black** with a slightly off yellow color from your previous selection.

11. Click the disclosure triangle to close the **Graphics** group. Open the **Text** group. There are five text elements, one for each text line onscreen. To change the text, select the **Title here** group. Press *F4* to go to the **Text** tab of the **Inspector**. At the bottom, change **Title info here** to **Motion 5**. Repeat this step for the subtitle layers. The following screenshot shows the **Format Pane** tab in the **Inspector** for the **Subtitle** group:

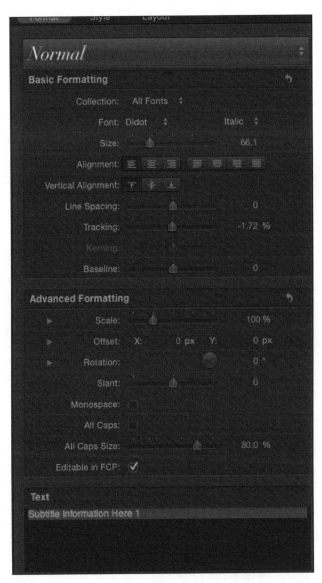

The following is a shot of the Canvas showing the template once all subtitle groups have been changed:

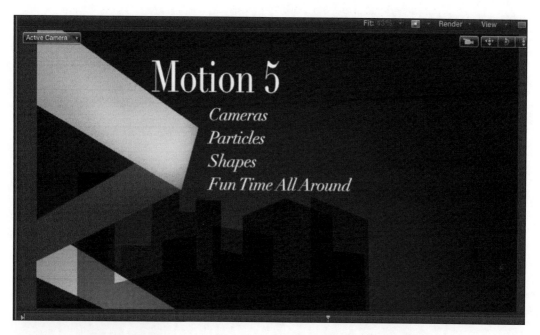

How it works...

When you open a template, you never switch the original file on the system. That's why in this recipe when you selected the template, Motion only gave you the option to open a copy. The original templates will never be overwritten.

There's more...

Motion also allows us to solo our layers.

Let solo be your friend

Having trouble differentiating what every item is? Here comes solo to the rescue. Simply select a group or layer and go to **Object | Solo** or press *Ctrl + S*. You can see that item all by its lonesome. To unsolo, go back to the **Object** menu and click **Solo** again.

 Motion is a big program but with a little practice you'll get better everyday!

Don't be intimidated

Motion is all about playing. If you didn't understand how everything worked in this recipe, relax. There is a lot of content in it we did not cover. Simply have fun by looking and playing with a few properties. With time, it's going to get easier and easier.

See also

▶   The *Moving and trimming layers in the Timeline and the mini-Timeline* recipe.

Keyboard customization

Sometimes trying to remember all the keyboard shortcuts from several applications can be a daunting task. We can easily customize our keyboard in Motion to suit our individual needs.

How to do it...

1.   With a blank Motion project open, go to the **Motion** menu and choose **Commands | Customize**. For those of you who use FCP X, the following interface should look very familiar:

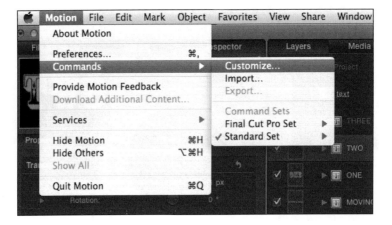

2. The keyboard is currently using the standard shortcuts that ship with Motion (shown in the next screenshot). In order to make changes, we need to duplicate the keyboard. Click on the **Keyboard Set** menu and choose **Duplicate**. Rename the keyboard to your liking.

3. Click on the letter _A_. Notice that in the **Key detail** field, all the commands associated with _A_ show up. One of them is **Record Animation**. Notice that it's color coated, allowing us to see what category it belongs to under **Command List**. The _A_ key in FCP X is the selection tool. Let's remap our keyboard to reflect that in Motion.

4. Click on the **Record Animation** field in the **No Modifier** column and drag it out of the box until you see a puff of smoke; now release your mouse.

5. In the **Command List**, choose **Tools**. Locate the **Edit** tool and drag this to the **Key Detail | No Modifier** section of _A_. Now, click **Save**.

6. Test out your newly-mapped keyboard by hitting _T_ to activate the **Text** tool followed by _A_ to jump back to the **Edit** tool.

There's more...

Motion ships with a Final Cut keyboard, which you can select anytime by switching from **Standard Set** to **Final Cut Pro Set**.

See also

▶ The *Looking under the hood – key preferences for your workflows* recipe.

Looking under the hood – key preferences for your workflows

Like Final Cut Pro X, Motion 5 has a number of preferences we can change to modify the way it works from its default settings. Let's look at a few key preferences we can change which may be able to assist us in our workflows.

How to do it...

1. With a blank Motion project open, go to frame 10 of your project by clicking *Shift* + the right arrow.

2. Press *Command* + *2* to open the **Library** tab.

3. Navigate to the **Content** folder near the bottom. Select **Particle Images | AquaBall** and click on the **Apply** button at the top of the window. The following screenshot shows the **AquaBall** image being added to the tenth frame in the mini-Timeline:

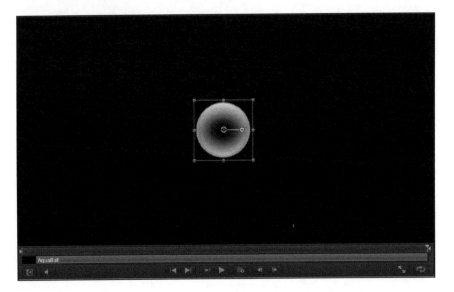

4. There are two default preferences at play here that we should be aware of. The first is that when you import a layer into Motion, it will always get added at the playhead position. When you're first starting to use the application, this can be very frustrating. Second, this was a still image and, by default, if you drag it 10 frames to the left, you'll notice it matches the length of the project. Let's change this now. Select the **AquaBall** image in the **Layers** tab and press *Delete*.

5. Go to the **Motion** menu and choose **Preferences**. Click on the **Project** tab.

6. Under the **Still Images & Layers** settings, notice that **Default Layer Duration** is set to **Use project duration** and **Create Layers at** is set to **Current frame**, as shown in the next screenshot. Set **Default Layer Duration** to **Use custom duration** and set the length to one second.

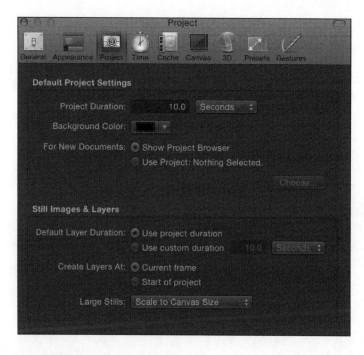

7. Set **Create Layers at** to **Start of project**.

8. Let's close the preference window. With your playhead still at 10 frames and the **AquaBall** visible in the **Library** tab, apply it to the project again. Notice its length and where it gets added, as shown here:

9. Go back to **Motion | Preferences** and change back the preferences to their defaults.

There's more...

We've only scratched the surface of some of the preferences available to us in Motion. Go back to the **Preferences** menu and get more familiar with some of the other preferences under the different tabs.

For instance, under the **Canvas** tab, the grid and ruler controls refer to items we can turn on under our **View** menu (**View | Show Rulers** and **View | Overlays | Show Grid**) to help us align objects in the Canvas.

See also

▶ The *Keyboard customization* recipe.

▶ The *Sequencing stills in the Timeline* recipe.

Sequencing stills in the Timeline

Sometimes, it is beneficial to be able to grab a group of stills and have them sequentially laid out in the Timeline with the click of a button. This recipe explains how we can set up our preferences and select multiple photos and perform this recipe in a flash.

How to do it...

1. Launch Motion. Select a Motion project, set **Preset** to **Broadcast HD 720p**, **Frame Rate** to **59.94**, and **Duration** to **20** seconds. Choose **Open**.

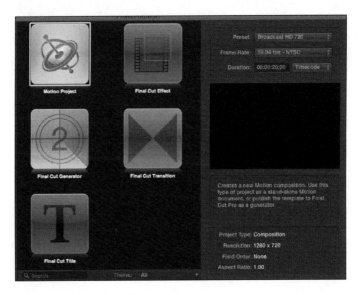

2. Go to the **Motion** menu and choose **Preferences**. Click on the **Project** tab.

3. Under the **Still Images & Layers** settings, notice that **Default layer Duration** is set to **Use project duration**. Change **Default Layer Duration** to **Use custom duration** and set the length to one second. Close **Preferences**.

4. Press *Command + 1* to navigate to the **File Browser** and locate the Chapter 1 exercise folder.

5. Turn off the **Collapse Image Sequences** icon on the lower-right corner of the **File Browser** so you can see all the photos. You should see 20 photos displayed; change from icon view to list view, as shown in the following screenshot:

6. Make sure your playhead is on the first frame of the project. Click the first photo and *Shift* + click the last one.

7. Drag the photos into the Timeline and try to align it with your playhead while holding down the *Shift* key. Wait for the pop-up window, and choose **Sequential**, as shown here:

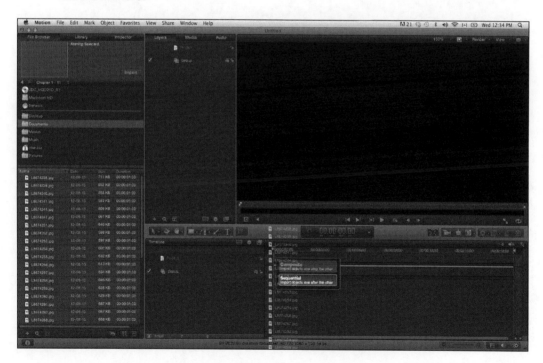

8. Press *Command + 1* to close the **File Browser** and *F5* to close the **Layers** tab. Drag upward between the Timeline and the Canvas to get a better view of the Timeline:

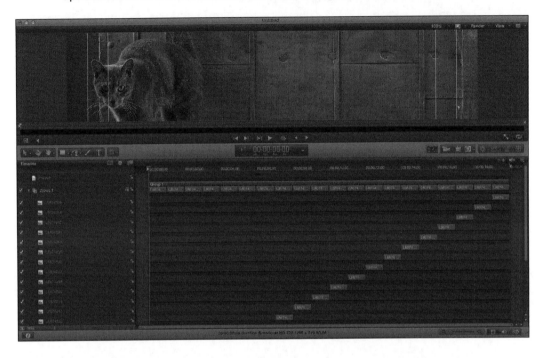

9. Change the **Layer** view in the Timeline from **Small** to **Mini** to fit more layers on screen, as shown here. Scroll down on the right-hand side to see more of them.

10. Press *Shift + Z* to fit the Canvas to the window and the Space bar to play it back. Notice how every second a photo appears until the project ends.

11. Go back to **Motion | Preferences** and change back the preferences to their defaults.

There's more...

At the start of this recipe, we chose to turn off **Collapse Image Sequences** when bringing in our photos. What happened is because some photos were named sequentially, Motion flagged this and thought we wanted to treat it as an image sequence. In the later chapters, we'll see how image sequences can be extremely useful in **Particles** and **Replicator** cells.

See also

▸   *Using an image sequence in a particle emitter, Chapter 7, Let's Make Particles.*

Managing the Layers tab

In some of the previous recipes, you may have seen that the **Layers** tab can become a very busy place. It's important as Motion graphic designers to feel comfortable where we're working. Let's look at a few tricks we can use to manage our **Layers** tab as we work in Motion.

How to do it...

1.   Launch Motion. Under **Composition**, select the **Pulse** category and choose **Pulse – Open**. Click **Open a copy**.

2.   The project has three groups comprising of various elements from the project. Press *Command + 1* to close the **File Browser** and *Command + 7* to close the Timeline, so that we can have a little more room to view our **Layers** tab.

3.   Let's play back the project to get a feel for it. Press the Space bar. This project consists of four different views of our animating circles and pulses.

4.   Let's look at this project a bit deeper. Go to the beginning of the project. Click the disclosure triangle for the **Text Elements** group, as shown in the following screenshot. Notice how the group is slightly less highlighted than the **Camera Light Graphics** and **Background Elements** groups. This indicates that at the current frame, this group doesn't exist. We get further confirmation of this by looking in our mini-Timeline and seeing the **Text Elements** group start a lot later. Press *Shift + I* to move to the in-point of the group.

Notice how the group now becomes highlighted but the **Subtitle** layer does not, as shown in the following screenshot:

5. Drag your playhead forward until you see the word **Subtitle** onscreen or go to frame 273. Notice it's now highlighted. Hit the disclosure triangle for the **Subtitle** group. Notice that there is a **Sequence Text** behavior on the text. (We will be going in depth with behaviors in *Chapter 3, Making It Move with Behaviors*, but right now think of it as what's causing the text to animate in). Sometimes when we add filters, masks, and behaviors to clips, our workspace in the **Layers** tab can get cluttered. We can easily turn off the visibility of these filters, behaviors, and masks at the bottom of the **Layers** tab. Press the gear icon (shown in the following screenshot) and notice how the **Sequence Text** disappears. Press it again so you can see it.

6. When we work, it's also advantageous to solo elements in the project. It allows us to focus our work rather than worry about hundreds of items. To see the layers in the **Text Elements** group by themselves, select it and click the square within the rectangle icon. Notice how the graphic disappears and the text moves slightly to the side. Click it again to unsolo it.

7. Close the **Text Elements** group and open the **Cameras Light Graphics** group. Notice there are four scenes in this group that correspond to the four circle and pulse animations that take place over time. Get a feel for when each scene starts and stops by looking in the **Layers** tab and in the mini-Timeline for when a group is highlighted.

8. Twirl open scenes four through one by clicking the disclosure triangle for each of them. This may cause some of the layers to go outside the view, and in order to see them you have to scroll. Instead, click the icon at the bottom-left of the **Layers** tab with the little head on it. Drag the slider to your right to resize the layers.

9. Close the **Camera Lights and Graphics** group.

See also

▶ *An intro to Text behaviors* in *Chapter 3, Making It Move with Behaviors.*

▶ *Changing the text format* in *Chapter 5, Let's Make Text.*

▶ *Changing the text style* in *Chapter 5, Let's Make Text.*

2
Looking at Motion's Library

In this chapter, we will cover:

- A brief tour of the Library tab
- Importing files from the Content library
- Applying a Glow filter to a layer
- Copying filters and applying filters to a group
- Controlling the filter order
- The power of cloning
- The power of blend modes
- Customizing a gradient generator
- Applying a blend mode to a gradient
- Adding a frame and changing a drop zone's content
- Adding a Flourish and applying filters

Introduction

As motion graphic artists and editors, we are constantly looking for content to bring into our projects and compositions. Some of this content can come from an onset location that we want to manipulate, while other content we create on the computer, such as text. What's amazing about Motion is that it ships with a library of content you can use *royalty free* in any of your projects. You already have some of the content you apply to images on hand, while other content you can create and use from scratch. The best part is that usually you don't have to look any further than in the Library to create breathtaking, broadcast-worthy visuals for a variety of different situations. Let's dive in to see the vast richness available for our projects.

A brief tour of the Library tab

Motion's **Library** is very similar to Final Cut Pro's **Media Browser**. Unlike the **File Browser** where we import material from outside of Motion, the **Library** contains filters, behaviors, generators, content, and presets available within Motion. It also gives us a gateway to a few external application libraries, such as iTunes and iPhoto. In this recipe, we'll have an overview of the **Library** tab.

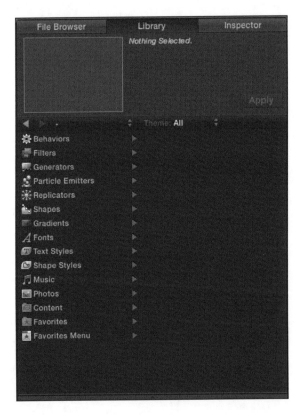

How to do it...

1. Launch Motion. Set the **Preset** to Broadcast HD 720p, **Frame Rate** to NTSC-DV, 29.97, and **Duration** to 10 seconds. Press **OK**.

2. Click on the **Library** tab located on the left-hand side of the interface. Take a second to look at all the categories that are displayed. Choose **Behaviors**. On the right-hand side, a list of subcategories display. Currently **All** is selected, and the content of that subcategory appears in the lower part of the window, as displayed in the following screenshot:

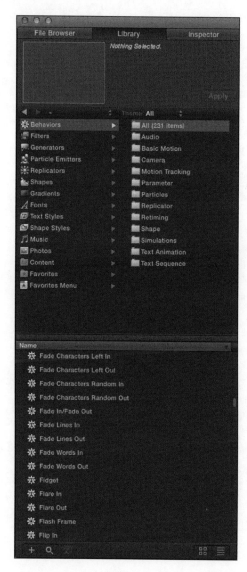

3. At the bottom of the **Library** tab, click on the magnifying glass icon. Similar to Spotlight on the Mac OS, we can now search in the subcategory. Type in `write on` in the search field. All the behaviors in the subcategory disappear except for the **Write on** behavior, as shown here:

4. Click on the **Content** category. At first, it appears that there is nothing inside. The **All** subcategory does not show any items. This occurs because we haven't cleared our search results and it just so happens there is no item by the name of **Write on** in the **Content** category. Click on the **x** icon in the search field to clear it. Now over 1300 items are displayed in the **Content** category. Click the spotlight icon again to close the search field.

5. Scroll down in the **All** subcategory until you can see **Atom 01**. Select it. In the upper part of the **Library** tab, a preview displays showing you it's animated:

6. Click on a few more items in the **Content** library to get familiar with some of the items available to you. In the next recipe, we're going to import some of them into our project!

See also

▸ The *Importing files from the Content library* recipe.

Importing files from the Content library

In the previous recipe, we had a brief tour of the **Library** tab and learned how we can easily search, select, and preview items. In this recipe, we'll import a few items into our project and see how to use them.

How to do it...

1. You can continue from the project you created in the previous recipe, or if you're starting here, launch Motion. Set the **Preset** to `Broadcast HD 720p`, **Frame Rate** to `NTSC-DV, 29.97`, and **Duration** to `10` seconds. Press OK.

2. Click on the **Library** tab and choose the **Content** category. On the right-hand side, select the **Background** subcategory.

3. As the subcategory implies, these items are meant to be used as backgrounds in your project. To change the way these items are being displayed, use the icon on the bottom right-hand corner with four squares. All the backgrounds are now displayed as icons. We can change the size of them by clicking on the duration slider, as shown in the following screenshot (next to the magnifying glass icon):

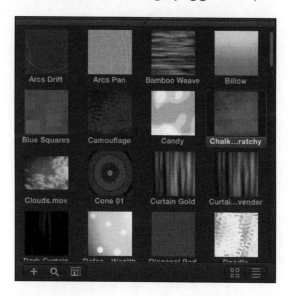

4. Click and select a few of the items below to view them in the upper window. Find and select **Chalkboard Scratchy**.

5. Make sure your playhead is at the beginning of the Timeline and the group in the **Layers** tab is selected. Click on the **Apply** button at the top of the **Library**, as shown in the following screenshot, to set the selected background as the background of your project. Select the Canvas and press *Shift + Z* to fit the video in the window. Press the Space bar to play the project.

6. We can even import content from our library while we are playing back our projects. Make sure your project is still playing. In the **Library**, select the group in the **Layers** tab. In the **Library**, under **Content**, select the **Symbols** subcategory. Scroll down and select **Radio Hazard**, as shown in the following screenshot:

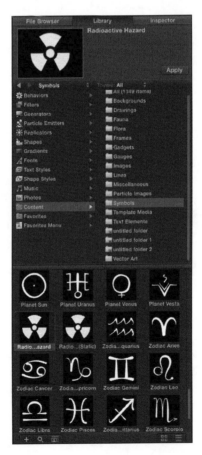

7. Click on the **Apply** button. The content is added to the group and starts at the beginning of the project, as shown here:

See also

▶ The *A brief tour of the Library tab* recipe.

Applying a Glow filter to a layer

For those of you from Final Cut X, applying effects to your projects is probably second nature but many of you may not realize that the vast majority of the effects in the **Media Browser** come directly from Motion. At any time, if you *Ctrl* +click or right-click these effects, you would see an option to open a copy of it in Motion, as shown in the following screenshot:

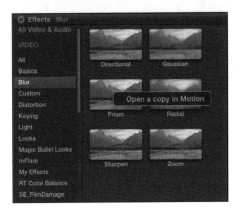

Let's see how easy it is to add a filter to a clip in Motion.

How to do it...

1. From this chapter's project folder, double-click and open the 02_03 project.. The project consists of an Aqua Ball from Motion's **Content** library. It has been scaled up in size. We want to add a filter to it. Make sure the Aqua Ball is selected in the **Layers** tab.

2. Click on the **Library** tab. Locate the **Filters** category and select it. Select the **Glow** subcategory. There are eight different glows to choose from, as shown in the following screenshot:

3. Select the **Light Rays** filter and click on the **Apply** button at the top of the **Library** tab. The filter is now applied to the Aqua Ball.

4. With the Aqua Ball selected, press *F3* to go to the **Filters** tab of the **Inspector**. Notice how the **Light Rays** filter is attached to your image. It seems to affect the brightest areas of the Aqua Ball. First, let's play with the **Mix** slider by dragging it to 0 and slowly back to 100, as indicated in the following screenshot:

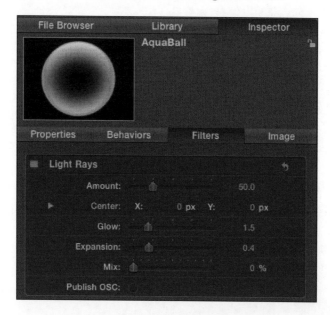

5. Experiment with each of the other parameter sliders to get a feel for the effect on the Aqua ball (threshold and radius have a greater effect than the other two parameters). I used 150 for **Amount**, 8 for **Glow**, and 2 for **Expansion**. The results can be seen in the following screenshot:

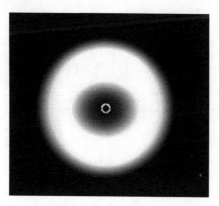

6. Turn the filter on and off to see the before and after of the results by clicking the blue square for the filter in the **Layers** tab.

There's more...

The magic of filters lies in our ability to keyframe them and create animation. Lucky for us, the majority of Motion parameters on filters are keyframable!

Keyframing filters

While the result of the previous example is a static effect, notice that if you hover your mouse over the right-hand side of any of the parameters in the **Filters** tab, a diamond shape pops up, as indicated in the following screenshot. Filters become even more powerful when we make variable changes to them over time. Keyframing is our tool for creating animation. Two keyframes at different places in time and with different values result in an animation. Filters can even be used as transitions between clips to create dynamic effects. We'll cover more of this in *Chapter 4, Making It Move with Keyframes*.

Don't sweat the filters

There are 132 filters in Motion's library! Don't sweat it if you don't know what each one does. Your desire to add filters and play with the parameters is all you need to discover all the options that are out there. So start exploring!

See also

▶ The *Copying filters and applying filters to a group* recipe.

▶ The *Controlling the filter order* recipe.

Copying filters and applying filters to a group

Motion 5 gives us incredible flexibility when we work with filters. By using simple copying and pasting procedures, we are able to easily move filters in between layers and groups.

How to do it...

1. From this chapter's project folder, open the `02_04` project.

2. The project consists of two Aqua Balls from Motion's library. One of them has a **Light Rays** filter on it, which we applied in the previous recipe. We would like to apply this filter to the other Aqua Ball, too.

3. Select the **Light Rays** filter in the **Layers** tab. Go to the **Edit** menu and choose **Copy**. Select the Aqua Ball without the filter and go to the **Edit** menu and choose **Paste**, as shown in the following screenshot:

4. Let's add a blur filter to both the Aqua Balls as well. Rather than apply a filter to each ball, we can apply the filter to the group they're both in. Select **Group 1** in the **Layers** tab. Click on the **Library** tab. Locate the **Filters** category and select it. Select the **Blur** subcategory. Select **Defocus** and click **Apply**. The **Blur** filter is now applied to both the Aqua Balls.

5. With **Group 1** selected, press *F3* to go to the **Filters** tab of the **Inspector**. The **Defocus** filter is attached to your group. Change a few of the parameters to see if you can increase the blur. I changed the **Amount** value to `20` and the **Shape** value to `Polygon`.

There's more...

Like any other application, you should get to know some keyboard shortcuts to speed up your workflow process.

Using Command + Command + C and Command + V when copying multiple filters

You can also copy a filter to multiple clips using *Command + C* to copy the filter, make a multiple selection on the clips you want to apply the filter to, and press *Command + V* to paste it to all of them.

See also

- ► The *Applying a Glow filter to a layer* recipe.
- ► The *Controlling the filter order* recipe.
- ► The *The power of cloning* recipe.

Controlling the filter order

Like any good recipe, the order in which we follow steps can make or break the meal we eat. The same can hold true for filters in Motion. In some instances, if we apply one filter before another, it can have a very different result than if the order was reversed. Let's take a look at a simple example where this applies.

How to do it...

1. Navigate to this chapter's folder and open the 02_05 project.

2. This project consists of an **Earth Transparent** layer from Motion's **Content** library. Click the disclosure triangle to reveal its filters and press *F3* to go to the **Filters** tab of the Inspector.

3. There are two filters on the layer. One filter was meant to colorize the earth map, while the other created a border around the map with a blue color. This problem arises because we added the **Colorize** filter *after* the **Border** filter, and this is affecting both the border and the layer. Select the **Simple Border** filter in the **Layers** tab and drag it up so that it's on top of the **Colorize** filter. Notice how the border now has its intended blue background, as shown in the following screenshot:

See also

▸ The *Applying a Glow filter to a layer* recipe.

▸ The *Copying filters and applying filters to a group* recipe.

The power of cloning

In the previous recipe, we saw how easy it was to copy and paste filters from one layer to another or to a group. Sometimes in a Motion graphics workflow, it's necessary to duplicate layers. A problem can occur when we want to change the filters on these layers. Both the duplicate and the original layers would each have to be changed manually. If you begin to change or manipulate filters several times, this can become a very tedious process. This is where cloning comes in handy. Any changes we make to filters on the original layer, the clone will follow along. As an added bonus, it also allows for better performance in Motion. Let's take a look at an example in action.

How to do it...

1. Open the `02_06` project from this chapter's project folder. This project consists of the **Arrow 01** group from Motion's **Content** library.

2. Click on the disclosure triangle for the **Arrow 01** group and reveal its content. Notice there are two filters on the group—a **Colorize** and **Trail** filter. Press *F3* to go to the **Filters** tab of the Inspector.

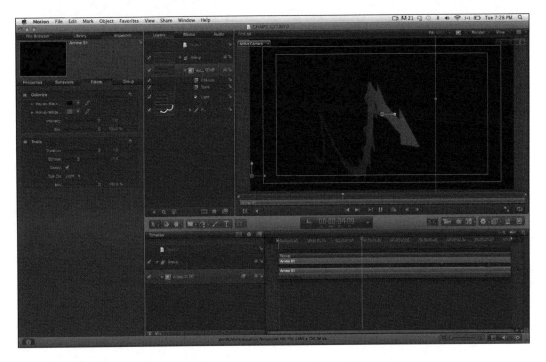

3. Press the Space bar to play back the project. Notice how the **Remap White** value on the **Colorize** filter has been turned to blue, and also notice how in the **Trail** filter, eleven echoes have been created lasting for a duration of one second.

4. Select the **Arrow 01** group in the **Layers** tab and go to the **Object** menu and choose **Make Clone Layer**, as shown in the following screenshot:

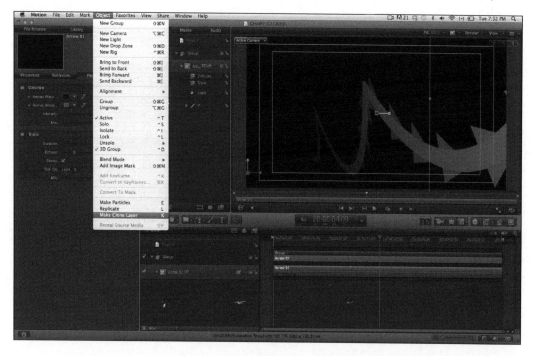

5. Notice that a new layer has been created just above the **Arrow** group, as shown in
    the following screenshot. Select **Clone** and press *F1* to go to the **Properties** tab of
    the Inspector. Change the **Position X** value to −400. Clones have independent **Scale**,
    Position, and **Rotation** properties from the original. Press the Space bar to play back
    and see the two arrows animate.

6. Stop the playback. Move to a frame where you can see both the arrows in the Canvas,
    or go to the one second and the thirty-fifth frame mark. Select the **Arrows 01** group
    and press *F3* to go the **Filters** tab of the Inspector.

7. Right-click or *Ctrl* + click the **Remap White** value and change the color to a red of your liking, as shown in the following. Under the **Trails** filter, set **Echoes** to **4**.

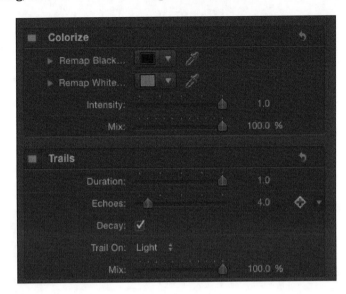

8. Press the Space bar to play back the project. Notice how the clone adopts the original group's filter changes, and you only had to switch one set of values!

There's more...

When we move our layer's **Position** co-ordinates, it's a good practice to know what the values mean.

Grid 101

Having a basic understanding of how **Position** co-ordinates work in Motion 5 can come in handy. When dealing with the x and y positions, we can easily break down our screen into four basic quadrants. The quadrants hold either positive or negative values. Here is a breakdown of the grid system in Motion 5; the same holds true in FCP X:

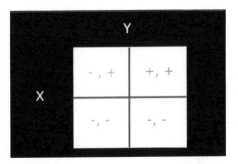

Clones and switching sources

If we are working with one layer in a project that has clones and later decide there may be another element that works better in its place, we can actually swap out the source. See the following example. In **Picture 1**, there was a photo of chalk that was cloned and scaled lower in size. The still picture of the ruler replaced the chalk and its clone. To achieve this, the ruler was dragged on top of the original chalk layer. The clone simply follows suit!

Picture 1

Picture 2

See also

▶ The *Copying filters and applying filters to a group* recipe.

The power of blend modes

When you're trying to develop looks for your images, blend modes can achieve exciting results. Blend modes are used in almost all imaging applications and truly are a foundation of motion graphics and compositing. While there is a ton of content about blend modes, such as Motion 5's user manual, sometimes it's better to see for yourself and experiment with a still image. Let's take a look at a few examples.

How to do it...

Let's create a new project and add a still from Motion's library:

1. Launch Motion. Set **Preset** to Broadcast HD 720p, **Frame Rate** to NTSC-DV, 29.97, and **Duration** to 10 seconds. Press **OK**.

2. Click on the **Library** tab. Go to the **Content** category and select the **Images** subcategory. At the bottom of the **Library** window, double-click the **Traditions** folder and select the **Watercolor 02** still image. In the preview area, you can see that the project's size is 2048 by 1362. That's much larger than our 1280 x 720 project.

3. Making sure your playhead is at the beginning of the project. Click on the **Apply** button to add the **Watercolor 02** image to the project. We're going to experiment with a few different types of looks with this abstract image by duplicating it and changing one of the layer's blending modes.

4. With **Watercolor 02** selected in the **Layers** tab, go to the **Edit** menu and choose **Duplicate**, as shown in the following screenshot. Select **Watercolor 02 copy**.

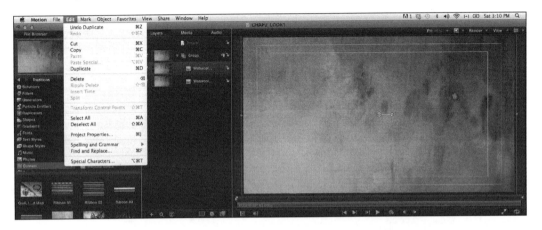

5. Click on the **Properties** tab of the **Inspector**. Under the **Blending** category, set **Blend Mode** to **Multiply**, as shown in the following screenshot. The **Watercolor 02 copy** image blends together with the original **Watercolor 02** image. **Multiply** looks at the darker colors in both images and multiplies them together. To see the before and after result, in the **Layers** tab, click on the checkmark next to **Watercolor 02 copy**. Click the empty box to turn the copy back on.

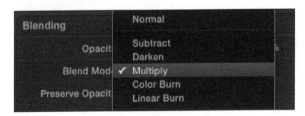

6. In the **Properties** tab, drag the **Opacity** slider up and down to see how this can be combined with the **Multiply** blend mode. Bring the **Opacity** slider back up to 100.

7. Set **Blend Mode** to **Add**. Notice how we receive a different effect. **Add** looks at the brighter parts of the image and adds them together.

8. Experiment with different **Blend Mode** values and **Opacity** settings to get a feel for some of the possibilities.

▸   The *Applying a blend mode to a gradient* recipe.

Customizing a gradient generator

Gradients are fun and easy to use. Some gradients in Motion can be applied to different types of objects. We can apply gradients to shapes, text, particles, and a variety of different objects to create cool looks. We can create other gradients from scratch. To do this, we need to generate the gradient.

How to do it...

1. Launch Motion. Set the **Preset** to Broadcast HD 720p, **Frame Rate** to NTSC-DV, 29.97, and **Duration** to 10 seconds. Press **OK**.

2. Click on the **Library** tab. Go to the **Generators** category. There are several generators for you to choose from. Choose **Gradient** and click **Apply**. Go to the **Window** menu and choose **Show HUD**, if it's not already showing. Use the following screenshot for reference:

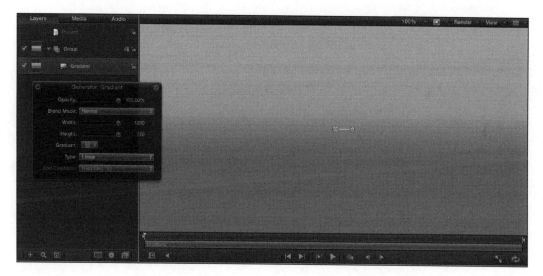

3. A great place to start customizing your gradient is by looking at the various presets that ship with Motion. Next to the word **Gradient** is an icon. Click it to reveal the gradient presets and select any random one. I choose **Dusk** as shown here:

4. Set **Type** to **Radial**. Press the **I** icon to go to the **Generators** tab of the Inspector. You can see that we have more options for our gradient here than in the HUD.

5. Click the disclosure triangle to the left of the word **Gradient**. Let's change the position of the radial gradient and then adjust its color setting.

6. Scrub the **Start Y** Value and drag it to -360. Set the **Y End** value to -1120.

7. In the gradient icon at the top, there are two parts to the line. The upper-most part contains the opacity tags for the gradient. The fact that they are both white means it's fully opaque. The bottom part contains the color stops for the gradient. Currently, this radial gradient consists of four colors. We're going to delete one of them. Click on the color tag on the left, drag it down, and release your mouse. You should see a puff of smoke quickly appear. Use the following screenshot for reference:

8. Drag the light purple color tag over a little to the left. We're going to change its color. Click on that color stop and notice how it loads in the **Color** window below. Use the following screenshot for reference. *Ctrl* + click the stop to the right of the word **Color** and adjust as desired.

There's more...

Here are a few quick tips on working with and adjusting your gradient.

Adding color and opacity stops

To add tags to the gradient, simply click the color or opacity line. Wherever you click on the line, a color stop will be added at that position. Click the upper white line to add opacity tags and click the lower colored line to add color tags.

We can also reverse a gradient's direction.

Reversing gradient colors

We can easily reverse the colors on a gradient by clicking on the appropriate button to the right of the tags, as shown in the following image:

See also

▶ The *The power of blend modes* recipe.

▶ The *Applying a blend mode to a gradient* recipe.

Applying a blend mode to a gradient

In this recipe, we're going to use a gradient generator and apply a blend mode to it so that we can enhance the sky in the image below it. While a still image is used in this recipe, this technique can be applied with moving footage as well.

How to do it...

We'll begin by navigating to this chapter's exercise folder on your drive.

1. Open the `02_08` project, which consists of a still image of a sky. Select the still in the **Layers** tab.

2. Click on the **Library** tab. Go to the **Generators** category. There are several generators for you to choose from. Choose **Gradient** and click **Apply**. Go to the **Window** menu and choose **Show HUD**, if it's not already showing.

3. Make sure the gradient is selected in the **Layers** tab. In the HUD, next to the word **Gradient** is an icon. Click it to reveal the gradient presets and select **Desert Sun**, as shown in the following screenshot:

4. With the gradient still selected in the **Layers** tab, *Ctrl* + click directly in the Canvas window. Choose **Edit Position** from the list, as shown. The gradient controls are now displayed on the screen:

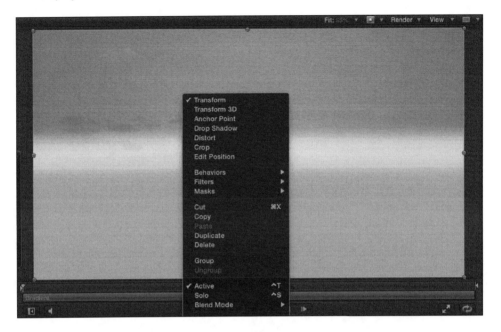

5. The gradient is going to be used as a filter for the following image. Press *Command + -* to zoom out on your Canvas. Drag the triangle controls to increase the spread and position of the gradient. Use the following screenshot for reference:

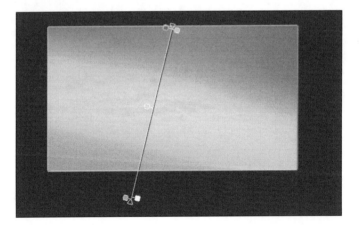

6. Press *Shift + Z* to fit the Canvas to your window. In the HUD, set **Blend Mode** to **Screen**. Slide down the **Opacity** value. Change the **Blend Mode** value to **Linear Burn**. Play with the **Opacity** and **Position** values of the gradient to suit your taste.

See also

▸ The *The power of blend modes* recipe.

▸ The *Customizing a gradient generator* recipe.

Adding a frame and changing a drop zone's content

Drop zones give us the ability to swap either video or a still in replace of a placeholder graphic. Drop zones are great in helping motion graphic designers automate their workflow. Let's say you have a news program that uses the same "Coming Next" animation every week, but the videos and still content in that animation constantly change. You can easily set up a drop zone, so that you can use that same graphic over and over again while literally dropping in video and stills to their respective places.

How to do it...

1. Launch Motion. Set the **Preset** to Broadcast 720p, **Frame Rate** to 29.97, and **Duration** to 10 seconds.

2. Click on the **Library** tab to open it. Go to **Content**. There are 1349 items to choose from. Click the magnifying glass at the bottom-left of the window. Type in Vertical.

3. Select any frame with an arrow in the middle of it and choose **Import**. Select the **Vertical** group and press *F1* to go to the **Properties** tab of the Inspector.

4. Decrease the **Scale** value to 50. Select the **Vertical** group and hit *Command + D* twice to make two copies.

5. In the **Layers** tab, select one copy and drag it to the left of the Canvas. Repeat the step for the other copy, but drag it to the right. We'll make sure they're precisely aligned in the next step.

6. Name each of the frames accordingly. Select all three and from the **Object** menu choose **Alignment | Distribute Horizontal Centers**. Go back to the **Object** menu and choose **Alignment | Distribute Vertical Centers**. Use the following screenshot for reference:

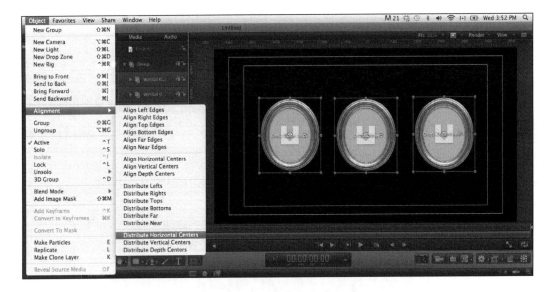

7. You may see that in the center of each frame, it says **Drop Zone** as long as the group is selected. Drop zones are meant to be replaced with stills or video clips. Let's add some sources to the drop zone. Click the disclosure triangle for one of the **Vertical** groups.

8. Let's navigate to our **File Browser** by pressing *Command + 1*. Make sure **Collapsed Image Sequences** is turned off, as shown in the following screenshot. Navigate to the cat pictures from this chapter's media folder. Select one you like.

9. Drag the picture from the **File Browser** onto the **Drop Zone** layer in the **Layers** tab and wait for the hooked arrow, as shown in the following screenshot. Release your mouse. Press *F4* to go to the **Image** tab of the Inspector, if it's not already displaying.

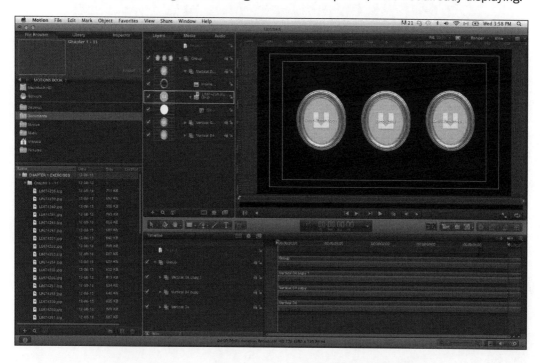

10. Scale and position the image in the frame to your liking. A sample is shown in the following screenshot:

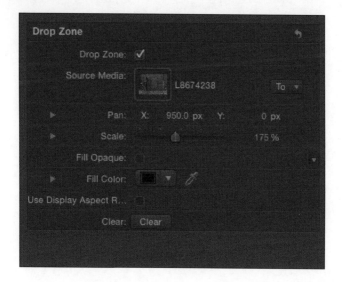

11. Repeat the preceding steps for the other two empty frames. Use the following screenshot for reference:

There's more...

Drop zones in Motion publish over to FCP X!

Drop zones for FCP X

You may have noticed in FCP X that certain transitions and templates have drop zones. We can create drop zones in Motion from the **Object** menu in any of our projects, as shown in the following screenshot. On top of this, we can save our project as a title, effect, or generator and manipulate that drop zone directly in FCP X. So, if you have a recurring show with the same intro animation and you need to continually update certain video segments, drop zones are for you!

Object	Favorites	View	Share
New Group			⇧⌘N
New Camera			⌥⌘C
New Light			⇧⌘L
New Drop Zone			⇧⌘D
New Rig			⌃⌘R

Anchor points

How does that image scale? It's all about the anchor point! To illustrate how anchor points work a bit more, try adding some text to you project by pressing the *T* key. Press *Esc* once it's entered to go back to the selection tool and then press *F7* to show the HUD. Change the size of the text and notice that when you scale it up, it scales from the lower-left corner. Press *Command + Z* to undo. Change the text alignment to center and scale it up again. Notice how the text scales from the center. Alignment acts as a text's anchor point and determines how the object scales and rotates.

See also

▶ The *Applying a Glow filter to a layer* recipe.

▶ The *Copying filters and applying filters to a group* recipe.

▶ *Spinning and throwing a ball* in Chapter 3, *Making It Move with Behaviors*.

▶ *An intro to Text behaviors* in Chapter 3, *Making It Move with Behaviors*.

▶ *Sequence Text* in Chapter 5, *Let's Make Text*.

Adding a Flourish and applying filters

The **Content** library in Motion is a great way to start to visualize some of the possibilities Motion has to offer. In this recipe, we'll be taking a look at some of the possibilities that are available with combining some content from Motion's library along with some filters.

How to do it...

1. Launch Motion. Set the **Preset** to Broadcast 720p, **Frame Rate** to 29.97, and **Duration** to 10 seconds. Click **OK**.

2. Click on the **Library** tab. Go to the **Content** category. There are 1349 items to choose from. Click the magnifying glass at the bottom-left of the window. Type in **Flourish**, as shown in the following screenshot:

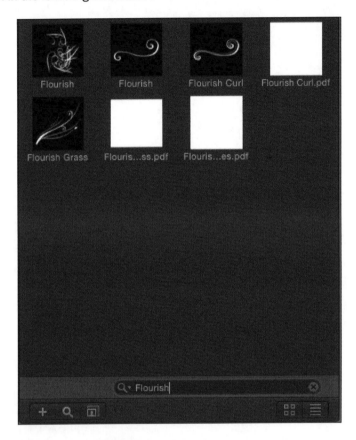

3. Select **Flourish** and click **Apply** to add it to the project.

4. Click the disclosure triangle to reveal the content of the **Flourish** group. It consists of an **Ornament** layer that is turned off and is referenced by a replicator. The replicator controls how many ornaments we see, while the **Sequence Replicator** behavior controls how the ornaments are being animated on screen. Clear the search field by clicking on the **x** icon in the search window.

5. Go to the **Filters** category. Go to the **Distortion** subcategory and select the **Mirror** filter. Drag it to the **Flourish** group. Notice how you can change the position of the **Mirror** filter directly in the Canvas by dragging the onscreen control.

6. Press *Command + 2* to go back to the **Library** and select the **Glow** subcategory. Select **Outer Glow**. Drag it on to the **Flourish** group. Press *F3* to go to the **Filters** tab. Set the **Radius** value to **4**, **Brightness** to **50**, and **Outer Color** to orange, as shown in the following screenshot. Press the Space bar to play back.

7. Let's add some text directly over the flourish and throw on a few behaviors to have it appear to be moving together. Make sure you're on the first frame of the project. Select the group in the **Layers** Tab. Type T to select the type tool, or select it from the toolbar by clicking on the *T* icon.

8. Type ORGANIC in the Canvas and press the *Esc* key to go back to the default selection tool. Press *F7* to bring up the HUD. Choose **Impact** as the font type, set **Size** to 121, and make sure the alignment is set to center, as shown in the following screenshot. Position it directly over top of the flourish in the Canvas.

9. *Option* + click the **Outer Glow** filter to copy it to the **Organic** text. Make sure **Outer Glow Copy** is selected, and in the HUD change the **Inner** and **Outer Color** values of the text to a purple and blue color of your liking. Use the following screenshot for reference:

10. Let's have the text start a bit later and have it fade in as well as grow on screen. With the **Organic** text selected, jump to one second and the tenth frame mark in your Timeline. Press the *I* key to trim the layer's in-point to that location.

11. Press *Command + 2* to go to the **Library** tab and select the **Behaviors** category. Select the **Basic** subcategory and drag the **Grow/Shrink** and **Fade in/Fade Out** behaviors to the **Organic** text layer in the **Layers** tab.

12. Press *F2* to go to the **Behaviors** tab of the **Inspector**. Set the **Fade In Time** value to 30 and the **Fade Out Time** value to 0.

13. Under **Grow/Shrink**, change the **Scale** value to **10**, as shown in the following screenshot. Press the Space bar to play back your project.

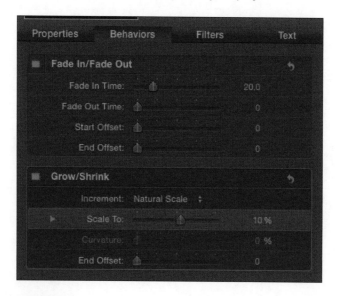

See also

▸ *Applying a Fade in/Fade Out and Grow/Shrink behavior to a still* in Chapter 3, *Making It Move with Behaviors*.

▸ *Changing the text format* in Chapter 5, *Let's Make Text*.

▸ *Changing the text style* in Chapter 5, *Let's Make Text*.

3
Making It Move with Behaviors

In this chapter, we will cover the following:

- ▶ Applying a Fade In/Fade Out and Grow/Shrink behavior to a still
- ▶ Customizing a Motion Path
- ▶ Spinning and throwing a ball
- ▶ Adding an Attractor and Attracted To behavior
- ▶ Adding Edge Collision and Gravity behaviors to a ball
- ▶ Creating Random Motion using the Randomize behavior
- ▶ Stop, Wriggle, Rate, and Quantize
- ▶ Using the Link behavior
- ▶ An intro to Text behaviors
- ▶ Writing on your shape's outline
- ▶ Creating constant and variable speed changes
- ▶ Holding and looping your animations

Introduction

If you've ever used FCP 7 or FCP X to animate the scale, position, or parameter of an effect on a video clip, you're probably familiar with the concept of **keyframing**. The idea of keyframing comes from the classical days of animation. A head animator would come in and draw two pictures, let's say a lizard at the beginning and end of a race. A junior animator would then be responsible for drawing every picture during the race. In Motion 5, consider yourself the head animator while Motion acts as the junior animator. Yet, on top of using keyframing as an option to animate, we also have behaviors.

Behaviors automate the keyframing process. In some cases, where we might have had to use hundreds of keyframes to mimic a reel-life simulation, we can use one behavior and change a few controls to perform that task immediately. In other cases, it aids us better than having to use keyframes, because certain behaviors have graphical user interfaces which help us visualize what they do. Behaviors are a very powerful motion graphics tool that will assist us throughout the animation process. They're also a ton of fun to use! Let's see some behaviors in action.

Applying a Fade In/Fade Out and Grow/Shrink behavior to a still

For those of you from Final Cut X, when in the **Video** tab of **Inspector**, we can easily set our **Crop** settings to **Ken Burns** and automatically get movement in our still images by setting the start and stop position for the effect. In Motion 5, these types of automatic animations come naturally when we use behaviors. Let's add some effects to a still and see it in practice.

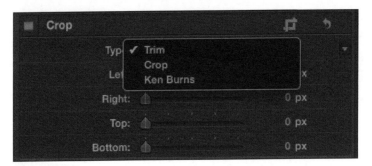

Getting ready

Locate the exercise folder for this chapter on your computer. Choose the 03_01 project and double-click to open it in Motion. The project is just a still picture of a cat that has been scaled to fit an NTSC – DV project. We're going to have this photo grow over time by using a behavior to animate it.

How to do it...

1. Press the *Command + 2* shortcut to go to the **Library**. Navigate to **Behaviors | Basic Motion | Grow/Shrink** as shown in the following screenshot. Select the behavior and notice that in the mini-Timeline, it's the same length as your still (in this case 10 seconds). We can always trim behaviors to be whatever length we want them to be.

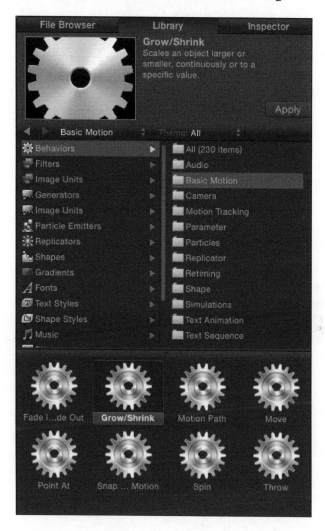

2. Navigate to **Window | Show HUD**. In the HUD, you'll see a square. Grab one of the corners and drag it outward. Notice that only one side gets scaled up as shown in the following screenshot. Press the Space bar to play back the animation. We can also see that the picture does not scale up uniformly. Press the *Command + Z* shortcut to undo.

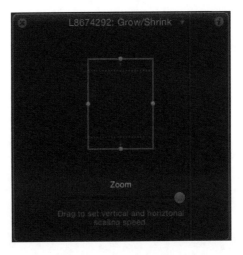

3. Let the project continue to play while you make the next change. Drag any of the corners and drag outward to scale up. Notice how the photo animation moves quicker the more you drag out. Now drag the square inward until it is inside the smaller square as shown in the following screenshot. Notice in the Canvas how the photo scales down. The further you drag in, the faster it scales down. Isn't it amazing how we've managed to do this all in real time!

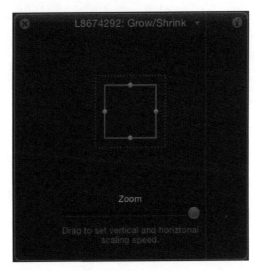

4. With the **Grow/Shrink** behavior selected in the **Layers** tab, press the *F2* key to go to the **Behaviors** tab of the **Inspector**. You also have the option of dragging the scale slider. A negative number shrinks the picture, and a positive number makes it grow. Let's add another behavior to the clip. The **Library** is a good place to get familiar with material because you may have noticed that when you click on an object a preview of it plays in the top-left corner. But just like FCP X, in Motion there are a ton of ways to do the same thing.

5. Make sure the still layer is selected. Just beneath the mini-Timeline on the right-hand side, you'll see a gear icon. This is another area we can find behaviors and add them to clips. Click on it and navigate to **Basic Motion | Fade In/Fade Out**. In the HUD, notice how it comes with a 20-frame Fade In at the beginning and Fade Out at the end of the clip. Increase the Fade In by dragging the triangle to the right-hand side. Make it 30. Decrease the Fade Out to 10. Press the Space bar to play back your project if you stopped it.

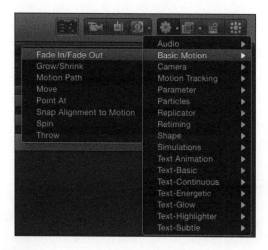

There's more...

We can cycle through various effects on a layer by pressing the *D* key.

The D key

In older versions of Motion, the **Heads Up Display** (**HUD**) used to be called the Dashboard. If you have a lot of behaviors on a clip, with your HUD displaying, you can hit the *D* key to cycle through all the behaviors without having to click on them.

Real-time playback

One of Motion's greatest perks is your ability to adjust behaviors and animations while playing back your project. Just like editing, where it's best to make editing decisions while playing back your project, animation works the same way! You can see if your project is maintaining real-time playback by looking in the upper-left corner of the Canvas. Just keep in mind the minute we start adding several filters and behaviors, this will slow everything down and you'll need to create a RAM preview.

FPS: 30

See also

► The *Customizing a Motion Path* recipe
► The *Spinning and throwing a ball* recipe

Customizing a Motion Path

The Motion Path behavior is very versatile. It creates a path for an object to travel along and is customizable.

How to do it...

1. Let's launch Motion and create a new Motion project with a **Preset** of **Broadcast 1080p**. Set **Duration** to 6 seconds.

2. Press the *Command + 2* shortcut to go to the **Library**. Go to **Particle Emitters** and select the **Pulsing Laser Star** as shown in the following screenshot. Click on **Apply**.

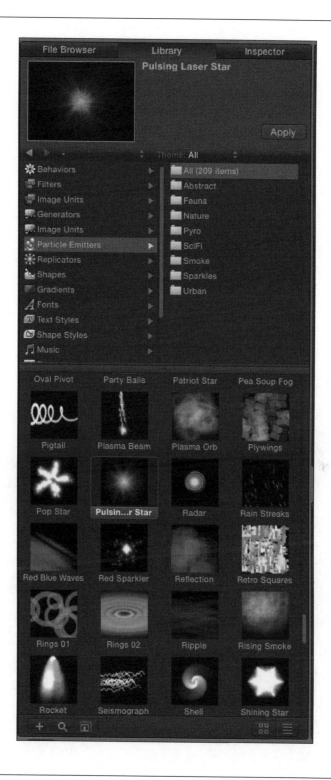

3. Press the Space bar to play back your project. It's a simple star that twinkles in the middle of your Canvas. We're going to make it travel along a path. Click the gear icon on the bottom-right corner of the Canvas and choose **Motion Path** under **Basic Motion** as shown in the following screenshot. Press the *F7* key to show the HUD if it's not already displayed.

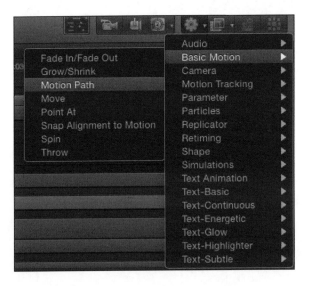

4. Zoom out on your Canvas by pressing the *Command + -* shortcut. Notice that with the **Motion Path** behavior selected, you can see a line in the Canvas that has two points; one point is in the center and the other is off-screen to the right-hand side. Press the Space bar to play back the project. Notice that the star travels from left to right.

5. In the HUD, change the value of **Direction** from **Forward** to **Reverse**. Make sure the project is still playing back. Drag the point offscreen to the lower-right corner of the Canvas and the middle point to the upper-left corner, as shown in the following screenshot:

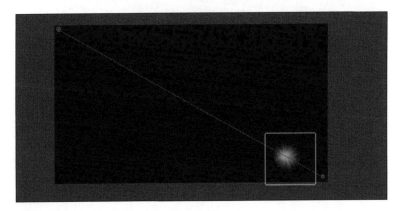

6. While still playing back, change the value of **Speed** from **Constant** to **Ease Both**. The star now slowly goes out of the first point and then slows down when entering the second point.

7. Change the value of **Loops** to **3** and the **End Condition** to **Ping-Pong**. Press the *Shift + z* shortcut to make your Canvas fit in the window.

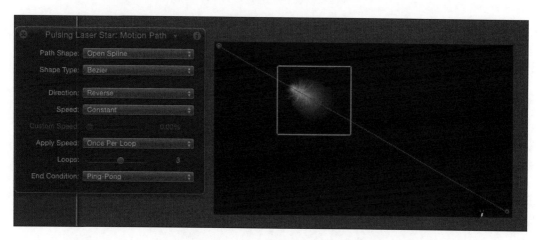

8. Double-click on the line once you are close to the first point and the end point. Two more points are added. Click on one of the newly created points and notice handles appear that will allow you to make a curved shape path. Drag the handles on each of the new points to make your own curved path. Click on any point and drag it across the line to change its position. *Option* + click a handle on any point to break them apart and customize you shape even more. Use the following screenshot for reference:

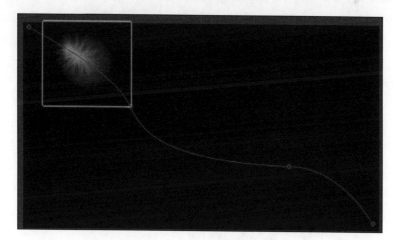

9. As a final step, change the value of **Path Shape** to **Rectangle**. Choose a few more path shapes to familiarize yourself with the options available to you. Customize the additional settings as you see fit.

There's more...

There's a lot of flexibility in Motion's behaviors to use custom shapes to create animation.

Using Geometry under Path Shapes

If you choose **Geometry** under **Path Shape** in the **Motion Path** behavior, you are asked to give it a source to use for your object to travel along. In **Library** under **Shapes**, there are 16 shapes you can use as the source as indicated in the following screenshot. Simply apply them to your project and then drag the shape in the source well for the path shape.

The Snap Alignment to Motion behavior

The **Snap Alignment to Motion** behavior is a great complement to Motion Path. Sometimes when you have objects following along a path, you want it to turn with the path. Take a look at the following screenshot. I added a text layer and used one of the characters from the Webdings font. I adjusted the path to make it curved and then applied the **Snap Alignment to Motion** behavior from **Basic Motion**.

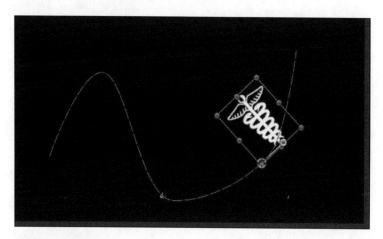

See also

▸ The *Applying a Fade In/Fade Out and Grow/Shrink behavior to a still* recipe

▸ The *Spinning and throwing a ball* recipe

Spinning and throwing a ball

This recipe continues our exploration of Motion behaviors.

How to do it...

1. Double-click to open the 03_03 project. This project consists of an **AquaBall** still image. This is taken right from Motion's **Library**.

2. With the **AquaBall** selected, go to the gear icon and choose **Throw** from under **Basic Motion** as shown in the following screenshot. Press the *F7* key to reveal the HUD.

3. Press the Space bar to play back the project. Nothing happens. In the HUD, we need to determine where we want the ball to go. Click and drag the center cross hair to the right-hand side until you see an arrow. Drag it till it touches the outermost edge of the circle. If the circle isn't moving fast enough to go offscreen, drag the zoom parameter to the right and than drag the arrow further to the right as shown in the following screenshot:

4. Stop the playback. Make sure you're on the first frame of your project. Decrease the Canvas size by pressing the *Command + -* shortcut. Select **AquaBall** in the Canvas and drag it until it's offscreen to the left-hand side. The ball now travels from offscreen left to offscreen right. If it's not, select the **Throw** behavior and try adjusting the zoom value in the HUD followed by the arrow.

5. Click on the **i** icon to go to the **Inspector**. Click on the disclosure triangle next to **Throw Velocity**. Adjust the x value to **250**. Press the Space bar to play back.

6. Let's reset the **Throw** behavior and throw the ball so it looks like it's falling away from us. Click the hooked arrow on the top-right corner of the **Behaviors** tab as shown in the following screenshot. Click on the **Properties** tab and set **Position** to 0, 0 and **Scale** to 400.

7. In the HUD, change the **2D** tab to **3D**. Click and drag in the center to get an arrow. Drag the arrow so that it faces away from you, as shown in the following screenshot:

8. In the **Inspector**, change the value of **Throw Velocity** of **z** to **-3000**. Play back your project. The ball is now thrown back in space. With the ball selected, in the **Layers** tab, go to the gear icon and choose **Spin** from **Basic Motion**. Press the *F2* key to go to the **Behaviors** tab. Under **Spin**, change the **Axis** to **y** and set the **Spin Rate** to 9 degrees. Finally, adjust the middle circle in the HUD display as you see fit. Pay attention to the changes that take place in the **Behaviors** tab, as shown in the following screenshot:

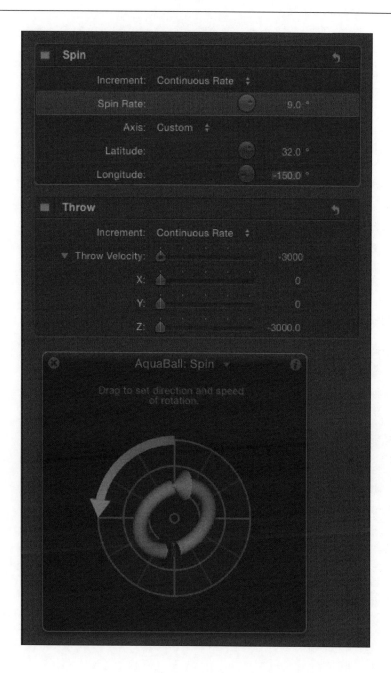

There's more...

The **Throw** behavior is a great introduction to the complex and never-ending world of 3D in Motion!

Z space and 3D

Through our simple change on **Throw Velocity**, we have started with the most basic introductions to the world of 3D. While x is left and right and y is up and down, z denotes depth. The further back an item is, the smaller the number it will be on z. That's why when we threw our ball -3000 pixels back it became really small.

See also

▸   This *Applying a Fade In/Fade Out and Grow/Shrink behavior to a still* recipe

▸   This *Customizing a Motion Path* recipe

Adding an Attractor and Attracted To behavior

Goodbye Basic Motion and hello Simulations! While Basic Motion behaviors are some of the most commonly used animation tools, we may also want to simulate real-life movement even further. That's where simulation behaviors come in. Gravity, Wind, Edge Collisions, and more are here to help give your projects that extra magic touch.

How to do it...

1.   Double-click to open the `03_04_Attractor` project.

2.   This project consists of one large arrow and six small ones. Press the Space bar to play back the project. You'll see that the large arrow moves from the top-left corner of the screen to the bottom-right corner. Stop and move back to the first frame of the project.

3.   Select the **Small Arrows** group and press the *Command + -* shortcut to zoom out on the Canvas to around 20 percent. You should be able to see the bounding box for the group as shown in the following screenshot, but by default, you can't see any of your objects offscreen:

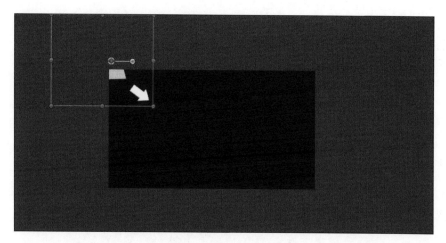

4. Navigate to **View | Show Full View Area**. You should now be able to see those missing arrows as seen in the following screenshot:

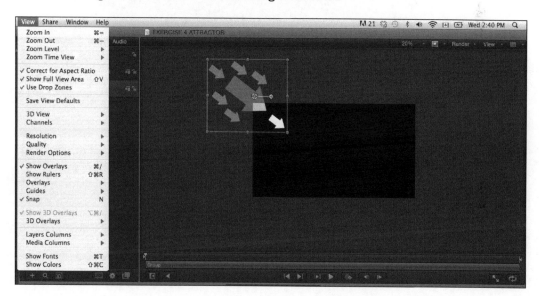

5. We want these small arrows to follow along with the big one. We're going to apply an Attractor behavior to the big arrow. Select the **BIG ARROW** group. Go to the gear icon just under the Canvas and choose **Attractor** under **Simulations**.

6. Play back the project again. Only two arrows seem to move; the arrow inside the **BIG ARROW** group and the small arrow in front of it. Stop the playback. Select the **Attractor** behavior and press the *F2* key to go the **Behaviors** tab. Increase the **Strength** to **100** and **Influence** to **2000**. Now the small arrows follow the big arrow, but the entire animation is springing back and forth.

7. If you look closely in the Canvas with the **Attractor** behavior selected, you can see that the path the group travels along is still the same. Since we've added the behavior to the group and not the **YELLOW ARROW** layer, it's also influenced by the behavior. In the Layers tab, drag the behavior from the group to the **YELLOW ARROW** layer.

8. Start the playback. Now the small arrows have stopped moving. In the **Behaviors** tab, change the the value of **Affect** from **Related Objects** to **All Objects**. The yellow arrow attracts the smaller ones as shown in the following screenshot. Adjust the other settings to get a feel for the parameters. When finished, navigate to **File | Open** and open the `04_04_Attracted_to` project from the exercise folder for this chapter.

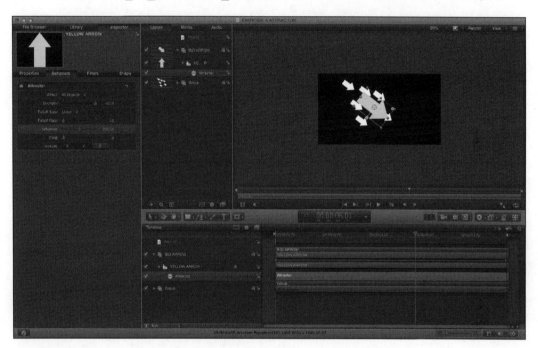

9. Press the Space bar to play the project. This project contains six ants; five small ones and a big one that has been animated using a **Motion Path** and the **Snap Alignment to Motion** behavior. We want the small ants to start offscreen and start following the big one at 1 second and 15 frames until the end of the project. Let's add an **Attracted To** behavior to the small ants to simulate this motion. First, stop the playback and drag the **ANT CHILDREN** group offscreen to the left. Hold down the *Shift* key to constrain the movement. Since the group won't start until later, let's trim the layers' in-point. Drag the in-point of the group in the mini-Timeline to 1 second and 15 frames as shown in the following screenshot:

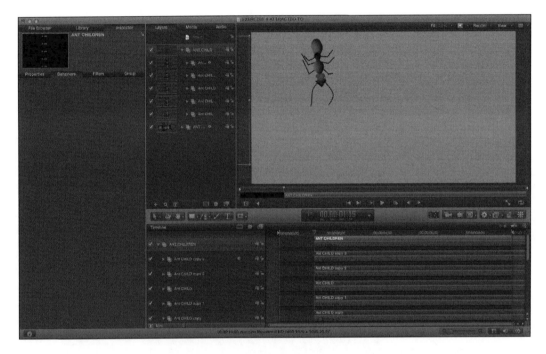

10. With the **ANT CHILDREN** group still selected, go to the gear icon and navigate to **Simulations | Attracted To**. Press the *F7* key to show the HUD.

11. You'll see that the **Object** well in the HUD is set to **None**. We need to feed it a source. Drag the **ANT KING** group into the source well, wait for the hooked arrow and release your mouse. Use the following screenshot for reference. Press the Space bar to play back. Navigate to **View | Show Full View Area** if you can't see the ants offscreen. They're staying still.

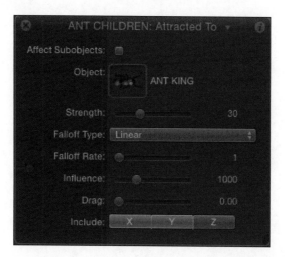

12. Press the Space bar to stop. Increase the **Influence** slider to **1500**. If you're having trouble adjusting the value in the HUD, go to the **Behaviors** tab. Play back the project again.

13. Increase the **Strength** to **60**, **Falloff Rate** to **2**, **Influence** to **6000**, and **Drag** to **1**. These parameters "push and pull" against each other, controlling how much and little influence the attracted object has on them.

14. Now the **ANT CHILDREN** group still doesn't turn with the motion path. Let's change that by adding **Snap to Alignment** behaviors to each one of them. Click on the disclosure triangle for the **ANT CHILDREN** group and select **Ant Child 1**. Go to the gear icon and select **Snap Alignment to Motion** from **Basic Motion**.

15. In the HUD, change the axis from **Horizontal** to **Vertical**. Select the behavior and press the *Command + C* shortcut to copy it. Select the remaining **ANT CHILDREN** and press *Command + V* to paste the modified behavior as shown in the following screenshot:

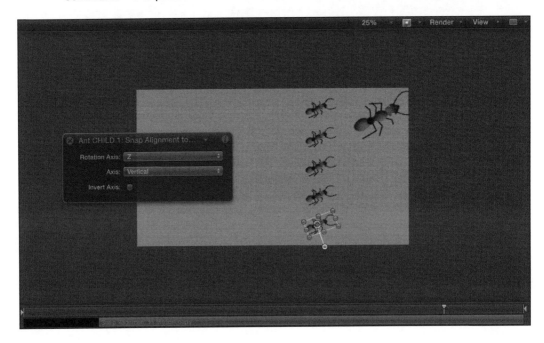

Simulation behaviors are very render intensive. It's best practice to stop the playback before trying to tweak them.

Stop the playback when tweaking Simulation behaviors

While it was easy to adjust Basic Motion behaviors and play them back in real time, simulations are render-intensive. It's a good habit to stop the playback and tweak your settings to avoid any small hiccups that Motion could encounter in trying to calculate all that data!

See also

▶ The *Adding Edge Collision and Gravity behaviors to a ball* recipe

▶ The *Creating Random Motion using the Randomize behavior* recipe

▶ The *Stop, Wriggle, Rate, and Quantize* recipe

▶ The *Using the Link behavior* recipe

Adding Edge Collision and Gravity behaviors to a ball

Combining simulation behaviors can create some complex animation. Let's take a look at how we can make a ball bounce around our Canvas.

How to do it...

1. Double-click to open the 03_05 project.

2. Press the Space bar to start the playback. This project consists of a 3D ball being tossed across the screen using the **Throw** behavior. Click on the disclosure triangle for the group to reveal its content. You can see the behavior along with the filters used to colorize the object. Let's add a little gravity to the ball so that it falls down.

3. Go to the gear icon just under the Canvas and choose **Gravity** from under **Simulations**. The **Throw** behavior is affected by gravity and the ball now falls down.

4. Press the *F7* key to reveal the HUD. Increase the **Acceleration** to a value of **100**. Notice how the ball falls down quicker as shown in the following screenshot:

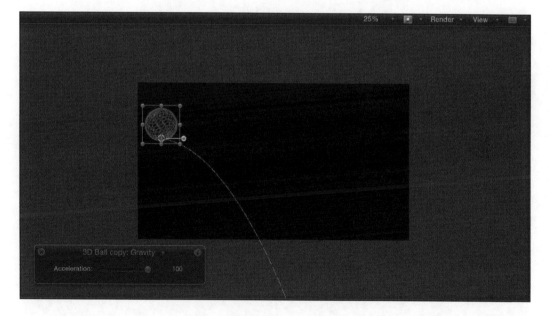

5. Press the *D* key a few times to cycle to the **Throw** behavior in the HUD and drag the arrow to the right-hand side to increase the throw velocity. Since the ball is being thrown more aggressively, gravity has a different effect. Experiment with different values for the **Throw Velocity** and **Gravity Acceleration**. Press the *F2* key to go to the **Behaviors** tab of the **Inspector**.

6. In the **Behaviors** tab, change the value of **Gravity Acceleration** to **2000** and under **Throw Change**, the **Throw Velocity** on **X** and **Y** to **1000**.

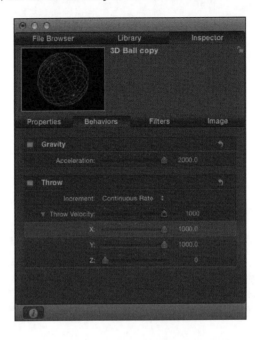

7. Select the 3D ball in the **Layers** tab. Go to the gear icon just under the Canvas and choose **Edge Collision** from under **Simulations**. Use the following screenshot for reference:

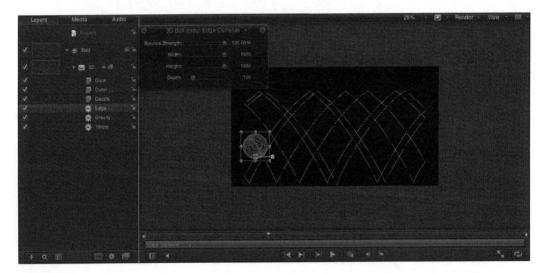

8. By default, the edges are set to the width of your project. In this case, it's 1920 by 1080. Play back your animation by pressing the Space bar and notice that as soon as the ball comes close to the edge, it will bounce away from it.

9. In the HUD, bring down the **Bounce Strength** to **50** and see how the ball slowly loses its bounce each time it hits the edges. Bring the **Bounce Value** up to **100**.

10. If the ball appears to not quite hit the edge, try increasing the height and width slightly. For **Width**, I used **2020** and for **Height**, **1180**. Use the following screenshot for reference:

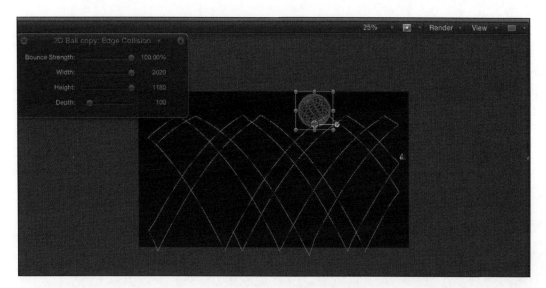

11. As a final step, select the 3D ball in the **Layers** tab. Go to the gear icon just under the Canvas and navigate to **Simulations | Align to Motion (Simulations)**. Notice how the ball rotates when it moves. Decrease the **Spring Tension** in the HUD to **50**. Try playing around with the other behavior settings to see the different results you can get.

See also

▶ The *Adding an Attractor and Attracted To behavior* recipe

▶ The *Creating Random Motion using the Randomize behavior* recipe

▶ The *Stop, Wriggle, Rate, and Quantize* recipe

▶ The *Using the Link behavior* recipe

Creating Random Motion using the Randomize behavior

Random Motion allows us to add a little variation to our projects. In fact, using **Randomize** under **Parameter** behaviors allows us to target a specific value. Let's see how this differs with a **Random Motion** behavior.

How to do it...

1. Double-click to open `03_06` from the exercise folder for this chapter.

2. Press the Space bar to play back the animation. It's three circular shapes being thrown across the screen. We're going to add a random simulation behavior to them. Stop the playback. In the **Layers** tab, select the **Purple**, **Blue**, and **Yellow** circles as shown in the following screenshot. Go to the gear icon just under the Canvas and choose **Random Motion** under **Simulations**.

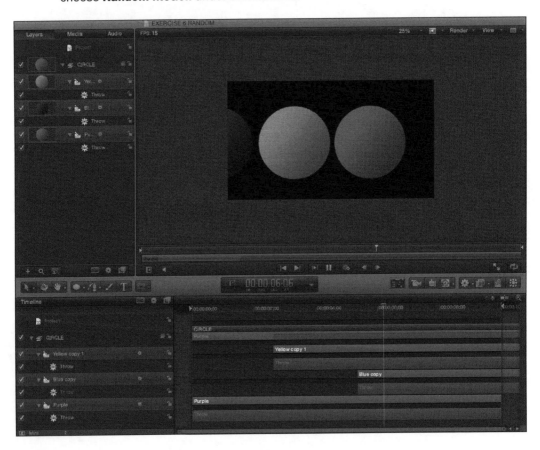

3. Play back the animation. You may notice that each of your circles has a subtle bit of randomization to it. To make the circles appear as if they are growing and shrinking, we're going to have the **Random Motion** behavior affect the z position. Select all three of the Random Motion behaviors by *Command* + clicking them, and then click on **Z** in the HUD to include it, as shown in the following screenshot:

4. Let's change the frequency and amount on each of the circles to different values so we can get a sense for how they affect our objects. On the **Blue** circle, select the **Random Motion** behavior. Press the *F2* key to go to the **Behaviors** tab. Set the **Frequency** to **1000** and the **Amount** to **200**.

5. On the **Purple** circle, select the **Random Motion** behavior. In the **Behaviors** tab, set the **Frequency** to **100** and the **Amount** to **600**.

6. On the **Yellow** circle, select the **Random Motion** behavior. In the **Behaviors** tab, set the **Frequency** to **1200** and the **Amount** to **500**. Play back the animation.

7. To get a closer look at what's happening with the **Purple** circle selected, go to the **Properties** tab by pressing the *F1* key. You'll see that the **Position** parameter is being controlled by the behavior. We can see this because of the gear icon to the right-hand side of the parameter, as shown in the following screenshot. The values randomize over time. The higher the frequency, the more often it changes; the higher the amount, the greater it changes.

8. Select all three of the **Random Motion** behaviors and press the *Delete* key to remove them from the circles.

9. So far, when we've added behaviors, there's been no say over which parameters are affected. Simply, we add the behavior to the object and change the settings. The beauty of parameter behaviors is that we can target which parameter we want. Let's say we want to randomize the position of our circle more frequently. With the **Purple** circle still selected in the **Properties** tab, *Ctrl* + click on the word **Position**. Navigate to **Add Parameter Behavior | Randomize** as shown in the following screenshot:

10. In the **Behaviors** tab, bring up the **Amount** to **30**, change the value of **Apply Mode** to **Add and Subtract** and change the value of **Frequency** to **20**, as shown in the following screenshot:

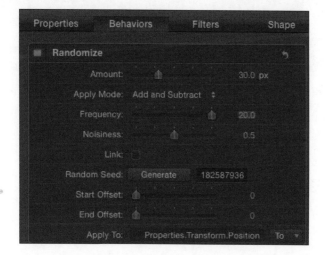

11. The **Add and Subtract** apply mode looks at your position and adds to or takes away from that number based on the amount you've specified. Try applying different random behavior parameter settings by adding the behavior to the other two circles' positions using the preceding method.

There's more...

Motion offers you a few ways to add parameter behaviors. Let's explore why adding them in the **Inspector** may be the most beneficial way.

Parameter behaviors are best added in the Properties tab

Parameter behaviors are the only behaviors we can add by *Ctrl* + clicking on the chosen parameter in the **Properties** tab. Like other behaviors, we can also add parameter behaviors to objects by going to the gear icon or from the **Library**. The problem with these two methods is we need to do an additional step because we haven't yet targeted a specific parameter. All we've targeted is the object that will be affected. When using the **Library** or gear icon, make sure to select the parameter you want to affect in the **Apply To** field in the **Properties** tab, as shown in the following screenshot:

See also

- ► The *Adding an Attractor and Attracted To behavior* recipe
- ► The *Adding Edge Collision and Gravity behaviors to a ball* recipe
- ► The *Stop, Wriggle, Rate, and Quantize* recipe
- ► The *Using the Link behavior* recipe

Stop, Wriggle, Rate, and Quantize

Now that we've been introduced to our first parameter behavior in *Chapter 2, Looking at Motion's Library*, let's look at a few more and see what they can do.

How to do it...

1. Open 03_06 from the exercise folder for this chapter.

2. Press the Space bar to play back the animation. It's four arrows travelling from left to right across the screen. We're going to add a different parameter behavior to all three and see the effects. Stop the playback. Move the playhead to the 5-second mark in the mini-Timeline. In the **Layers** tab, select the **S** layer. Press the *F1* key to go to the **Properties** tab. *Ctrl* + click on the word **Position**. Navigate to **Add Parameter Behavior | Stop**. Start the playback. The arrow stops dead in its tracks at 5 seconds and remains there till the end of the animation.

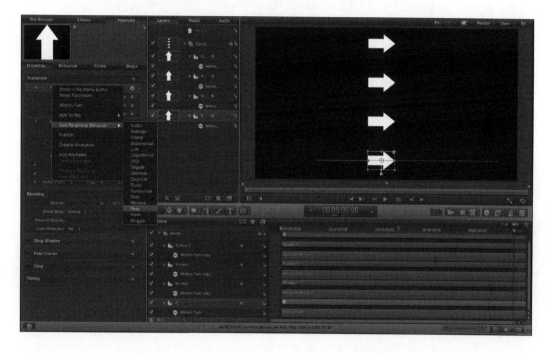

3. Select the **W** layer. Press the *F1* key to go to the **Properties** tab. *Ctrl* + click on the word **Position** and navigate to **Add Parameter Behavior | Wriggle**.

4. Click on the **Behaviors** tab in the **Inspector**. Change the value of **Amount** to **50**, the **Apply Mode** to **Add and Subtract**, and the **Frequency** to **0.5**. **Wriggle** is very similar to the **Randomize** behavior as shown in the following screenshot. It wiggles the arrow on its position coordinates by adding and subtracting to its original position value. Play back the animation.

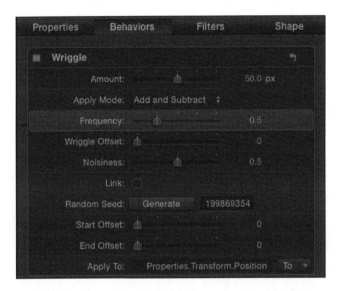

5. Select the **R** layer. Press the *F1* key to go to the **Properties** tab. *Ctrl* + click on the word **Position** and navigate to **Add Parameter Behavior | Rate**.

6. Click on the **Behaviors** tab in the **Inspector**. Change the value of **Rate** to **20**. Notice how the path the arrow travels along moves slightly quicker as well as projects upward. Press the *Command + Z* shortcut a few times until the **Rate** behavior is removed. Again, press the *F1* key to go to the **Properties** tab. *Ctrl* + click on the letter **X** under **Position** and navigate to **Add Parameter Behavior | Rate**.

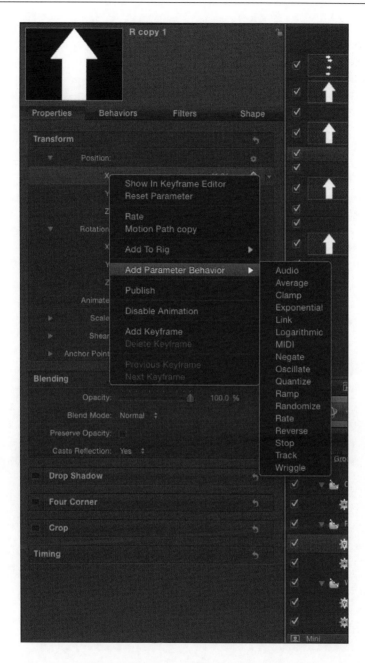

7. Change the value of **Rate** to **20**. Start the playback. Notice how when we only select **X** the rate only affects the speed of travel to the left and right.

8. In the **Layers** tab, select the **Q** layer. Press the *F1* key to go to the **Properties** tab. *Ctrl* + click on the word **Position**. Navigate to **Add Parameter Behavior | Quantize**.

9. Click on the **Behaviors** tab in the **Inspector**. Increase the **Step Size** to **100**. Notice that the arrow seems to jump from point to point rather than follow a smooth path of travel.

10. Select the **S** layer and navigate to **Object Menu | Solo**. Continue this for each layer to get a sense for the animation by itself as you play back. Change the values for each parameter behavior to get a sense for how they work.

Wriggle is one of my favorite parameter behaviors.

There's a lot to the Wriggle behavior

The **Wriggle** behavior is great not only for making changes to position, but also for a whole lot of other parameters too. One of my favorite things to do when working in 3D is add a light to a scene and add a **Wriggle** behavior to the intensity value so the light appears to be flickering. Take a look in the `03_07_Bonus` project in the exercise folder for this chapter. I added a **Wriggle** parameter behavior to the intensity and color values of **Light**.

See also

▶ The *Adding an Attractor and Attracted To behavior* recipe

▶ The *Adding Edge Collision and Gravity behaviors to a ball* recipe

▶ The *Creating Random Motion using the Randomize behavior* recipe

▶ The *Using the Link behavior* recipe

Using the Link behavior

The Link behavior allows you to link the parameter values of one object to another. Let's take a look at two examples for how the link behavior can be used to aid us in our workflow.

How to do it...

1. Under the exercise files of this chapter, open the `03_08` project by double-clicking on it.

2. This project consists of three layers. The background map that is scaling up uses a **Grow/Shrink** behavior. The two compasses remain static in the foreground.

3. We want both compasses to rotate by the same values as the project plays. Select **Compass 02** in the **Layers** tab and press the *F1* key to go to the **Properties** tab.

   Ctrl + click the word **Rotation** and navigate to **Add Parameter Behavior | Link** as shown in the following screenshot. Press the *F7* key to show the HUD.

4. The **Link** behavior in the **Layers** tab is turned off. This is because it needs a source to link to. Click-and-drag **Compass 01** and drop it into the **Source Object** well in the HUD. Once it's added, you will see a picture of the compass in the well and the **Link** behavior will turn on, as shown in the following screenshot:

5. The next task is to tell the behavior which parameter to link to. Since we *Ctrl* + clicked on the word **Rotation**, Motion assumes that you want to link the rotation of the source object to the rotation of the target object (the one you added the behavior to). To see how they're connected, select the **Compass 01** layer and click on the gear icon under the Canvas. Navigate to **Basic Motion | Spin**.

6. In the HUD, drag the arrow on the outer circle to about 11 o'clock as shown in the following screenshot:

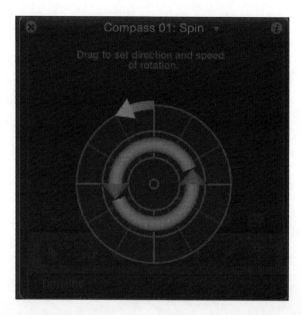

7. Press the Space bar to play back the animation. Notice how both the compasses now rotate by the same amount. Let's say we wanted to have **Compass 02** rotate the other way and by a slightly higher amount.

8. Select the **Link** behavior in the **Layers** tab and press the *F2* key to go to the **Behaviors** tab. Double-click on the number next to **Scale** and enter -2. The compass now spins in the opposite direction twice as fast.

9. Let's look at another example where we can apply the **Link** behavior to text objects. Essentially, what we want is for one text object to scale up and the other text object to scale down. Save your current project by pressing the *Command* + S shortcut. Navigate to **File | Open** and navigate to the exercise folder of this chapter and choose the 03_08_Link_Scale project.

10. Press the Space bar to play back the animation. There are two text objects in the **Layers** tab. One scales up and down over time and the other stays stagnant on the screen. We want the still text layer to move in the opposite direction.

11. While you may think **Scale** is the parameter to link, it's not. Let's try it anyway. Select the **I Get Small** layer and press the *F1* key to go to the **Properties** tab of the **Inspector**. *Ctrl* + click the word **Scale** and navigate to **Add Parameter Behavior | Link**. Press the *F7* key to show the HUD if it's not displayed.

12. Click-and-drag the **As I Get Big** text to the **Source Object** well in the HUD. Release your mouse when you see the hooked arrow.

13. Press the **i** icon in the HUD to go to the **Behaviors** tab of the **Inspector**. Double-click on the **Scale** field number and type -1. For **Scale**, a negative number flips the object, as shown in the following screenshot. In order to have the **I Get Small** text scale in the opposite direction, we're going to link the **Z** position parameters of the two text objects. Think of **Z** as depth. A negative number is further back in the Canvas and a positive number is closer.

14. In the HUD, click on **Target Parameters** and navigate to **Properties | Transform | Position | Z** as shown in the following screenshot. Repeat this step for **Compatible Parameters**. Press the Space bar to play back the project. Your **I Get Small** text now scales in the opposite direction from the **As I Get Big** text. Set the **Scale** to -1 if needed.

See also

▸ The *Adding an Attractor and Attracted To behavior* recipe

▸ The *Adding Edge Collision and Gravity behaviors to a ball* recipe

▸ The *Creating Random Motion using the Randomize behavior* recipe

▸ The *Stop, Wriggle, Rate, and Quantize* recipe

An intro to Text behaviors

So far, the behaviors we've added in Motion have had no restrictions. It means we can apply them to any movie, still, PSD file, or Text object, and it will work. The next few behaviors we'll be exploring are restrictive, meaning you can only apply them to particular objects. For instance, particle behaviors can be applied to particles and text behaviors can only be applied to text. While there's an entire chapter dedicated to text, here's a sneak peak at animating text with behaviors.

How to do it...

1. From the exercise files of this chapter, open the 03_09 project by double-clicking on it.

2. Press the Space bar to play back the project. It's a simple text object with a lightly-animated gradient background from the **Library**. Let's animate this layer in and out using some blur behaviors.

3. Go to the gear icon under the Canvas and navigate to **Text Basic | Blur In**.

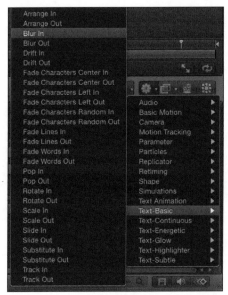

Selecting a text behavior from the behavior icon underneath the Canvas

4. Play back the animation. The text blurs in. With the **Blur In** behavior selected in the **Layers** tab, notice in the mini-Timeline that the behavior is 1 second and 10 frames long. Unlike the majority of behaviors we've added in previous exercises, a lot of text behaviors are simply meant to bring your text in and out of the screen, so they are much shorter in length.

5. Let's have our text blur offscreen as well. Select the text again and click on the gear icon underneath the Canvas. Navigate to **Text Basic | Blur Out**.

6. Play back the animation. Notice how the text animation blurs in and then blurs out at the same time. By default, text behaviors start at the beginning of the text layer. All we need to do is move the behavior. Select the **Blur Out** behavior. In the mini-Timeline, move your playhead to the last frame of the project. Press the *Shift +]* shortcut to move the out-point of the **Blur Out** behavior to where your playhead is, as shown in the following screenshot:

7. Let's add one behavior that will animate your text for the entire project length. Press the *Command + 2* shortcut to go to the **Library** and navigate to **Behaviors | Text Sequence**. Double-click on the **Text-Continuous** folder as shown in the following screenshot. Drag the **Quiver** behavior to the text in the **Layers** tab. Play back the project. Press the *F2* key to go to the **Behaviors** tab and change some of the values under the **Randomize Sequence** section to your liking. Play back the project again.

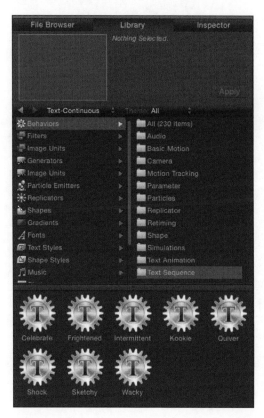

There's more...

All the text behaviors you see in Motion come from one behavior!

It all began with Sequence Text

There are a lot of text behaviors in Motion but the funny thing is one behavior created them all. Under the **Text Animation** category, there is a behavior called **Sequence Text**. This behavior will allow you to recreate any animation from Motion's text behaviors.

You can get a good grasp of all the text behaviors by previewing them in the **Library**.

Don't forget the Library to preview your animations

Can you see the word for a text behavior and don't know what it does? Go to the **Library** and preview the animation in the upper-left corner by selecting it, as shown in the following screenshot:

See also

▶ *Adding and trimming multiple text behaviors in Chapter 5, Let's Make Text*

▶ *Saving your favorite text animations and styles in Chapter 5, Let's Make Text*

Writing on your shape's outline

Motion gives you the ability to draw and erase shape outlines easily. Maybe you want to draw on an animated line over a map to animate the path of travel. Let's see how we can use this.

How to do it...

1. From the exercise files of this chapter, open the `03_10` project by double-clicking on it.

2. The project consists of a simple circle and square. Let's apply a **Shape** behavior to draw these objects on the screen. Select the **Rectangle** layer and click on the gear icon under the Canvas. Navigate to **Shape | Write On** as shown in the following screenshot:

3. Nothing happens. That's because the **Write On** behavior will only work on the outline, not the fill of a shape. Press the *F4* key to go to the **Shape** tab of the **Inspector**. Under the **Style** pane, turn off **Fill** and turn on **Outline** as shown in the following screenshot. Play back the animation.

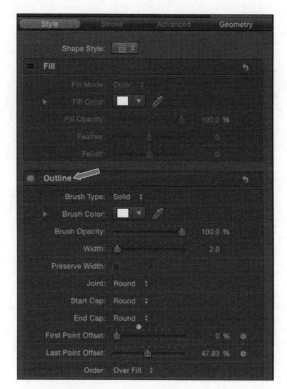

4. The **Rectangle** layer is drawn onscreen over the length of the project. Stop the playback. Select the **Write On** behavior in the **Layers** tab and move your playhead to 2 seconds in the mini-Timeline. Press the *O* key to trim the out-point of the behavior. Play back the animation and notice the outline being drawn over 2 seconds.

5. Let's spice up the look of the outline. Select the **Rectangle** layer and press the *F7* key to bring up the HUD. Click on the icon next to **Shape Styles** and select **Frost Heavy** from under **Garnish** as shown in the following screenshot. Increase the **Width** of the outline to 16.

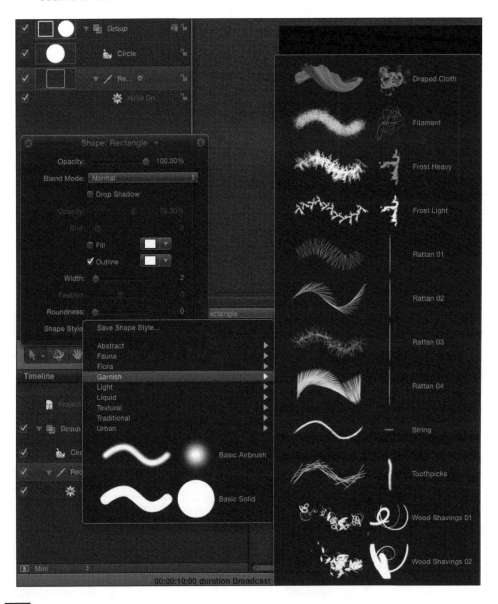

The outline is now a **Frost Heavy** texture as shown in the following screenshot. Your system may slow down if you try to play back. If it does, press the *Command + R* shortcut to create a RAM preview.

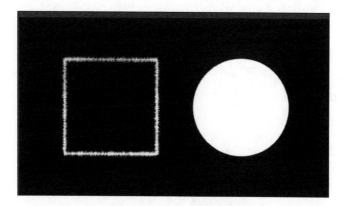

6. Let's add another **Write On** behavior to the **Circle**. Rather than selecting the behavior from the gear icon, *Option* + click on the existing **Write On** behavior from the **Rectangle** and drag it to the **Circle** in the **Layers** tab.

7. Select the **Circle**, and in the HUD, turn off **Fill** and turn on **Outline**. Increase the **Length** to 16 and the **Roundness** to 20. Click on the icon next to **Shape Style** and choose **Frost Light** from under **Garnish**.

8. Select the **Write On** behavior under the **Circle** and change the value of **Shape Outline** to **Draw and Erase**, the **Direction** to **Reverse**, and the **Speed** to **Ease Both**. Move to 5 seconds on the mini-Timeline and press the *O* key to trim the behavior's out-point. Use the following screenshot for reference:

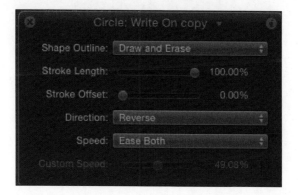

9. Press the *Command + R* shortcut to create a RAM preview and then the Space bar to play back the animation. The circle draws on and erases off over a span of 5 seconds.

See also

▶ *The relationship between shapes and Paint* in *Chapter 6, Paint and Masks*

▶ *Using shape masks* in *Chapter 6, Paint and Masks*

Creating constant and variable speed changes

Final Cut Pro X allows you to make speed changes by simply clicking on a clip and going to the **Retime** menu as shown in the following screenshot. In Motion, applying speed changes is similar, but rather than a **Retime** menu, we have the **Behavior** menu to which we apply a speed behavior to the full clip or a portion of a clip.

Getting ready

Locate a clip you would like to adjust the look of on your computer by adding some speed adjustments to it. Launch Motion. Select a Motion project with settings suitable for your footage. Choose **Open**. Use the *Command + 1* shortcut to go to the **File Browser**. Navigate to your footage and import it into your project.

How to do it...

1. Select the clip in the **Layers** tab and go to your gear icon underneath the Canvas. Choose **Set Speed** from under **Retiming** as shown in the following screenshot:

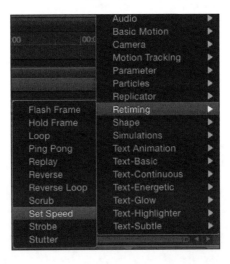

2. Press the *F7* key to show the HUD. The clip has already been slowed down to 50%. 100% represents the actual speed of a clip. To speed it up, set the **Speed** to **300%**. If you're having trouble getting to the exact percentage, *Option* + click to the right or left of the scroll wheel to move one increment at a time. Play back your project.

3. Let's say that we wanted the clip to play faster at the beginning of the clip, slow down for a pivotal moment, then play back at normal speed. To achieve this, we're going to use three speed behaviors. First, trim back the out-point of your first behavior just before you want to slow it down by dragging it.

4. *Option* + click and drag the behavior in the **Layers** tab to make a copy.

5. Name the first behavior as `Fast` and the second one as `Slow`. Select the **Fast** behavior and move to its out-point by using the *Shift + O* shortcut. Select the **Slow** behavior and use the *Shift + [* shortcut to move its in-point to the playhead.

6. In the HUD, change the value of **Speed** to **20**. Drag the out-point of the behavior to encompass the whole action you're trying to slow down. Increase the **Ease In** and **Ease Out** time to **30**.

7. Select the **Fast** behavior and press *Command + C* to copy it and *Command + V* to paste it. Move it down in the Timeline right after the **Slow** behavior finishes. Select the **Fast Copy** behavior and move it to the end of the Timeline and press the *O* key to trim the out-point to the playhead. Play back your animation.

See also

▶   The *Holding and looping your animations* recipe

Holding and looping your animations

Sometimes you may just want a video clip to repeat itself over and over again. At other times, you may need to hold the end frame of a clip or an action in the middle of the clip. We can use the **Retiming** behavior to achieve these desired results.

Getting ready

Locate a clip you would like to adjust the look of on your computer. Launch Motion. Select a Motion project with settings suitable for your footage. Choose **Open**. Press *Command + 1* to go to the **File Browser**. Navigate to your footage and import it into your project. Play back your project. Find a frame you want to hold and move to that frame.

How to do it...

1. Select the clip in the **Layers** tab and go to your gear icon underneath the Canvas. Choose **Hold** from under **Retiming**.

2. Play back your project. The **Hold Frame** behavior gets added right where your playhead is and lasts to the end of your project. Let's make it only 1 second. Select the **Hold Frame** behavior and use the *Shift + I* shortcut to move to the in-point of the behavior.

3. Press *Shift + Command + A* to deselect everything and press *Shift + = + 1 + .* to move your playhead 1 second forward. Select the **Hold Frame** behavior and press the *O* key to trim its out-point to your playhead as shown in the following screenshot:

4. Let's try to loop the video clip we have three times. First, select your **Hold Frame** behavior and press the *Delete* key on your keyboard.

5. We need to find out how long our clip is and then increase our project length to three times that amount. To find out the exact length of the clip, go to the **Media** tab behind the **Inspector** and look at the duration for your clip as shown in the following screenshot:

6. Click on the arrow in the time field underneath the Canvas and choose **Show Project Duration**. Double-click on the time field and change the project duration to fit the time you need. Use the following screenshot for reference:

7. Click on the **Layers** tab and select your clip. Go to the gear icon under the Canvas and navigate to **Retiming | Loop**. Select the clip. In the mini-Timeline, move the playhead to the end of your project and press the *O* key to extend the clip and the behavior for the full project duration.

8. The only thing left to decide is how often we want the animation to loop. By default, it's set to loop the video every 30 frames. Let's say your video is 10 seconds long and your project is set to 29.97 fps; we would set the value of the loop behavior to 300 frames so it goes through the whole video. Select the **Loop** behavior. Press the *F2* key to go to the **Behaviors** tab of the **Inspector** and adjust the **Loop Duration** to your desired setting.

See also

▸   The *Creating constant and variable speed changes* recipe

4
Making It Move
with Keyframes

In this chapter, we will cover:

- ▶ Moving a still's anchor point and keyframing its scale

- ▶ Deleting and disabling keyframes

- ▶ Keyframing a group

- ▶ Autokeyframing multiple parameters on a shape

- ▶ Working with multiple parameters in the Keyframe Editor

- ▶ Moving keyframes in the Keyframe Editor

- ▶ Reversing keyframes

- ▶ Understanding and changing the interpolation

- ▶ Converting behaviors into keyframes

- ▶ Combining keyframes and behaviors – animating a Photoshop file

- ▶ Combining keyframes and behaviors – animating a clock

Introduction

Keyframing is the change of an element's attribute in space and time. In Motion, attributes can also be thought of as a layer's parameters. If you went through the last chapter, you'll realize how helpful behaviors are to the animation process, but with the option to keyframe, your workflow becomes even more flexible. Maybe you feel more comfortable working with keyframes coming from other applications, or you may want to customize your animations beyond the values a behavior gives you. Regardless of the reason, keyframing in Motion will allow you to create dynamically rich animated projects.

Moving a still's anchor point and keyframing its scale

FCP X and Motion both allow you to animate stills using keyframes. Let's look at how similar the process is between the two applications. As we dive deeper into the chapter, we'll see the rich features Motion has to take your animations above and beyond FCP X's capabilities when it comes to animation.

How to do it...

1. Launch Motion and set the **Preset** to Broadcast 720p, **Frame Rate** to 29.97, and **Duration** to 10 seconds. Press *Command + 1* to go to the **File Browser** and locate the Chapter 4 - Exercise folder on your computer. Open the 04_01 subfolder and select the photo inside it. Choose **Import**. The photo should be in the middle of the Canvas, as shown in the following:

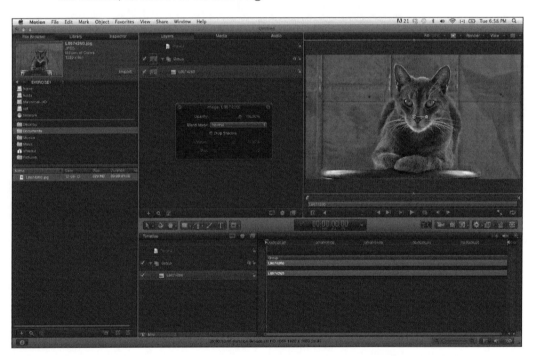

2. We want to zoom in on the cat's right eye slowly over time. While we can easily keyframe the scale and position to achieve this effect, we're going to adjust the anchor point of the image to determine what point we will scale into. Be default, on still images and video, the anchor point is located in the middle of the object. Let's change it by using the **Anchor Point** tool. In the **Layers** tab, click the arrow to the right of the selection tool to get access to the tools underneath and choose **Anchor Point**, as shown in the following screenshot:

3. Drag the red and green arrow to position the anchor point over the cat's right eye. Use the following as your guide:

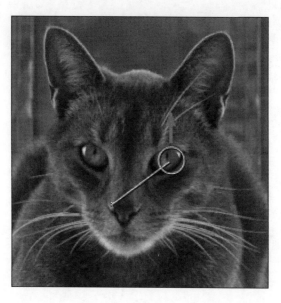

4. Press *Shift + S* to jump back to the selection tool. To see the effect this change has had on the clip, select the photo in the **Layers** tab and press *F1* to go to the **Properties** tab of the **Inspector**. Scrub the scale value to see where it scales into. Press *Command + Z* to undo the change and do the same for rotation; press *Command + Z* to undo that change as well.

5. Let's now keyframe the scale to have the image grow over time. Before we begin, here are a couple of general rules of keyframing in Motion:

   - You need at least two keyframes at different points in time and with different values to have animation

   - Once we add a keyframe to a parameter, if we adjust that parameter's value at a later point in time, an additional keyframe will be added automatically

6. In the **Properties** tab, make sure you are on the first frame of the project. Hover your cursor just to the right of the scale number until you see a diamond pop-up. Click on the diamond; you'll see that it's highlighted, as shown in the following screenshot. This indicates that a keyframe has been added at this point in time.

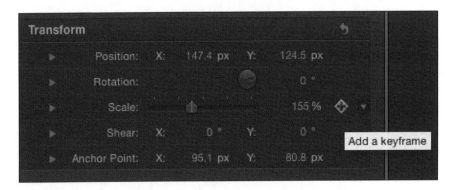

7. Move to the end of the mini-Timeline and scale up your still 50 percent more from the previous value. Notice that once you adjust the value, a keyframe is automatically added for you, as you can see in the following screenshot of the highlighted icon:

This can also be seen in the Timeline at the bottom of the screen, as shown here:

8. Play back the animation and notice how the picture scales up and moves in on the cat's right eye.

There's more...

You can easily move between keyframes on a selected object by using *Option + K* to move to the previous keyframe and *Shift + K* to the next keyframe. The same can be achieved in the **Inspector**. You'll notice on keyframed parameters that you'll be able to see the diamond shape. To the left and the right are arrows that allow you to move back and forth between the keyframes, as shown in the following:

In Motion 5, we can also see all the keyframes on a layer displayed in the Timeline without having to go to the **Keyframe Editor**. On top of this, you can easily drag a keyframe to another point in time. When dragging, if you hold down the *Shift* key while approaching your playhead, the keyframe will snap to that position:

See also

▸ *Applying a Fade in/Fade Out and Grow/Shrink behavior to a still* in *Chapter 3, Making It Move with Behaviors*.

▸ The *Keyframing a group* recipe.

▸ The *Deleting and disabling keyframes* recipe.

Deleting and disabling keyframes

When you first begin animating with keyframes, you may add one, two, or even hundreds of keyframes by accident! Also, you might want to toggle the animations you create on and off to see how your video looked before and after the animations. Let's look at a few ways we can achieve that.

How to do it...

1. Locate the `Chapter 4` folder and navigate to the `04_02` project. Double-click on it to open.

2. Play back the project by pressing the Space bar. This is the same picture of the cat used in the last recipe, except keyframes have been added to **Opacity** and **Rotation**. At the beginning of the animation, the image fades in from black, and over the 10 second duration, the picture scales and rotates slightly. We can identify all the keyframe parameters in the **Properties** tab by looking for any number that is highlighted in red. See this for yourself by pressing *F1* with the still selected, using the following screenshot as a guide:

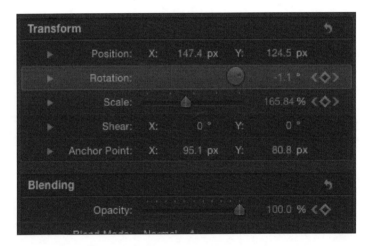

3. Let's say we want to temporarily disable an animating parameter such as **Opacity**. Make sure your playhead is at the one second mark in the mini-Timeline. In the **Properties** tab, to the right of the diamond next to **Opacity**, click on the downward arrow (the **Animation** menu) and select **Disable Animation** (shown in the following screenshot). A disable parameter is identified by a dash in the **Properties** tab. Play back the animation once and see that the still no longer fades in at the beginning. Disabling an animation does not delete any keyframes from the parameter. To enable the opacity animation again, simply go back to the **Animation** menu and choose **Enable Animation**. Play back the animation and see that the fade-in appears again.

4. When you want to delete a keyframe, we've got a few options. Let's say we no longer want our image to rotate. In the **Properties** tab, make sure we are on the first rotation keyframe. Go to the **Animation** menu and choose **Delete Keyframe**. Move to the last keyframe and this time just click the diamond and notice that the keyframe disappears.

5. Press *Command + Z* a few times to bring back both keyframes on rotation. Let's say that we want to delete all keyframes from the **Transform** properties. Rather than having to click on every single keyframe, we can reset all the parameters. Click the hooked arrow at the top-right of the **Transform** window to reset all the values. You can see the reset arrow in the following screenshot. Both **Scale** and **Rotation** have been reset, but **Opacity** remains animated.

6. To reset **Opacity**, click on the hooked arrow to the right of the **Blending Properties**. Now no parameters have keyframes.

7. Press *Command + Z* a few times until all the keyframes come back.

There's more...

You've got tons of options for deleting keyframes, even in the Timeline.

Selecting and deleting keyframes in the Timeline

You can also select and delete keyframes in the Timeline. Simply select the keyframe under the layer and press *Delete* from your keyboard. Keep in mind that if two or more parameters are keyframed at the same position in time, they will all be deleted.

While a lot of keyframing can be done in the **Inspector**, for fine-tuned animations we go to the **Keyframe Editor**.

For more control, proceed to the Keyframe Editor

For fine control over your keyframes and individual values, we need to look beyond the Timeline and the **Properties** tab. Here comes the **Keyframe Editor**. We can access it from the **Window** menu, by pressing *Command + 8*, *Ctrl* + clicking a keyframe in the Timeline, or clicking on the keyframe icon at the bottom-right of the Timeline. In the **Keyframe Editor**, we can copy and paste keyframes, see how various keyframed parameters interact with one another, and get an understanding of how Motion interpolates the values between your keyframes. We'll see more of the **Keyframe Editor** in the next few recipes, but for a sneak-peek, have a look at the following screenshot:

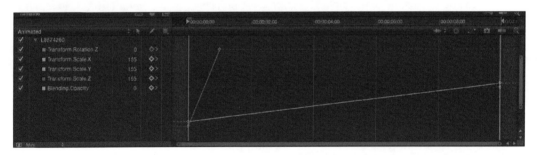

In the **Keyframe Editor**, the lines you see between keyframed parameters represent interpolation.

Interpowhat?!?! ......Interpolation explained

Interpolation is the path of travel between two keyframes. Basically, as an animator, you add keyframes and Motion interpolates the values in the middle. As we'll see, not all interpolation is the same. For instance, some values you keyframe, such as scale, are automatically given a linear interpolation, meaning the rate of speed does not change between keyframes. On other values such as position, the interpolation will be Bezier or have curves, so the rate of speed changes over time. This is to try and mimic the way things move in real life. Rarely do objects travel along straight, linear paths. Take your car, for instance. When you start driving at a green light, your car slowly makes its way up to the speed limit. When it stops, your car slows down before coming to a rest.

Keyframing a group

We can keyframe groups the same way we keyframe layers. The advantage of keyframing groups is that if we have a bunch of layers or objects that are related, we can keyframe just the group the layers are in rather than keyframe each layer individually. Let's take a look!

How to do it...

1. Open the `04_03` project in this chapter's exercises folder.

2. Play back the project. This project consists of a radial gradient background, some smiley faces, text, and animated arrows. We want to animate all the elements in this project on and offscreen together. Select the group and press *F1* to go to the **Properties** tab of the **Inspector**.

3. Move to the one-second mark on your Timeline. Next to the word **Scale**, in **Transform** properties, click the diamond icon to add a keyframe, as shown in the following screenshot. Move to the end of the Timeline and change the **Scale** value to **120**. A new keyframe is automatically added.

In the following screenshot, we see a view of our window's display after the preceding changes have been made:

4. Let's have the full group rotate and scale down from offscreen. With the group still selected, move to the beginning of the project. Enter 2500 for **Scale**. A keyframe is added automatically. Play back the animation. The group now scales from 2500 to 100 over one second and slams into place. We would like the group to gradually slow down before reaching 100.

5. Press *Command + 8* to bring up the **Keyframe Editor**. Drag up in between the Timeline and **Keyframe Editor**, so you have more space. Make sure the group is selected. Over to the left, we can see that we've added keyframes to all the scale values (x, y, and z.). With your mouse, draw a square around the second keyframe, as shown in the following screenshot:

Right-click the keyframe and from the menu choose **Ease In**. Refer to the following image and notice the curve on the second keyframe. Play back the animation. You should see that the group scales and slows down when approaching the second keyframe.

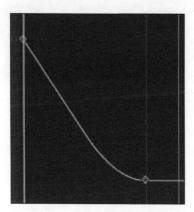

6. Move to the one-second mark in the Timeline. Click the disclosure triangle next to **Rotation**. Add a keyframe for the rotation **Y** parameter in the **Properties** tab by clicking on the diamond icon to the right of the **Y** parameter. We're not going to change the value here because this is where we want it to land.

7. Move to the beginning of the project and type in `45` for the **Y** rotation. A keyframe is automatically added. Draw a square around the second **Y** rotation keyframe in the editor. Right-click and choose **Ease In**. Play back the animation.

8. Let's have the group animate offscreen right. Move to the five-second mark in the Timeline. In the **Properties** tab, click on the diamond icon next to **Position** to add a keyframe.

9. Move to six seconds and scrub the **X** position value until the group is offscreen right. A keyframe is automatically added. I entered a value of `2250`. Play back the animation. The following screenshot shows a selected frame at the end of the animation:

There's more...

While we can move a keyframe's position by dragging in the Timeline or the Keyframe Editor, we can also move keyframes by selecting them and typing in a value to move them. For instance, to move the second **Rotation Y** keyframe in this recipe, select it in the **Keyframe Editor** and type in *Shift + = + 1 + .*, as indicated in the following screenshot. The keyframe moves one second forward. To move a keyframe back, select it and type – and the number you want and a period to force seconds. You can also move groups of keyframes in this way.

The **Keyframe Editor** can become a very busy place, very quickly. You can easily hide keyframes by clicking on the checkmark next to a parameter in the **Keyframe Editor**. If you *Option* + click the arrow, you will solo it, as shown here:

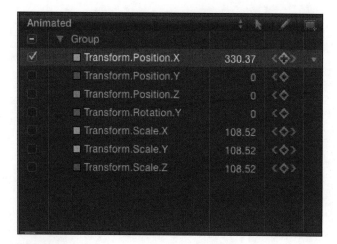

See also

▶ The *Moving a still's anchor point and keyframing its scale* recipe.

▶ The *Deleting and disabling keyframes* recipe.

Autokeyframing multiple parameters on a shape

Besides keyframing in the **Properties** tab, we can also use the Canvas by dragging objects and turning on the **Record Keyframes** feature.

How to do it...

1. Open the 04_04 project from this chapter's exercises folder.

2. Play back the project by pressing the Space bar. This project consists of a movie file with a spinning cube.

3. Under the Canvas, click on the **Record Keyframes** button or press *A*. Select the cube in the *Layers* tab. Press *F1* to go to the *Properties* tab of the Inspector. You should see every parameter marked in red, as shown in the following screenshot, indicating that **Record Keyframes** is turned on:

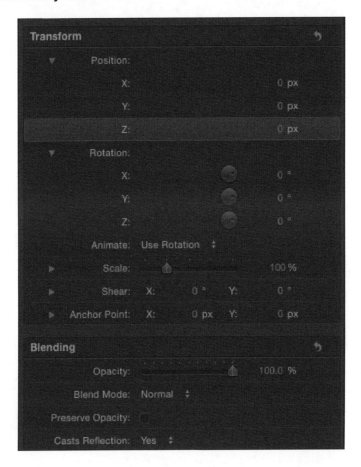

4. At the beginning of the Timeline, drag the cube down to the left and offscreen. Press *Command + -* to zoom out of the Canvas a bit. Move to the end of the Timeline and drag the cube up and to the right offscreen, as displayed in the following screenshot. The motion path becomes visible. Unlike previous recipes, when **Record Keyframes** is turned on, we don't have to add any keyframes for animation to occur. The system automatically adds them for us.

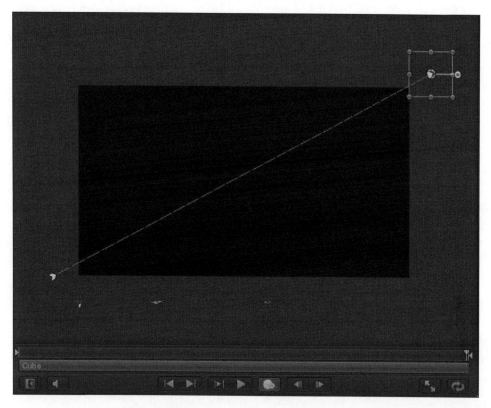

5. Click in the Canvas and type 3 + . and hit *Return* to move to the three-second mark in the Timeline. Drag the bounding box around the cube in the Canvas down a touch to create another keyframe. Let's also have the cube scale up and then back down over the length of the animation.

6. While still at the thee-second mark, *Shift* + drag one of the corner circles to scale the cube up to 130. You can see the **Scale** value appearing in the upper-left side of the Canvas.

7. Press *Shift* + *K* to move to the next keyframe. *Shift* + drag one of the corner circles of the bounding box down to 80. Now, play back the animation. The cube travels along the path and scales up to 130 and back down to 80. Let's see another method of working with **Record Keyframes**.

8. With the cube selected, press *F1* to go to the **Properties** tab of the Inspector. Press the hooked arrow in the top-right corner to reset all the **Transform** values. The cube jumps back to its original center position in the Canvas.

9. Double-click the **Record Keyframes** button to go to its properties. In here, we have options for keyframe thinning, as shown in the following screenshot. If we were to play back our project, we could record keyframes on the fly. Let's set **Keyframe Thinning** to **Reduced** in order to minimize the number of keyframes that will be added when we move the cube across the screen during playback with our mouse. Press **OK** to close the window.

10. We're going to animate the cube during playback. First, move the cube to the top-left corner of the screen. We want to move the cube in a zigzag fashion across the screen for the duration of the project until it reaches the bottom-right corner. Make sure your playhead is at the beginning of the project and **Record Keyframes** is still on. Select the cube in the Canvas. Press the Space bar to play back and start animating the cube for six seconds. Use the following screenshot for your reference:

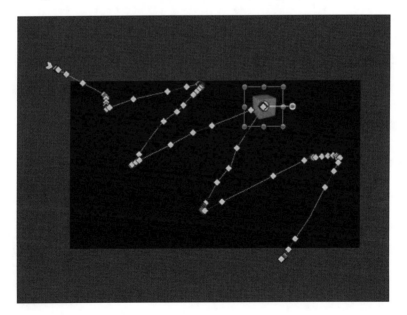

11. If you are unhappy with the results, press *Command + Z* to undo your animation. Start from the beginning and try again. You can also smooth out the animation by removing some unnecessary keyframes. Simply click on those keyframes in the Canvas with the cube selected and press *Delete*.

There's more...

Turning **Record Keyframes** on can be disastrous to your project if you're not aware of it. It also doesn't help that the *A* shortcut key is a shortcut for the position tool in FCP X and is also a shortcut to record keyframes in Motion. Be *very* careful of this button and look at the preceding recipes, so that you easily know how to delete keyframes from your project.

See also

► The *Moving a still's anchor point and keyframing its scale* recipe.

► The *Deleting and disabling keyframes* recipe.

► The *Keyframing a group* recipe.

Working with multiple parameters in the Keyframe Editor

It's all fine and dandy working with keyframes in the **Properties** tab, but when we want to see keyframes in relation to one another, we need to go to the **Keyframe Editor**. Let's take a look at a few methods so that we can work with it efficiently.

How to do it...

1. Launch Motion. From the **Project Browser**, select the **Decode | Decode Open** template. Choose **Open a copy in Motion**.

2. Press *Shift + Z* in the Canvas to fit the project to the window. Press the Space bar to start playback. This project consists of a lot of text that decodes onscreen as a camera flies and rotates through it to reveal the final title and subtitle. We want to get a better understanding of how the camera moves through the text by looking at its keyframes in the **Keyframe Editor**.

3. Press *Command + 8* to bring up the **Keyframe Editor** and drag in between it and the Timeline to increase its size, as shown in the following screenshot. Select the **Camera** from the **Layers** tab to reveal all of its animated properties.

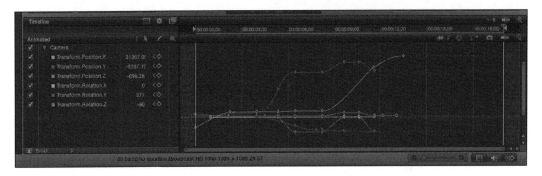

4. Click on the arrows to the right of the word **Animated** to choose **All**. It reveals every parameter you can keyframe. Wow, there's a lot! We'll go into more detail about this in the later chapters. For now, just switch back to **Animated**.

5. Move the playhead to the beginning of the **Keyframe Editor** and press *Shift + K* a few times to move forward keyframe by keyframe. This will give you a sense of how this camera was keyframed. Move all the way to the last keyframe.

6. Since our camera has been rotated in space, **Position X** now controls how close we are to the final text (we'll also see more of this in the upcoming chapters). Let's say we want to punch in on it a little. It's always a good practice to solo parameters in the **Keyframe Editor** to focus on what we're working on, so *Option* + click the checkmark next to **Transform.Position.X** to turn off the visibility of all the other animated parameters in the editor. Change the value on the last keyframe to 32000 to punch in on the text a bit more, as shown in the following screenshot. Play back the animation to see the change. *Option* + click the checkmark next to **Transform.Position.X** to turn on visibility for all the other keyframed values.

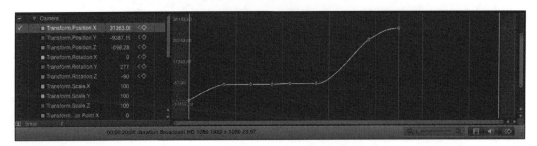

7. *Option* + click on **Transform.Rotation.Y** to solo it. Press *Option* + *K* several times to move backwards over the keyframes until you land on the third **Rotation Y** keyframe from the beginning, as seen in the following screenshot. With your mouse, scrub the number value back and forth to get a sense of how you can change the rotation. Adjust this value to 16. *Option* + click the checkmark next to **Transform.Rotation.Y** to see all the other animated values. Now, play back the animation.

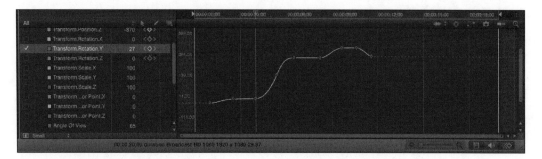

8. Click the arrows to the right of the word **Animated** and choose **Position**. Navigate through the keyframes using *Shift* + *K* and *Option* + *K*, and adjust the values to your own liking.

There's more...

Sometimes your keyframes may appear too close together and may not spread out over the entire length of the window. To easily get our animation curves to stretch to the length of a window, simply click the button (shown in the following screenshot) in the top-right corner of the window. The visible curves will now fit to its length.

See also

▶ The *Moving keyframes in the Keyframe Editor* recipe.

▶ The *Reversing keyframes* recipe.

▶ The *Understanding and changing the interpolation* recipe.

Moving keyframes in the Keyframe Editor

As animators, we will constantly be adjusting and moving keyframes in order to fine-tune our animations. Let's look at some ways of doing this in the Keyframe Editor.

How to do it...

1. Open the 04_06 project from this chapter's exercises folder.

2. Press the Space bar to play back the animation. This animation has a camera that goes across a series of vines that sprout onscreen, eventually revealing text. We want to extend the animation so it takes a second longer before coming to a rest.

3. Select **Camera** in the **Layers** tab and click the disclosure triangle to reveal its content, and notice that it's being controlled by a behavior. If we want to extend the animation, we simply extend the behavior.

4. Select the **Ramp Position X** behavior and press *Shift + O* to move to its out-point.

5. Double-click in the **Current Time** field and type *Shift + = + 1 + .* to move one second forward, as shown in the following screenshot. Press *O* to extend the behavior to this point.

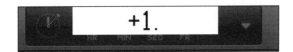

6. Play back the animation. You may notice that everything looks great, apart from the fact that now the text wipes onscreen too early. Click the disclosure triangle, next to the **Text Elements** group in the **Layers** tab, to reveal its content. Select the **Rectangle (for mask)** layer and press *Command + 8* to open the **Keyframe Editor**, as shown in the following screenshot. This mask is being used to animate the text onscreen. Let's move its keyframes to start one second later.

7. Draw a box around the keyframes to select them all, and type *Shift* + = + *1* + . and hit *Return* to move the keyframes to start a second later. Play back the animation to see that the text now "pops" onscreen instead of wiping on behind the vine. This is a case where the rectangle mask finishes earlier than the keyframes. Move to the last keyframe on the mask and drag the out-point of the mask in the mini-Timeline to make sure it lasts until the animation is finished.

8. Play back the animation and notice how the vine now wipes onscreen one second later as intended. Let's see another example of copying and pasting keyframes. From the **File** menu, choose **Open** and navigate to the 04_06_02 project. Click **Open**.

9. Play back the animation. The project consists of an atom that rotates forward over the first second and rotates backward over the next. We want this rotation to repeat for the entire project.

10. Select **Atom 1** in the **Layers** tab and press *Command + 8* to bring up the **Keyframe Editor**.

11. The only parameter with keyframes is **Rotation**, so click and draw a bounding box around the last two keyframes. Press *Command + C* to copy them.

12. Move to the three-second mark and press *Command + V* to paste them.

13. Repeat this step one more time. Copy the second and the third keyframe, and go to the five-second mark to paste the animation. Play back the project. Compare your results to the following screenshot:

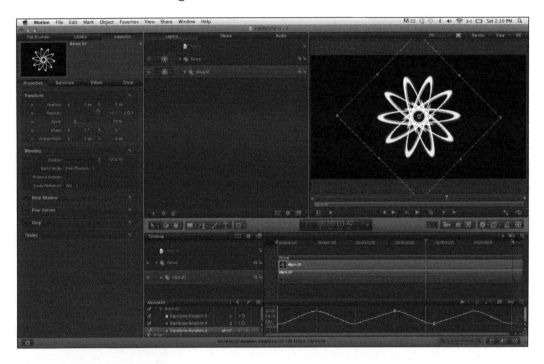

How it works

As we've seen in this recipe, we can easily copy and paste keyframes to different places in time. Perhaps you would like to have a longer fade-in, for an animation to end on a beat of music, or you'd like your objects to scale up quicker over time. Moving keyframes will change the speed and flow of our layer's animation. If you went through the recipes in *Chapter 3, Making It Move with Behaviors*, think of changing the distance between keyframes, such as trimming or extending the length of a behavior.

There's more...

While we copied and pasted keyframes in this recipe, there's nothing stopping you from dragging a keyframe in the editor. Just note, when dragging keyframes, that you can easily change the values if you drag up or down. As a tip, hold down the *Shift* key as you drag to constrain movement to the direction you're going. Alternatively, use the Timeline to drag and this will ensure that apart from the position, no other keyframe values change.

See also

- ► The *Working with multiple parameters in the Keyframe Editor* recipe.
- ► The *Reversing keyframes* recipe.
- ► The *Understanding and changing the interpolation* recipe.

Reversing keyframes

Every once in a while, we may look at an animation and say: "That would look so much better if it was played in the opposite direction". That's where reversing keyframes comes in. We can select a series of keyframes and easily reverse them to flip the animation.

How to do it...

1. Open 04_07 from this chapter's exercises folder.

2. Press the Space bar to play back the animation. It's a book from Motion's **Content** library. The **Opacity, Position, Scale**, and **Rotation** parameters have been keyframed. We're going to reverse the **Rotation** and **Scale** keyframes, so that it animates in the opposite direction.

3. Press *Command + 8* to bring up the **Keyframe Editor**. On the left-hand side of this editor, click on the word **Animated** and choose **Rotation** from the drop-down menu. Now, only the **Rotation** keyframes show in the graph.

4. Press *Command + A* to select both the **Rotation** keyframes in the editor. *Ctrl* + click on one of the keyframes and choose **Reverse Keyframes**, as shown in the following screenshot. Play back the animation and see that it now rotates in reverse. Let's repeat this for **Scale**.

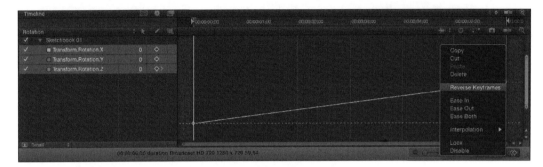

5. Click on the word **Rotation** and select **Choose** from the resulting drop-down list. Press *Command + A* to select all the visible keyframes. *Ctrl* + click on any one keyframe and from the list choose **Reverse Keyframes**. Press *Command + A* to select the **Scale** keyframes again. *Ctrl* +click any one of the keyframe and choose **Ease Both**.

6. Play back the animation and see how the graph has curves as we leave and come into each of the keyframes, as shown in the following screenshot. As a final step, we're going to copy and paste the two **Opacity** keyframes to the end of the animation, and then reverse them so they fade in instead of out.

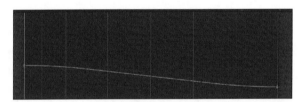

7. Click on the word **Scale** in the **Keyframe Editor** and from the resulting drop-down list, choose **Opacity**. Drag a rectangular marquee around the **Opacity** keyframes and press *Command + C* to copy them to the pasteboard.

8. Move to the five-second mark and press *Command + V* to paste them. Select the two keyframes you just pasted by dragging around them.

9. *Ctrl* + click on any one of the keyframes and choose **Reverse Keyframes**. Use the following screenshot for reference:

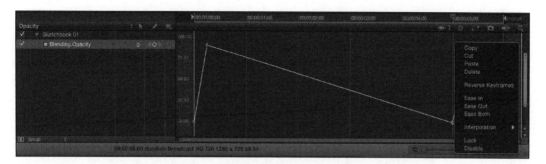

10. Play back the animation and see the book now fades in and out.

There's more...

So far, the majority of keyframes we've changed or added have been in the **Properties** tab. We can also keyframe filters and use them to create transitional effects. We can achieve this by changing the **Mix** value from 100 to 0 or vice-versa. Try adding a **Glow** filter and play with the **Mix** value to add a transitional type effect. Reverse the keyframes using the steps just explained in this recipe.

See also

▸   The *Working with multiple parameters in the Keyframe Editor* recipe.

▸   The *Moving keyframes in the Keyframe Editor* recipe.

▸   The *Understanding and changing the interpolation* recipe.

Understanding and changing the interpolation

The way your objects travel from one keyframe to another can vary depending on the interpolation set between the two images. The default interpolation varies depending on the parameter you have selected. In most situations, this would either be set to **Bezier** or **Linear**. Let's look at some of the ways we can change the path of travel using different types of interpolation that are available to us in the **Keyframe Editor**.

How to do it...

1. From this chapter's exercise files, open the `04_08` project.

2. This project consists of a `Butterfly.mov` file, which is too short for our project. Luckily, we may be able to try and loop the animation to prepare the file for keyframing. With the `Butterfly.mov` file selected in the **Layers** tab, press *F1* to go to the **Properties** tab of the Inspector.

3. At the very bottom of the **Properties** tab is the **Timing** pane. With your mouse, hover over to the right of the word **Timing** and click on the word **Show** to reveal the content of the pane. Use the following screenshot for your reference:

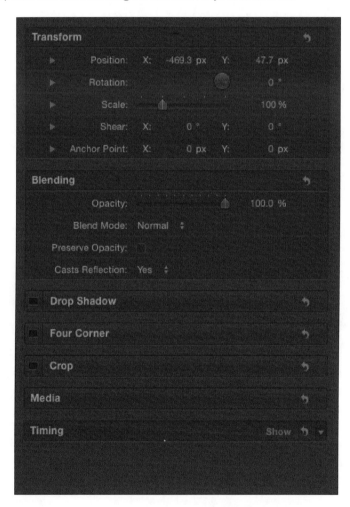

4. Set **End Condition** to **Loop**. We need to tell Motion how long we want the end duration to be. Move to the end of the mini-Timeline and with the **Butterfly** file still selected, Press *O* to extend it. Notice that in the **Properties** tab, the end duration was set to 280 frames.

5. Move to the beginning of the project with your playhead. In the **Properties** tab, click the diamond icon to the right of the word **Position** to add a keyframe. Go to the end of the project and in the **X** value, type 470 to reposition the **Butterfly** file. A keyframe is automatically added, as shown here:

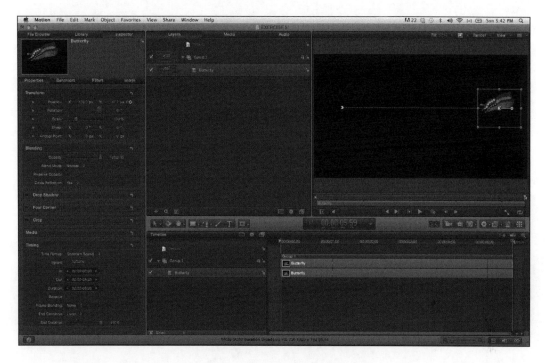

6. Press *Command + 8* to open the **Keyframe Editor**. Drag up in between the **Keyframe Editor** and the Timeline to create more space. *Option* + click the check mark for **Position Y** to solo it.

7. Click on the **Fit Visible Curves in Window** icon (it looks like a graph). Click the first keyframe in the editor and notice that a handle appears just to the right. This is known as a **Bezier interpolation**. The great thing about Bezier is we can manipulate the path our object goes along any way we see fit. Drag the path handle for this keyframe slightly down to create a curve in it.

8. Select the second keyframe and drag its handle slightly up. Notice how the **Butterfly** animation slowly comes out of the first keyframe before getting to full speed and slowly comes to a stop at the last keyframe, as seen in the following screenshot:

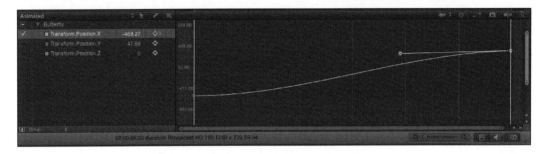

9. Select both keyframes in the editor by clicking and dragging a marquee around them. *Ctrl* + click either one and choose **Interpolation | Continuous**, as shown. Notice how both the curves look very similar. Click on one of the keyframes and notice that there are no handles to manipulate with continuous interpolation.

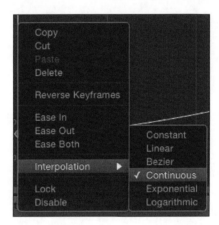

10. Let's look at a few more types of interpolation. Move to the three-second mark. Click the hollow diamond next to **Position X** in the editor to add a keyframe. Press *Command + A* to select all the visible keyframes. *Ctrl* +click any keyframe and choose **Interpolation | Constant**. Your graph should look similar to the one shown in the following screenshot. Play back the animation. Notice how the **Butterfly** animation stays in place until the next keyframe and then jumps to the next position.

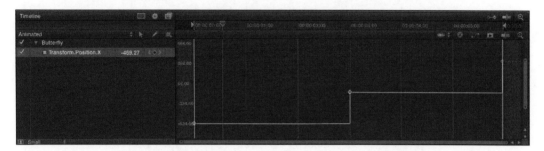

11. *Ctrl* + click the first keyframe and choose **Interpolation | Exponential**. Play back the animation. *Ctrl* + click the first keyframe again and choose **Interpolation | Logarithmic**.

See also

▶ The *Working with multiple parameters in the Keyframe Editor* recipe.

▶ The *Moving keyframes in the Keyframe Editor* recipe.

▶ The *Reversing keyframes* recipe.

Converting behaviors into keyframes

Sometimes we may want a little more control from our behaviors beyond the listed parameters that we can tweak. The great thing is we can convert behaviors into keyframes for more manual control any time we want.

How to do it...

1. From this chapter's exercise files, open the 04_09 project.

2. Press the Space bar to play back the project. It's a ball that has been animated to fade in, grow, and jump from side to side.

3. Select the ball and press *F1* to go to the **Properties** tab of the Inspector. Notice how a gear icon appears next to every property that's being controlled by behaviors. In this case, it's **Scale**, **Opacity**, and **Position**, as indicated in the following screenshot:

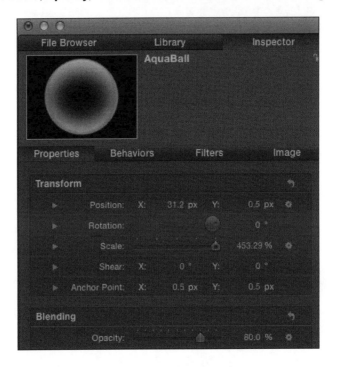

4. We want to have the ball ease in and out when it jumps from point to point, and there doesn't appear to be an option to switch this in the **Behaviors** parameters. Stop playback and with the **AquaBall** selected, choose **Object | Convert To Keyframes**.

5. Press *Command + 8* to bring up the **Keyframe Editor**. Scroll up the window so that you can see the graphs clearly, as shown here:

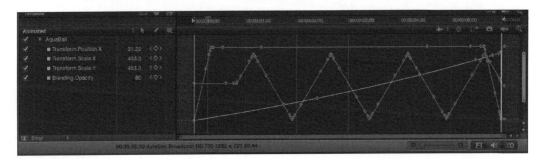

6. There may be more keyframes created than you had intended. If there are too many, simply select the unwanted keyframes and press *Delete*. You can also right-click a keyframe and choose **Delete** from the menu, as shown:

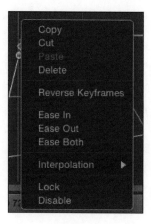

7. *Option* + click the checkmark next to **Position X** to solo it. Try to remove as many keyframes around the peaks that we don't need. The next screenshot shows quite a few that you might not want. Try marquee-selecting multiple keyframes to help you save some time. Make sure not to select the peaks.

8. *Shift* + click each of the keyframes at the peak of the graph to select them. Right-click any one of them and choose **Ease Both**. Look to see how the graph changes. Play back the animation. Repeat the preceding two steps for the lower ends of the graph.

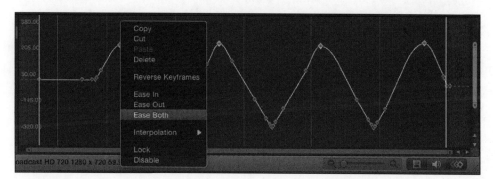

9. *Option* + click the **Position X** parameter in the **Keyframe Editor** to unsolo it. Turn off **Position** and **Opacity** by clicking the checkbox, so only **Scale X** and **Scale Y** can be seen. Let's say we want the ball to scale up a bit, hold its value for a second, and then increase to its final value.

10. Make sure both **Scale X** and **Scale Y** are selected. Draw a square around one of the middle keyframes and press *Command* + *C* to copy it.

11. Move one second forward from the keyframe you just selected and press *Command + V*. Draw a box around the previous keyframe and *Ctrl* + click. Choose **Interpolation** | **Linear** as shown in the following screenshot. Play back the project.

There's more...

See the word for a text behavior and don't know what it does. Go to the **Library** tab and preview the animation in the upper-left corner once selecting it.

See also

▶ *Applying a Fade in/Fade Out and Grow/Shrink behavior to a still* in Chapter 3, *Making It Move with Behaviors*.

Combining keyframes and behaviors – animating a Photoshop file

Okay, we've gone through the recipes of keyframing and also behaviors in the last chapter, so now it's time to bring it all together. We're going to animate a Photoshop file using both keyframes and behaviors to create a simple animation on screen. Let's get started!

How to do it...

1. From this chapter's exercise files, open the 04_10 project.

2. The project consists of a Photoshop file that was imported with multiple layers. Our goal is to animate the little ninja you see in the following image and have him jump onscreen while bobbling his head. We'll then have a spear fall into his hands as he adjusts them to fighting position. Eventually, we'll want both the spear and ninja to end up where the ninja currently is.

3. Move to the one-second mark on the Timeline. Select the **Ninja** group. Press *F1* to go to the **Properties** tab of the Inspector and add a keyframe by clicking on the diamond next to **Position** and **Rotation**, as shown here:

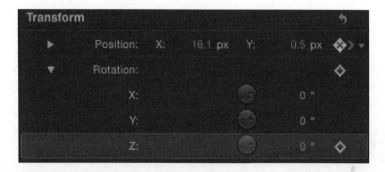

4. Move back to the beginning of your Timeline by pressing the home key on the extended keyboard or drag your playhead. Change the **Position** value of **X:** to 440 and of **Y:** to 740 and the **Rotation** value to 720. Play back the animation. Our ninja rotates and jumps onscreen. Awesome!

5. Let's have him land a bit more softly on the ground. Press *Command + 8* to open up the **Keyframe Editor**. Draw a square around the keyframes at one second to select them. *Ctrl +* click anyone of them and choose **Ease In** from the menu.

6. With the **Ninja** group still selected, move to the end of the Timeline. Set the **X** position value to -450. The ninja lands and then slowly moves to the left. Let's make his head move a bit with a **Parameter** behavior.

7. Select the **Head** group. Click the disclosure triangle next to **Rotation** in the Inspector. *Ctrl +* click **Rotation Z** and choose **Add Parameter Behavior | Wriggle**.

8. In the **Behaviors** tab, set the number to 1, **Apply Mode** to **Add**, and **Subtract** and the **Frequency** to 1.

9. Jump to the two-second mark in the Timeline. Select the **Spear** layer. Press *F1* to jump to the **Properties** tab of the Inspector. Add a keyframe for **Position** and **Rotation** by clicking the diamonds next to the values.

10. Move to the two-second and the thirty-frame mark. Twirl down the **Rotation** values and type 360 in **Z** rotation. Change the **Position** values to of **X:** to 16 and of **Y:** to 134. Play back the animation.

11. Move to the three-second mark. We're going to keyframe the movement of the left arm and attach the right arm to move with it using a **Link** behavior. Select **Right Arm** in the **Layers** tab. In the **Properties** tab, add a keyframe to **Z Rotation**. Move to four seconds and change **Z Rotation** to 30.

12. Select **Left Arm**. *Ctrl* + click the letter **Z** under **Rotation** and choose **Add Parameter Behavior | Link**.

13. In the **Layers** tab, select **Right Arm** and drag it to the source well on the **Link** behavior in the **Behaviors** tab. Refer to the **Properties** tab in the following image for reference. Play back the animation and notice how both arms move together:

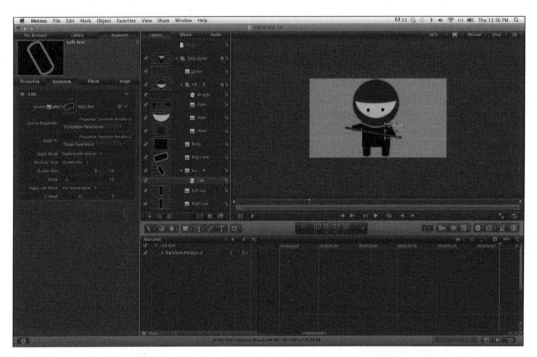

14. Select the **Spear** layer. Move to three seconds in the Timeline and add a keyframe for **Z Rotation** and **X Position**.

15. Move to four seconds and change the **X Position** to 20 and **Z Rotation** to 372. Play back the animation.

16. As a final step, select the **Eye** layer. *Ctrl* + click the word **Scale** in the Inspector and choose **Add Parameter Behavior | Wriggle**. In the **Behaviors** tab, set the number to 5, **Apply Mode** to **Add**, and **Subtract** and the **Frequency** parameters to 1.

There's more...

In order for the arms to rotate around the Ninja's shoulders, the anchor points on the arms were moved. This was achieved using the same method we used to move in on the cat's eye in the first recipe of this chapter. We'll see more about this in the next recipe.

See also

- ▸ The *Moving a still's anchor point and keyframing its scale* recipe.
- ▸ The *Combining keyframes and behaviors – animating a clock* recipe.
- ▸ *Using the Link behavior* in Chapter 3, *Making It Move with Behaviors*.

Combining keyframes and behaviors – animating a clock

Let's take a look at another example of combining keyframes and behaviors by animating a clock's minute and hour hand while linking some text to rotate along with the clock.

How to do it...

1. From this chapter's exercises folder, open the 04_11 project. This project consists of a clock from Motion's library that contains separate layers for the hour and minute hand. There are also two text layers, as shown in the following image. We want the text to rotate along with the clock's hand. In order to achieve this, we're going to move both of the texts' anchor points to the center of the clock.

2. On the toolbar, click and select the **Anchor Point** tool located underneath the selection tool, as shown in the following screenshot. Select the **Hour Text** layer and use the green and red arrows to move the anchor point to the center of the clock. Repeat this step for the other text layer.

3. Press *Shift + S* to go back to the selection tool. Let's keyframe the minute hand so that it rotates twice around the clock. Select the **Minute Hand** layer and press *F1* to go to the **Properties** tab of the Inspector. Make sure the playhead is at the beginning of the mini-Timeline. Click the disclosure triangle for **Rotation** and add a keyframe for **Z Rotation**.

4. Move to three seconds and change the **Z Rotation** value to -1080. Press *Command + 8* to open the **Keyframe Editor**. *Ctrl +* click the last **Z Rotation** keyframe and choose **Ease In**.

5. Let's say we're not sure if we want the clock to rotate around three times. We want to keep options available in case we change our mind without having to go and redo every animation. Say hello to the **Link** behavior. The **Link** behavior will allow us to link the **Z Rotation** for all of our objects. If we change the keyframes on the hour hand, it will pass on to the linked layers. Let's link the hour hand first. Select the **Hour Hand** layer. In the **Properties** tab, *Ctrl +* click **Z Rotation** and choose **Add Parameter | Link**, as shown in the following screenshot:

6. Press *F7* to show the HUD. Drag the **Minute Arm** layer straight into the source well. Move the playhead to the beginning of the mini-Timeline and play back the animation. The hands are linked but they're moving at the same rate. In order to correct this, we're going to play with the **Link** behavior's **Scale** value.

7. In the **Behaviors** tab, change the value of **Scale** to 0.083. To come up with this number, we divide 1 by 12 (representing the number of hours on the clock). Scrub the animation and see the clock hands move as they're supposed to.

8. Select the **Hour Text** layer. Press *F1*. In the **Properties** tab, *Ctrl* + click **Z Rotation** and choose **Add Parameter | Link**. In the HUD, drag the **Hour Arm** layer straight into the source well.

9. Select the **Minute Text** layer. Press *F1*. In the **Properties** tab, *Ctrl* + click **Z Rotation** and choose **Add Parameter | Link**. In the HUD, drag the **Minute Arm** layer straight into the source well.

10. Let's see it all come together. Select **Minute Arm**. In the **Keyframe Editor**, select the last **Z Rotation** keyframe and press *Command + X* to cut it. Move to six seconds and press *Command + V* to paste it. On the left-hand side of the **Keyframe Editor**, double-click the **Z Rotation** value and set it to -2160, as shown in the following screenshot. Play back the animation.

11. As a final step, select the **Master** group. Click on the gear icon to the right-hand side of the Timeline and choose **Basic Motion | Grow/Shrink**. Change the value in the **Behaviors** tab or HUD as you see fit.

See also

▸ *Using the Link behavior* in Chapter 3, *Making It Move with Behaviors*.

▸ The *Moving a still's anchor point and keyframing its scale* recipe.

▸ The *Combining keyframes and behaviors – animating a clock* recipe.

5
Let's Make Text

In this chapter we will cover:

- ▶ Changing the text format
- ▶ Changing the text style
- ▶ Changing the layout and creating text on a path
- ▶ Adding and trimming multiple text behaviors
- ▶ Sequence Text
- ▶ Using the Transform Glyph tool
- ▶ Saving your favorite text animations and styles
- ▶ Using vector images from the Special Characters library
- ▶ Using videos and textures to fill text
- ▶ Creating a lower third for FCP X

Introduction

Today, in a world of increased communication through video, text plays a vital and important part. As technology has advanced, the need and desire to create more sophisticated and organic flowing text has increased tenfold. For example, when you turn on the TV tonight, pay attention to some of the commercials and how text behaves in them. Text is used as a way to communicate key messages to our audience whether it be as simple as a lower third or as elaborate as a kinetic text animation.

Whatever your text desire may be, Motion has an intricate set of parameters to make all of your text dreams come true. Its workflow not only allows us to create but also save our favorite designs. On top of this, Motion's elaborate set of behaviors dedicated to text allow us to have instant animation.

This chapter will give us a basic overview of how to format and make stylistic changes to our text. We will also look at built-in animators and text generators available right in Motion's library. Let's dive right in!

Changing the text format

The **Format** pane of text has several options available to us before we even begin to explore the style and layout options of our text. Let's explore some of these features.

Getting ready

Launch Motion and choose a **Broadcast 720p, 29.97** project with a **10 second** duration. Press *Shift + Z* to fit the Canvas window.

How to do it...

Let's create some text and head to the **Inspector** to change its format.

1. Press **T** or select the **T** icon on the toolbar to select the text tool as shown in the following screenshot. Click somewhere close to the center of the Canvas. Type `Playing With Text` and press *Esc* to exit the text entry mode. Use the dynamic guides to help you center your text on the screen. Press *F7* to show the HUD.

2. While we could switch our text in the **Format** pane, it's actually beneficial to do it in the HUD. Click and hold down the font menu (just above the alignment options). Scroll through the various options as shown in the following screenshot and notice how your text updates immediately in the Canvas. Select **Al Bayan** and press *F4* to go to the **Text** tab of the **Inspector**. In the first tab we see the **Format** pane.

Abadi MT Condensed Extra Bold
Abadi MT Condensed Light
Academy Engraved LET

Accidental Presidency

Adobe Arabic

Adobe Caslon Pro

Adobe Devanagari

Adobe Fan Heiti Std
Adobe Fangsong Std
Adobe Garamond Pro
Adobe Gothic Std
Adobe Hebrew
Adobe Heiti Std
Adobe Kaiti Std
Adobe Ming Std
Adobe Myungjo Std
Adobe Naskh

Adobe Song Std

Al Bayan

AlternateGothic2 BT

Ambule BT

American Typewriter

Andale Mono

Apple Braille

Apple Chancery

Apple LiGothic

Apple LiSung
Apple Symbols

AppleGothic

AppleMyungjo

Arial

Arial Black

Arial Hebrew

Arial Narrow

Arial Rounded MT Bold

Arial Unicode MS

Ayuthaya

3. At the very top of the **Inspector** is an option to change the style of our text with a preset. Click on the word **Normal** at the top of the **Format** pane and choose **Gold Leaf** as shown in the following screenshot. You'll notice the word gets filled in with a gradient. Style presets are a combination of parameters from all the text panes that we'll look at in greater detail in later exercises.

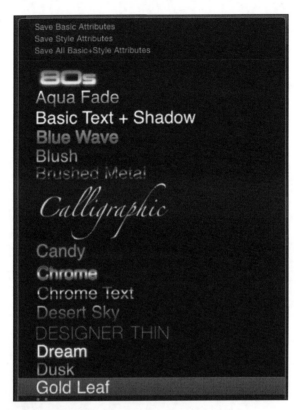

4. Change the value of **Text Alignment to Center** and **Tracking** to 5. Reposition the text in the center of the Canvas. Add a keyframe next to tracking on the first frame of the project by clicking the diamond shape, as shown in the following screenshot:

5. Move forward to 3 seconds and change the **Tracking** value to -2. An additional keyframe is added automatically. Move to the first frame of the project and play back the animation.

6. In the **Advanced Formatting** section, scrub both the slant and rotation values. Notice that when you scrub rotation, each of the individual characters are affected, unlike the **Properties** tab where rotation would affect the entire word.

7. We can also change the text position by playing with **Offset** in the **Advanced Formatting** section. At the 4 second mark, add a keyframe by clicking on the diamond shape next to **Offset**.

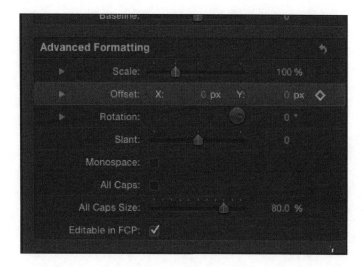

8. Go to 6 seconds and scrub the **X** value to the right until the text is offscreen. Move to the beginning and play back the animation.

There's more...

Keyframes allow us to use animation, but don't forget about behaviors.

Text behaviors

While we created some subtle animation using keyframes, don't overlook text behaviors. They create animation for your text without having to use keyframes. There are hundreds of them and you can preview them at any point by going to the **Library**.

Text presets allow for quick and sophisticated design.

Saving text presets

While we had a glimpse of some of the text presets available, keep in mind you can also save your own for later use. This will come in handy for your projects where you need to create consistent stylized text.

It's important to make sure the audience can see your text.

Safe zones

Not all TV screens are made alike. This is why we have safe zones. You can turn on Motion's safe zones by going to the **View** menu above the Canvas. The innermost rectangle refers to the text safe margin. This will ensure that your text will appear on majority of the television screens.

See also

▶ The *Changing the text style* recipe

▶ The *Changing the layout and creating text on a path* recipe

Changing the text style

After you initially format your text, it's time to look at the stylizing options available. Motion has a **Style** pane with four sections to help you get your desired color and look finalized.

Getting ready

Locate the exercise folder for this chapter and navigate to the 05_02 project. Double-click on it to open it.

How to do it...

Like text format, to change the text style, we head to the **Inspector**:

1. Press *F4* to go to the **Text** tab and click on the **Style** pane. While we have access to changing the face color in the HUD, we don't have options to change the fill type. Change the value of **Fill** from **Color** to **Gradient** as shown in the following screenshot:

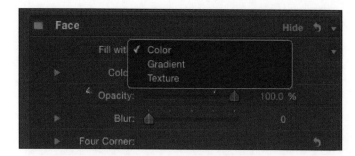

2. Click on the disclosure triangle next to **Gradient**. From the gradient preset styles choose **Dawn**. Click on the blue color stop to load it in the color well. Switch the color to a more vibrant blue. Drag the middle color stop over to the right to increase the blue influence over the letters. Use the following screenshot for reference:

3. Now that we have made these adjustments, we could save it as a preset for later use. From the preset menu choose **Save Preset** and type in Dawn (alternate).

4. The great thing about Motion's **Style** pane is its flexibility to mix several parts of our text together or work with them separately. For now, turn off the face of our text by clicking on the blue square. Click on the empty square next to the word **Outline** to activate it. Change the value of the **Color** from white to black and the **Width** to 2.

5. Turn back on the face of our text. Make sure the outline is set to be **Under the face**.

6. Let's add a glow to all of our text, but rather than use the **Style** pane option we're going to use a filter. From the filter icon choose **glow – glow**.

7. Press *F3* to go to the **Filters** tab and increase the **Glow** to 50.

8. As a final step, activate **Drop Shadow** by clicking on the empty square. Change the value of **Distance** to 10 and **Blur** to 7 as shown in the following screenshot. Deactivate **Face** and **Outline** to see how the drop shadow looks by itself.

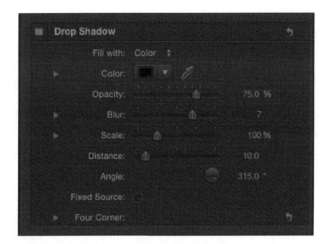

9. Under **Drop Shadow**, click on the disclosure triangle next to **Four Corner** and change the bottom left **X** position to 15. See how you can change the other corners by playing with the values.

There's more...

We can also achieve this effect by adding a texture to our text.

Adding textures

We can add any texture to the **Face** and **Outline** of our text. A texture can be a still image or even a movie file. All we need to do is make sure we have the texture we want to use in the **Layers** tab. With it, select the texture from the appropriate section and drop the texture into the source well. As a final step, turn off the texture in the **Layers** tab.

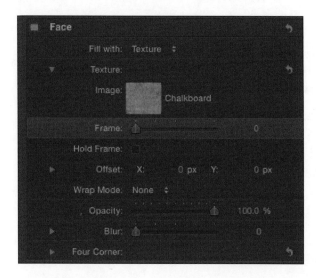

Changing the render quality for better playback

You may have noticed the quality of the video was not as sharp as the other projects. This is because the render quality has been turned down for better playback. At anytime, you can go to the render menu and choose a different resolution and quality to have a faster playback. Keep this in mind for render-intensive projects. Since you're reading this book, it's going to happen sooner rather than later.

Setting the play range to a smaller value than your project length can make all the difference.

Changing the play range

Rather than playing your whole project, sometimes it's better to isolate a section we're working on so that Motion doesn't have to play back the entire animation. Simply drag the play range handles to your desired location. Use the following screenshot for reference. Press the Space bar and notice your project will only play between your two designated points.

Loading your project to RAM may be necessary in order to ensure you are seeing an accurate preview.

When you need to see it in real time, use your RAM

In the last exercise, our projects didn't play back in real time. In order to do that, we need to go to the **Mark** menu and choose an option under **RAM Preview**, as shown in the following screenshot. This will use our computer's memory to create temporary files in order to play back our full project or play our range in real time. Just note, as soon as you make a change, **RAM Preview** will be lost!

See also

▶ The *Changing the text format* recipe
▶ The *Changing the layout and creating text on a path* recipe

Changing the layout and creating text on a path

Sometimes we want text to follow along a path for a variety of different reasons. We may want text to travel across the edges of a shape or wrap to the pages of a book whose perspective is not flat to the screen. Whatever the reason may be, playing with text on a path in Motion is fun.

Getting ready

Open the `05_04` project in your `Chapter 5` folder. This project consists of a sketch book from Motion's library.

How to do it...

We're going to create some text and try to have it match our book's perspective.

1. Press *T* to select the **Text** tool and on the left side of the book type `Chapter 5 - Let's Make Text`. Press the *Esc* key to exit the text entry mode and press *F7* to show the HUD. Change the value of **Font** to **Tahoma**, make it **Bold** and set the size to `31`. Choose a dark blue color of your liking by keeping *Ctrl* pressed and clicking on the color well. Center align the text and move it back over the book. Use the following screenshot for reference:

2. We're going to change the perspective of our text to make it seem like it's in the book. Make sure the text is selected in the **Layers** tab. Press *F1* to go to the **Properties** tab of the **Inspector**. Click on the disclosure triangle next to **Rotation**. Change the value of **X** to -30.

3. Press *F4* to go to the **Text** tab of the **Inspector** and click on the **Layout** pane. Under **Layout Controls** change **Layout Method** to **Path**, as shown in the following screenshot. At the very bottom of the **Layout** pane are the path options. We can have the text go a long a circle, rectangle, or even feed it our own custom shape. For now we're going to leave the default as **Open Spline**.

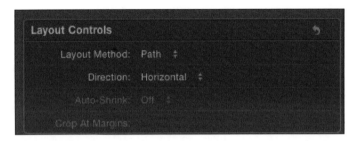

4. In order to adjust the path, double-click on the text in the Canvas. Move the control points that appear and wrap the text to the book.

5. Play with the offset value to center the text on the left side of the book. Notice we can easily keyframe this to animate our text along the path.

6. Let's try a different path shape. Change value of **Path** from **Open Spline** to **Closed Spline**. Click on the empty square to add a checkmark next to **Inside Path**. Drag the text back on the left side of the book. Use the following screenshot for reference:

See also

▶ The *Changing the text format* recipe
▶ The *Changing the text style* recipe

Adding and trimming multiple text behaviors

Let's explore some of the behaviors Motion has to offer us for the text.

Getting Ready

Open the 5_05 project from the exercise folder for this chapter. Play back the project. It consists of a background and three pieces of text that come on screen one second after each other.

How to do it...

We're going to start by having our text come from different directions offscreen to onscreen.

1. Click on the disclosure triangle to open the **Text** group in the **Layers** tab. Select the **Ready** text and press *Command + 2* to go to the **Library**. **Navigate to Behaviors | Text Sequence | Text Basic**. Select the **Slide In** behavior and click on **Apply**.

2. Move to 1 second on the mini-Timeline. Press *Command + Option + O* to trim the out-point of the play range. Play back the animation. Press *Command + -* twice to zoom out on the Canvas. Click and drag the red arrow until it's offscreen left as shown in the following screenshot. Press *F2* to go to the **Behaviors** tab of the **Inspector**.

3. Click the disclosure triangle for controls, and under unit size change it from Characters to Word.

4. *Option* + click the **Slide In** behavior in the **Layers** tab and drag it to the **Set** text. Double-click on the **Slide In** behavior on the **Ready** text layer and rename it Slide in from left. Double-click on the **Slide In** behavior on the set text layer and rename it Slide in from right.

5. Select the **Slide in from right** behavior. Drag the red arrow right across the screen till it's no longer visible.

6. *Option* + click on the **Slide In from left** behavior from the **Ready** text layer and drag it to the **Go** text. Move to 3 seconds on the mini-Timeline. Press *Command* + *Option* + *O* to trim the play range to the playhead. Play back the animation so far.

7. Let's finalize our animation by having each of our text behaviors dolly out of the screen. Select the **Ready** text. Select the gear icon underneath the Canvas and choose **Text Energetic | Dolly Out** as shown in the following screenshot. Move to 5 seconds. Select the **Dolly Out** behavior in the **Layers** tab and press *Shift +]* to move its out-point to 5 seconds. Press *F2* to go to the **Properties** tab of the **Inspector**. Under the **Dolly Out** behavior, click on the disclosure triangle for controls and under **Unit Size** change it from Characters to Word.

8. *Option* + click and drag the **Dolly Out** behavior to the **Set** text and repeat the step for the **Go** text.

9. Move to 5 seconds and 25 frames. Select the **Dolly Out** behavior on the **Set** text and press *Shift +]* to move the behavior's out-point to this location. Move to 6 seconds and repeat the earlier step for the **Go** text. Press *Option + X* to reset the play range and play back the animation. Great work!

How it works...

Text behaviors preceded by the word *Out* are meant to animate the text off screen. By default, when you apply them to text they are always added at the beginning. Make sure you don't forget to move the behavior in the mini-Timeline to where you want your text to animate out so you can achieve your intended result.

See also

▶   The *Applying a Fade In/Fade Out and Grow/Shrink behavior to a still* recipe in Chapter 3, *Making It Move with Behaviors*

▶   The *Sequence Text* recipe

Sequence Text

There is one text behavior that rules them all! It couldn't be said better when we look at Sequence Text. All the animations you see in the various categories started from Sequence Text. Let's see how we can make some custom text animations!

Getting ready

Double-click on the 05_06 project from the exercise folder for this chapter. This project consists of a background and some static text. We're going to customize an animation to have the text come on and off the screen while exploring some of the various options available to us by using sequence text.

How to do it...

Let's begin by adding the **Sequence Text** behavior.

1. Select **Text** in the **Layers** tab and press *Command + 2* to go to the **Library**. Select **Behaviors | Text Animation | Sequence Text**. Click the **Apply** button.

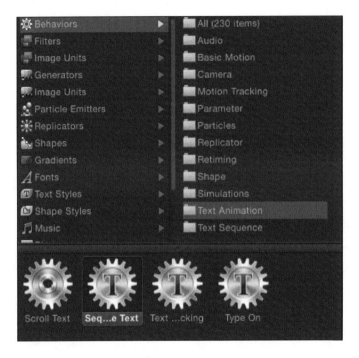

2. With the text still selected, press *F2* to go to the **Behaviors** tab of the **Inspector**. At first, the sequence text has no default animation. We need to pick a parameter we want to change. After adjusting the value, **Sequence Text** will ramp from the value we specify to the state our text is in now.

3. From the parameter menu, go to **Add | Format | Position** as shown in the following screenshot. Under **Position**, change the **Y** value to 220. Play back the animation. The text drops in character by character over the entire length of the project. Let's change a few of the settings.

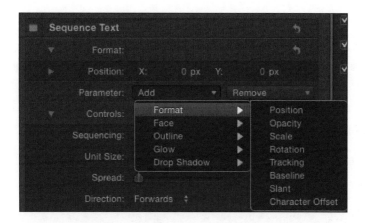

4. Move to 1 second. Select the **Sequence Text** behavior and press O to trim the out-point to the playhead. Under **Controls**, change the value of **Spread** to 6 and the **Direction** to **Backwards**. Play back the animation to see how the text reacts.

5. Change the value of **Direction** back to **Forwards**, **Spread** to 2, and change the value of **Unit Size** to **Word**. Also change the **Speed** to **Ease Both**.

6. From the **Parameter** menu, choose **Add | Format| Opacity** and **Add | Face | Blur**. Change the **Opacity** value to 0 and the **Blur** value to 30 as shown in the following screenshot. Play back the animation.

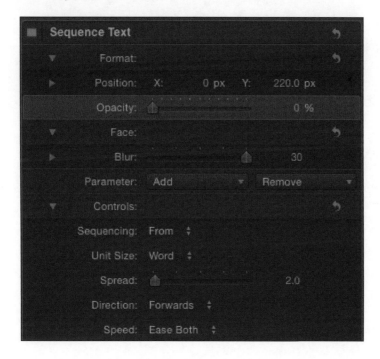

7. Select the **Sequence Text** behavior in the **Layers** tab and press *Command + D* to duplicate it. Move to the end of the project. Press *Shift +]* to move the duplicate behavior to the playhead. Rename it to `Sequence Text Out`. In the **Behaviors** tab, with the **Sequence Text Out** behavior selected, change the position of the **Y** value to `-220`, **Sequencing** to **To**, and **Direction** to **Backwards**. Play back the animation.

There's more...

Once you master Motion's sequence text, you can put those skills to use in FCP X. In the text library within FCP X, you'll find **Custom** text, as shown in the following screenshot. It has most of the control settings that Motion's Sequence Text has.

See also

▸ The *Applying a Fade in/Fade Out and Grow/Shrink behavior to a still* recipe in *Chapter 3, Making It Move with Behaviors*

▸ The *Adding and trimming multiple text behaviors* recipe

Using the Transform Glyph tool

The **Transform Glyph** tool allows us to adjust the individual characters of our text with ease and precision directly in the Canvas. Combine it with the Sequence Text behavior and we can make our animations come to life by dragging our text to where we want it to start.

Getting ready

Double-click on the 05_07 project from the exercise folder for this chapter folder. Play back the animation. This project consists of an animated alarm clock and some text.

How to do it...

We're going to begin by changing the size of a few characters.

1. Underneath the **Selection** tool, select the **Transform Glyph** tool as shown in the following screenshot:

2. Press *F7* to bring up the HUD. Click on the letter **M** in the Canvas. Adjust its scale in the HUD to around 190, as shown in the following screenshot. *Option* + click to the left and right of the slider to increase the size by one. Repeat this step for the letter **R**:

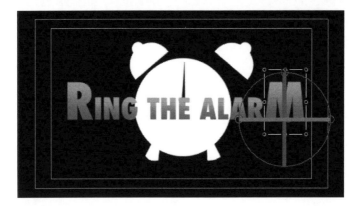

3. Select **Ring the Alarm** in the **Layers** tab. Go to the gear icon to the right of the Canvas and select **Text Animation | Sequence Text**. Move to 2 seconds in the mini-Timeline and press *O* to trim the behavior's out-point. Press *Command + Option + O* to move the play range out-point to the playhead. Move to the beginning of the project.

4. Click on the letter *R*. Press *Command + -* a few times to zoom out on the Canvas. In the HUD, change the value of **Unit Size** value to **Line**. Hold down the *Shift* key and click on the top circle. Drag the text to the right to rotate it by 45 degrees on the x axis.

5. Select the blue arrow and drag it to the right to move your characters offscreen. Change the **Speed** to **Ease Both**. Play back the animation. Try changing the value of **Unit Size** to **Word** and the value of **Direction** to **Random**. Play around with the settings until you're happy with the animation. Use the following screenshot to help guide you:

Saving your favorite text animations and styles

As a motion graphics designer, you have a responsibility to work efficiently. One way to save time is to save your favorite animations for future use. Let's take a look at how we can save our own animations that we can use over and over again.

Getting ready

Under the exercise folder for this chapter, folder open the `05_08` project. This project consists of a background and text layer. The project is 3D so it allows us to add lights that interact with our scene! We'll learn about this later but for now take a second to explore and see how this project was constructed.

How to do it...

We're going to save the text style and basic attributes associated with this text so that we can easily apply it to other text layers that we might have in our project.

1. Select the **Imagine** text and press *F4* to go to the **Text** tab of the **Inspector**. Go to the **Format** pane at the very top under the **Style Presets** menu click and choose **Save All Basic + Style Attributes** as shown in the following screenshot. Name the preset `BGothic, Grad, Glow and Shadow`.

2. Press *Command + 2* to go to the **Library**. Select **Text Styles**; note that your preset is saved as shown in the following screenshot. Turn off the **Imagine** layer and turn on the **Apply** layer by clicking on the checkmark box next to it in the **Layers** tab. Drag the preset over to the **Apply** text. Look how easy that was compared to adjusting all the settings again!

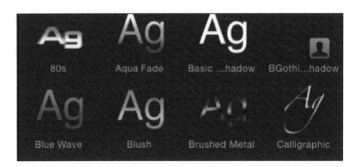

3. Let's see how we can do this with text behaviors we create with sequence text! Go to the **File** menu and open the 05_08_01 project. Play back the project. Take a second to explore the various filters, behaviors, masks, and lights that were used to make the project. If you're going through this book chronologically, you'll find out more about this in the later chapters.

4. We want to copy the **Sequence Text** behavior from the **Imagine** text to apply to clips in the Timeline. *Option* + click the checkmark next to **Imagine** to solo it. Move to 4 seconds in the Timeline. Select the behavior on the **Imagine** text and press *F2* to go the **Behaviors** tab. Both scale and position have been adjusted on the **Sequence Text** behavior to create the animation you see. Press *Command + 2* to go to the **Library**. Select **Favorites** and drag the Sequence Text from the **Layers** tab directly into the **Favorites** folder. Rename it Scale 400 and Z Position Move.

5. Create a new project, add some text, and apply the preset behavior to it from the **Library**! How easy was that! Use the following screenshot for reference:

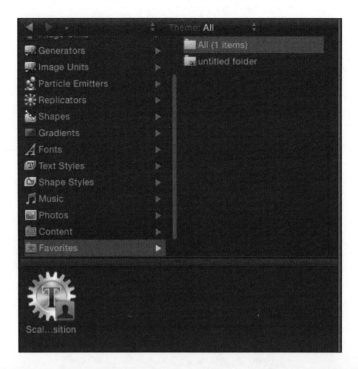

Using vector images from the Special Characters library

We can't talk about text without talking about the vector images that are available to us through **Special Characters**. It opens up a world of motion graphic possibilities as we can fly in on these images with cameras, and put them in replicator and particle systems, creating complex animations.

How to do it...

We start with creating a new project for this exercise.

1. Create a **720p** project, **10 seconds** long at **30** FPS.

2. Press *T* to select the type tool and click somewhere close to the center of the Canvas. Go to the **Edit** menu and select **Special Characters** from the list as shown in the following screenshot:

3. Under **Symbols**, go to **Miscellaneous**, and locate the skull and crossbones image (the location of these images may be different depending on your current operating system). With the image selected, click on **Insert** located on the bottom-right of the window. Press the *Esc* key to exit the text entry mode and then *F7* to bring up the HUD.

4. Change the value of **Size** to 288, center align your image, and drag it into the Canvas to center it to the screen using your dynamic guides to help you. While we can't scale the image any further in the HUD, we can scale this value infinitely in the **Format** pane of the **Text** tab. Press *F4* to go there.

5. Change the value of **Size** to 500. Go to the **Style** pane and change the color to a gradient of your liking and add any additional changes you want. Use the following screenshot for reference.

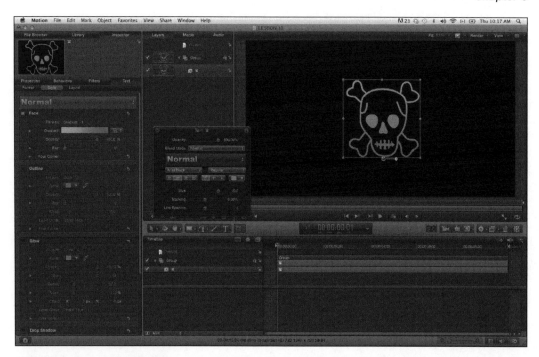

There's more...

Some of the icons available to you under the **Special Characters** library are also available under the font **Webdings**. Select the **Type** tool and **Webdings** as a font. Spell out the alphabet. Do it again, this time pressing *Option* before the letter. Use the following screenshot for reference to see some of the available graphics:

Using videos and textures to fill text

We're going to take a quick look at how we can fill our text with something other than a solid or gradient color by using video. In this exercise, we're going to apply a blend mode on our text to achieve the desired result.

Getting ready

Find a piece of video and create a project based on its dimensions, frame rate, and duration. Go to **File Browser** and navigate to the location where the file is. Make sure you're on the first frame of your project and select **Import** to bring it in.

How to do it...

Let's begin by creating some text.

1. Select the text icon in the toolbar underneath the Canvas and type out MOVING FORWARD. Press *Esc* and *F7*. Select a nice, thick font such as **Aerial Black** as shown in the following screenshot:

2. Select the text and press *F1* to go to the **Properties** tab. From the pop-up list under **Blending Mode**, select **Stencil Luma**. Your image is now contained in the text. If it seems to have got lost on the screen, try duplicating the text by pressing *Command + D*.

3. On the duplicate, change the value of **Blending Mode** to **Normal**. Press *F4* to go to the **Text** tab and click on the **Style** pane. Turn off the **Face** option and turn on **Outline**. Select a width and color of your liking. Use the following screenshot for reference:

4. Making sure all layers are in the same group, select the **Group** layer, press *Command + 2* to go to the **Library**, and under **Behaviors** select **Basic Motion |
Grow/Shrink**. Click on **Apply** to add it to the **Group** layer and tweak it to your liking. Play back your animation.

There's more...

We can achieve a similar effect by filling the face of our text with a texture. Under the **Style** pane and under **Face**, Select **Texture** as the **Fill With** option. Drop the video into the source well that appears and then turn off your video clip in the **Layers** tab. Use the following screenshot for reference:

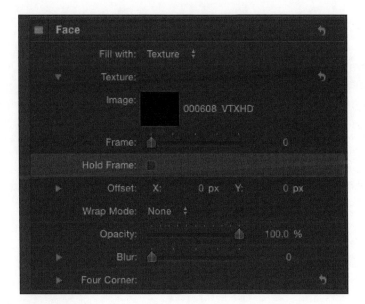

See also

▸ The *Using image masks* recipe in *Chapter 6, Paint and Masks*

Creating a lower third for FCP X

Sometimes you may want to use something from Motion in one of your FCP X projects. It's very common to have projects where we need to utilize the same text design across the project making slight tweaks to it along the way. This exercise is a preview to *Chapter 11, Publishing your Work to FCP X*, which goes into much greater detail about publishing and rigging your work for FCP X.

Getting ready

Under the exercise folder for this chapter, open the 05_12 project. Play back the project. A lower third moves from offscreen to onscreen while some placeholder text fades in. It then stays static and disappears offscreen again. What you may not see is that it's set up to be used in FCP X. If you take a look at the project extension right above the Canvas, you'll notice it's a .moti file. When creating this project, I chose to save it as Final Cut Title in order to have it available in FCP X'S media browser.

How to do it...

Let's get a closer look at this project.

1. In the **Layers** tab, open up the **Lower Third Contents** group and then the **Lower Third Bars** group. There are four still layers in here that have all been masked in order to create a textured lower third bar. The ultimate goal here was to allow someone the option to choose which bar they would like to use in FCP X. A rig was set up in order to achieve this.

2. To see the rig, select **Bars Pop-Up** in the **Layers** tab and look at the **Widget** tab of the **Inspector**. Press *F4* if it's not visible. Under **Bars Pop-Up**, go through each of the four different types of background bars. Make sure your playhead is at a place where the text has animated on the screen. The **Opacity** parameter of each still layer was added to the rig. You can see that the **Opacity** value was set to 0 or 100 depending on whether that layer was selected or not. Use the following screenshot for reference:

3. Before we make this available in FCP X, there's one more thing to look at. At the top of the Timeline, you may have noticed these two green triangular marks and the section in between them identified by an orange highlight. These are known as **Optional Build In** and **Optional Build Out** markers. They were created to allow the user in FCP X to increase or decrease the length of the text animations. It also prevents the middle section from getting highlighted due to the unnecessary change in speed.

4. Let's bring it into FCP X. From the **File** menu, select **Save**. Name the template as My Lower Third. Save it to the **Lower Thirds** category and create a new theme called **Custom Lower Thirds**. Make sure **Use Unused Media** is unchecked and **Save Preview Movie** is checked. Click on **Publish**.

5. Open FCP X and create a new project. Navigate to your **Title Browser**. Go to the **Lower Thirds** category on your left and find your text. Drag it in to the Timeline. Select the text in the Timeline and click on the **i** icon to go to the **Inspector**. Click on the **Title** tab and change between the **Bars-Pop Up** states. Play back the animation. Uncheck **Build In** and play back the animation again. Congrats, you've just completed another chapter!

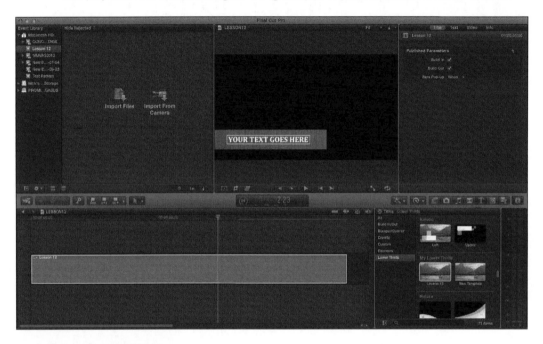

See also

▸ The *Opening and changing text from FCP X in Motion* recipe in *Chapter 11, Publishing Your Work to FCP X*

▸ The *Publishing parameters versus publishing rigs 101 – part 1* in *Chapter 11, Publishing your Work to FCP X*

6
Paint and Masks

In this chapter, we will cover the following:

- ▸ Using the Paint Stroke tool
- ▸ Changing Shape Style and Width Over Stroke
- ▸ Using Sequence Paint
- ▸ The relationship between shapes and Paint
- ▸ Using shape masks
- ▸ Creating a garbage matte for a green screen
- ▸ Adding video to a television screen
- ▸ Applying multiple masks to an image and changing mask modes
- ▸ Using image masks
- ▸ Creating an advanced logo effect with shapes and masks

Introduction

Paint is an extremely fun and versatile tool in Motion. It allows us to use a collection of built-in brush strokes in all of our motion graphics projects. Whether we're accentuating text, creating an organic pattern across the screen, or animating strokes to bring us in a scene, Paint gets the job done.

Using the Paint Stroke tool

Let's take a look at some of the basics the Paint tool has to offer. The Paint tool is located on the toolbar just to the right-hand side of the Pen tool. You can also select it by pressing the *P* key.

Getting ready

Launch Motion and choose a project with a **Preset** of **Broadcast 720p** and a **Frame Rate** of **29.97** with a **Duration** of 10 seconds. Press *Shift + Z* to fit the Canvas window. Press the *T* key or click on the **T** icon on the toolbar to select the Text tool and click somewhere close to the center of the Canvas. Type The Paint Tool and press the *Esc* key to exit the text entry mode. Use the dynamic guides to help center your text on the screen. Press the *F7* key to show the HUD. Pick a font and size of your liking.

How to do it...

Now that your text has been formatted, it's time to paint some strokes onscreen.

1. Press the *P* key to select the Pen tool or click on the brush icon to the left of the Text tool. With your HUD displaying, change the width of your stroke to 15.

2. Choose a blue color. Set the **Pen Pressure** to **Width** and the **Pen Speed** to **Nothing**. Make sure **Write On** is selected. Now with everything set, make sure your playhead is at the beginning of the mini-Timeline.

3. Draw out your Paint stroke underneath the text. Nothing is shown immediately. Press the Space bar to play the project.

 Unlike the **Write On** behavior we've used in the past, notice that the shape is written onscreen based on the speed at which you drew the stroke. If we wanted to customize the speed, we would need to change the behavior settings.

4. Select the **Write On** behavior. In the HUD, change the **Speed** from **Recording** to **Natural**. Move your playhead to 3 seconds on the mini-Timeline and trim the behavior to extend to this point as shown in the following screenshot:

5. Select the **Paint** layer and press the *F4* key to go to the **Shape** tab of the **Inspector**. Notice under the **Style** pane that **Fill** is turned off and **Outline** is turned on as shown in the following screenshot. A paint stroke is simply an outline. We'll see in later exercises how we can create paint outlines using the Line tool.

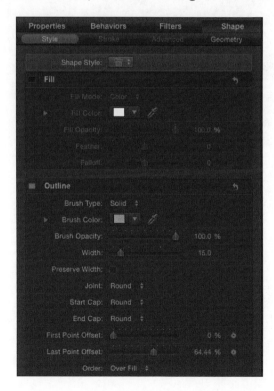

6. As a final step, click on the **Geometry** pane under the **Shape** tab of the **Inspector**. You'll notice your shape is a series of control points. If our objective was to straighten out the paint stroke, we could match all of our Y coordinates to the same number. Click on each Y coordinate for each point and make the values match. You can use the *Tab* key to navigate to each coordinate. Change the **Shape Type** to **Linear**, as shown in the following screenshot:

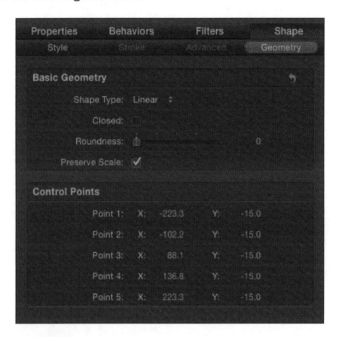

There's more...

Under the **Selection** tool in the toolbar is an **Edit Points** tool as seen in the following screenshot. If you have a **Paint** layer selected, with this tool you can adjust the control points of your paint stroke directly in the Canvas. Please note that it works on gradients and masks as well.

Changing Shape Style and Width Over Stroke

After you initially format your paint, it's time to look at the stylistic, stroke, and advanced options available to you to create extremely organic paint strokes across the screen.

Getting ready

Open the 06_02 project from the exercise folder for this chapter. This is a version of the project we created in the previous exercise. Play back the project and stop the playhead after the paint stroke has animated onscreen or at the 3 second mark.

How to do it...

1. Press the *F7* key to show the HUD. While we chose a solid line stroke in the last exercise, Motion ships with a ton of pre-set brush strokes. Some of them are pre-animated; others can be animated with the **Write On** behavior.

From the **Shape Style** menu, choose **Iron Filings** from under **Textural**, as shown in the following screenshot:

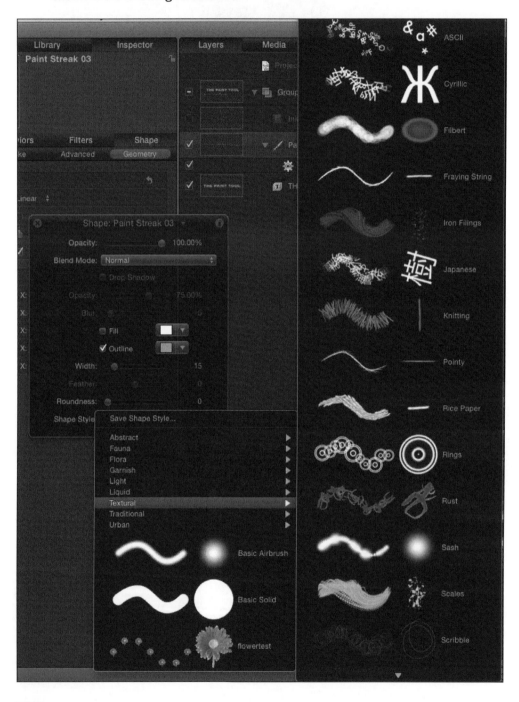

2. Press the *F4* key to open the **Inspector**. Select the **Stroke** tab. There are a lot of settings in here. One thing you can do is vary the length of the spacing and width across the stroke. Let's see how we can do that by using the **Width Over Stroke** property. Click on the disclosure triangle next to it in the **Inspector** to reveal a graph as shown in the following screenshot:

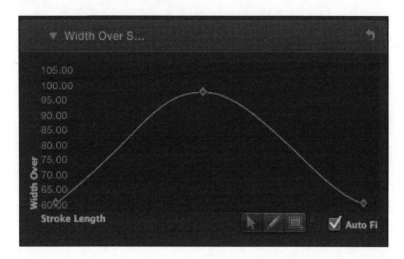

3. If you look in the Canvas and compare it to the graph, you'll notice the edges of the stroke are thinner than the center. Let's say we want to reverse it so the edges are thicker and the center thinner. Drag the keyframe on the left-hand side edge up to the number 300. Do the same for the keyframe on the right-hand side. Look at the results in your Canvas and compare it with the following screenshot:

The following is a screenshot of the graph after we've made the mentioned changes:

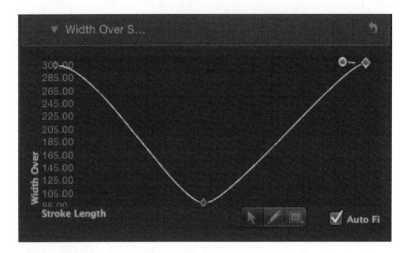

4. We can also add keyframes by clicking on the line to vary the stroke even more. Drag the middle keyframe up to 200. Double-click in between the first and second keyframe. Drag the point underneath the middle point to around a value of 100. Adjust the Bezier handles to taste. Repeat this step to add a point between the final two keyframes. Use the following screenshot for reference:

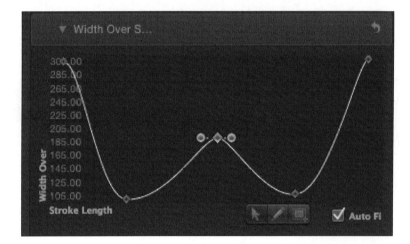

There's more...

Here are a few pointers to customize your paint strokes for a more automated workflow.

Saving paint strokes as presets

You can save any of your paint strokes as a preset just like text. From the **Shape Style** menu in the HUD or **Inspector**, simply choose **Save Preset** and give your setting a name. Besides your being able to select these presets from the Paint tool, they are also saved in the Library.

There are also a ton of creative possibilities available for what you can use as a source for your brush. This is a tip on using a still image or even a movie file as the source.

Using a still image or MOV file as a stroke source

Motion offers a variety of possibilities for the different stroke sources you can use. For instance, you can bring in a Photoshop logo or PNG file into your project and, in the **Shape** tab under the **Style** pane, drop that logo into the **Brush Source** well as indicated in the following screenshot. Try doing it with text and movie files too. Just make sure to bring it into your project first and turn it off if you're only using it for the brush stroke.

Using Sequence Paint

To take your brush stroke animations to the next level, look no further than Sequence Paint. Like Sequence Text, all prebuilt Paint animations come from this behavior. In this exercise, we'll look at some of the options available to us with this behavior.

Getting ready

Open the 06_03 project from the exercise folder of this chapter.

How to do it...

In this exercise, we're going to animate some brush stokes on top and underneath some text.

1. Press *Shift + Z* if necessary to fit the project to the Canvas window. Play back the project. The play range has been set to play the first 3 seconds of the project. The text grows over time while the brush stroke is waiting to be animated. Select **Paint** in the **Layers** tab and click on the gear icon underneath the Canvas. Select **Sequence Paint** from under **Shape**, as indicated in the following screenshot. Trim the behavior so it ends at 2 seconds.

2. Press the *F2* key to go to the **Behaviors** tab of the **Inspector**. If you went through the recipe on **Sequence Text** in the previous chapter, some of these parameters will look familiar to you. Let's add a few parameters to animate the text. From the **Add Parameter** list, choose **Color**. Click on the color well and choose a red color of your liking. Play back the animation. The stroke animates to the color red. Change the **Sequencing Parameter** to **From**. Now it goes from the color red.

3. From the **Add Parameter** list add **Position** and **Scale**. Change the Scale to **0** and the Position X to **-600** and **Y** to **-430** as shown in the following screenshot. Change the **Spread** to **20**.

If you play back the animation, you should see the text animating similar to the following screenshot:

4. The text animates from the lower-left corner of the screen to its original position over 2 seconds. Let's smooth out the animation by easing the values. Change **Reversal** to **Ease in/Out**. As a final step, let's duplicate the brush stroke, move the copy, and animate it from the opposite direction.

5. Select the **Paint** layer and press *Command + D* to duplicate it. Move the copy of the paint stroke above the text using your Canvas controls. You can hold down the *Shift* key to constrain its movement to just up and down. Press the *F2* key to go to the **Behaviors** tab of the **Inspector**. Change the **Position** values to 600 and 430 for **X** and **Y** respectively. Play back the animation and compare it to what you see in the following screenshot:

The relationship between shapes and Paint

When you start to dig deep and look under the hood of Motion, you'll start to see that several different tools and systems that exist are derived from the same engine. Nothing could be more true about shapes and Paint. Let's take a look to see how they're related.

How to do it...

In this exercise, we're going to create a shape and see how we can turn it into a brush stroke.

1. Launch Motion and choose a project with a **Preset** of **Broadcast 720p**, **Frame Rate** of **29.97**, and with a **Duration** of 8 seconds. Press *Shift + Z* to fit the Canvas window. Select the **Line** tool underneath the **Rectangle** tool on the toolbar as shown in the following screenshot. Make sure you're at the beginning of the project.

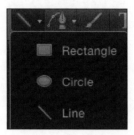

2. Drag a line across the screen, holding down the *Shift* key to keep it straight. Press the *Esc* key to go back to the Selection tool and the *F7* key to bring up the HUD.

3. Change the line to a color of your choosing and notice in the following screenshot how the icon next to the **Line** in the **Layers** tab is the same icon next to the layers we painted on in the previous recipe.

4. With the **Line** selected, press the *F4* key to go to the **Shape** tab of the **Inspector**. From the top of the **Style Pane** under **Shape Style**, navigate to **Abstract | Ideal Form**. Notice under the **outline** section that the brush source is filled with an image that happens to be the cubes from "Ideal Form". This is exactly how we filled the objects we painted on the screen in the previous recipes. Increase the **Width** to 61 and the **Spacing** to 110 to see this better.

5. All of the options available for Paint are available for the line we just created. Go to the **Stroke Pane** in the **Inspector**. Change the **Stroke Color Mode** parameter to **Color Over Stroke**. The cubes fill with a gradient. From the **Gradient** preset menu that you can see in the following screenshot, choose **Sundown**. Increase the **Color Repetitions** to **100**.

6. Click on the disclosure triangle for **Spacing Over Stroke**. Double-click on the **Line** a few times to add a few keyframes. Adjust it to vary the spacing in between the cubes. See the following screenshot as reference:

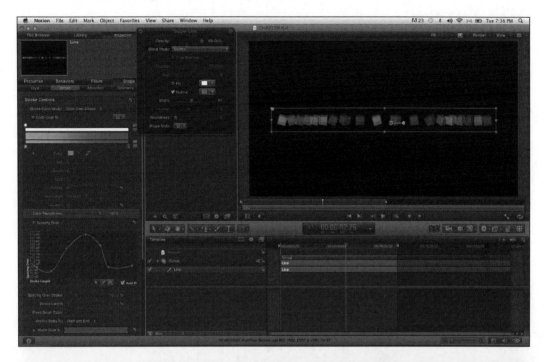

Using shape masks

While we can use Motion's shape tools to create shapes, every once in a while it's nice to use shapes to conceal or mask part of an object. Let's see how we can use our shape mask tools in Motion to do that in a practical situation.

Getting ready

Open the 06_05 project from the exercise folder of this chapter. The project consists of a frame from Motion's library and a picture of a cat we've used in previous exercises. We would like the cat picture to fit the frame of the oval picture. The best way to achieve this is to use the Circle Mask tool.

How to do it...

By adding the Circle Mask tool to the the picture, we'll be able to mask out the part of the image we don't want.

1. Select the **Circle Mask** tool from the toolbar. You'll find it to the right-hand side of the Text tool and underneath the **Rectangle Mask**, tool as shown in the following screenshot:

2. Draw out an oval shape, roughly the size of the oval frame. Adjust the position and size of the mask to get it in place as shown in the following screenshot:

3. Press the *F7* key to bring up the HUD. Click on the box next to **Invert Mask**. This allows us to easily reverse our selection for those instances where we want to discard what's inside the mask and keep what's on the outside. Click on the box again to disable inversion.

4. Increase **Feather** to `154` and change the color of your mask as desired.

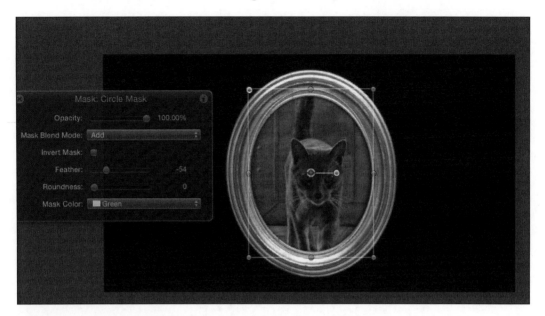

There's more...

There are limitations to the items that you can draw masks on in Motion. Items such as text cannot have a mask on them. To get around this limitation, simply place the **Text** layer within a group and mask the group.

Creating a garbage matte for a green screen

One of the first steps when you're dealing with green screens is to mask out the unwanted areas of your image before applying a Keyer filter to remove the green. This allows the Keyer filter to work a little less hard because it has fewer colors it needs to remove. Let's see how we can easily add a mask using the Bezier Mask tool within Motion.

Getting ready

Locate a piece of green screen footage preferably a shot with little to no camera movement. Create a Motion project that matches the resolution settings, frame rate, and duration of your clip. Make sure you are at the beginning of your project and bring the clip into the Canvas by importing it from the **File Browser**. Play back the clip and become familiar with your shot. The object here is to make a mask around what you want to keep. If the subject is moving, it would be best to find a frame where the action of your subject is the most extended (that is, when their hands or feet extend out from where they are standing). Once you've identified the frame, move your playhead to that location and select the clip.

How to do it...

Let's add a garbage mask around our clip using the Bezier Mask tool.

1. Select the **Bezier Mask** tool from the toolbar as shown in the following screenshot:

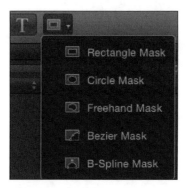

2. The **Bezier Mask** tool allows you to draw a custom mask shape. With your mouse, click on a point just outside where your subject is. Continue to click and add points around your subject as shown in the following screenshot. If you click-and-drag, you can bend the points rather than have them as linear.

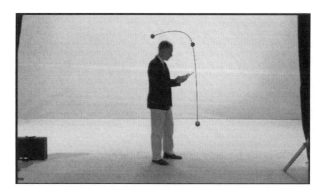

3. When you come back to your first point, hover your mouse over it and notice how a closed-fill circle appears. Click on it in order to close the shape.

4. Play back the project to make sure your subject does not get cut off. If it does, adjust the control points in the Canvas. You can also select the mask in the **Layers** tab and go to the **Inspector** by pressing the *F4* key to adjust the control points there, as shown in the following screenshot:

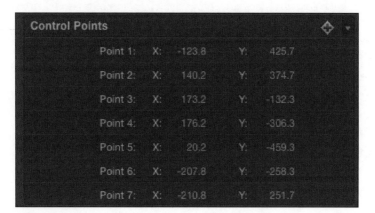

There's more...

If your green screen subject moves a lot, you can easily keyframe the control points of your mask by turning on **Record keyframes** in the Canvas by pressing the *A* key. Simply move frame-by-frame throughout the project and adjust your control points accordingly. Please note that *all* changes you make will be recorded.

See also

▸ The *Using shape masks* recipe of this chapter

▸ *Keying a green screen* in *Chapter 9, Motion Tracking and Keying*

Adding a video to a television screen

If you ever go to work in a visual-effects house, one of the first things they'll want you to do is screen replacement. This usually involves motion tracking. Let's see it in action.

Getting ready

From the exercise files for this chapter, double-click on the 06_07 project. There are two layers in the project; a still of the TV screen and a movie file. You can temporarily disable the visibility of the still by clicking on the check mark next to it in the **Layers** tab. Our goal here is to mask out the center of the TV screen and replace it with the video clip that we will scale down and rotate so that it fits. As a bonus step, we'll bring back in some of the black color from the screen to make the shot more realistic.

How to do it...

Let's find the **Bezier Mask** tool to choose the selection we need to remove.

1. Select the **Bezier Mask** tool from the toolbar as shown in the following screenshot. Press *Command* + = to zoom in on your Canvas so that we can add precise control points.

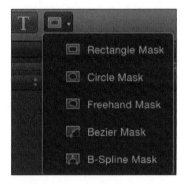

2. Click around the TV screen in order to enclose the portion we want to remove. Click on the first point you created in order to close the mask as shown in the following screenshot:

3. Right now, we have selected the portion of the shot we wish to remove. To reverse this, press the *F7* key to bring up the HUD. Click on the square next to **Invert Mask** to reverse the selection. Add a small amount of feather to help blend the shots together, as shown in the following screenshot. Tweak your control points around the mask to make your selection as precise as possible.

4. Select the movie file and zoom out on your Canvas by pressing *Command + -*. Click-and-drag one of the outer circles of your clip to scale down your object while holding down the *Shift* key to constrain the size. Reposition the clip so it fits in the TV screen and rotate it along the z axis so it matches the perspective.

5. Select the **TV screen** layer and press *Command + D* to duplicate it. Select the **Bezier Mask** on the duplicate and, in the HUD, click on the checkmark next to **Invert Mask** to reverse the selection. Now select the TV screen copy and bring down its **Opacity** to **50**. Make more changes as you see fit.

See also

▸ The *Using shape masks* recipe

▸ *Match Move Four Corner* in *Chapter 9, Motion Tracking and Keying* recipe

Applying multiple masks to an image and changing mask modes

Sometimes it's necessary to apply multiple masks to an image to get your desired selection. At other times, multiple masks can be used to animate and reveal only specific portions of your image, creating dynamic motion graphics. Let's see some of the options available to us when we start combining multiple masks on a clip.

Getting ready

From the exercise folder of this chapter, double-click on the `06_08` project file. Play back the project; it's a scenic shot of a beach. Our objective is to combine several masks across the image to make it appear as though we're looking at the image through the window of a jail cell. We'll achieve this by adding one mask and duplicating it several times. We'll use different mask modes to control the interaction between the masks.

How to do it...

1. Select the clip **Rectangle Mask** tool from the toolbar. You'll find it to the right-hand side of the Text tool.

2. Click-and-drag a narrow **Rectangular Mask** from the top-center of the screen to the bottom. Press the *F7* key to bring up the HUD and click on the empty square next to **Invert Mask**, as shown in the following screenshot:

3. Select the **Rectangular Mask** and press *Command + D* to duplicate it. Move the duplicate over to the right-hand side and don't be alarmed when you don't see anything. The reason we can't is because of the default mask blend mode and the fact that both masks are inverted. In the HUD, change the duplicate mask's blend mode to **Subtract** as shown in the following screenshot. Then, click the checkmark next to **Invert Mask**.

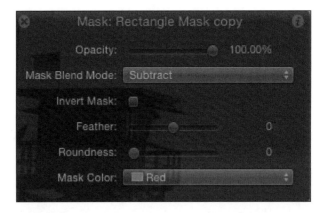

4. Select **Rectangle Mask Copy** and press *Command + D* eight times. Select each copy and spread them out across the screen; the alignment doesn't have to be exact.

5. In the **Layers** tab, click on the first mask and *Shift* + click on the last to have all ten selected. Go to the **Object** menu and choose **Align Top Edges** from under **Alignment**. Go to the **Object** menu again and choose **Distribute Horizontal Centers** from under **Alignment**.

6. As a final step, select the **Movie** layer and, from the toolbar, grab the **Rectangle Mask** tool. Draw a rectangle across the entire image encompassing the top and bottom of the lifeguard house. In the HUD, change the value of **Mask Blend Mode** to **Intersect**. Use the following screenshot for reference. We see our image only where each of our mask layers intersect.

There's more...

A lot of commercials with motion graphics require adding and animating masks. Watch some commercials in the next few days and see if you can point out where masks were applied.

See also

▶ *Combining keyframes and behaviors – animating a Photoshop file* in Chapter 4, *Making It Move with Keyframes*

▶ The *Using shape masks* recipe in this chapter

Using image masks

Motion has the flexibility to allow us not only to create masked shape selections but also to mask any object or group in the **Layers** tab. Let's take a look at how we can achieve this.

Getting ready

Under the exercise folder of this chapter, double-click on the 06_09 project file. Play back the project; it's a series of animated blurred circles moving across the screen from right to left. In this project, there is also a **Video clip** layer that has been turned off. Click on the empty square next to it to turn it on. Our goal is to have our video play with the circles onscreen. We can use either the luminance or transparency of the **Bokeh** group to achieve this.

How to do it...

We're going to add an image mask to the **Video** layer in this project.

1. Select the **Video** layer and from the **Object** menu choose **Add Image Mask**, as shown in the following screenshot. An image mask becomes applied to the video image but it needs a source.

2. Drag the **Bokeh** group over the top of the image mask in the **Layers** tab and release your mouse when you see a hooked arrow. Notice the **Bokeh** group is turned off automatically. Motion assumes that, when you use an object or group as an image mask, you don't want to see it on the Canvas.

3. Play back the clip and notice how the video only appears in the circles. Try experimenting with different sources from Motion's **Library** to see the different type of results you can get.

There's more...

If your image mask source does not contain an **Alpha** channel (a fourth channel of information on a video clip that creates transparency), which is the default mode, simply change it to **Luminance** to see if you get your desired result. This effect depends on the contrast in your footage. For example, a quick way to create a reflection is to use a black-and-white gradient as a source for an image mask while setting the mode to **Luminance**, as shown in the following screenshot. Anything covered by black in the image will be masked out, anything covered by gray will be partially transparent, and anything covered by white will be fully opaque.

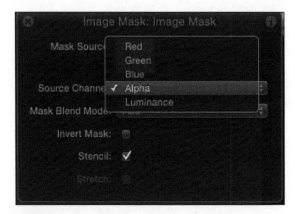

See also

▸ The *Using videos and textures to fill text* recipe in *Chapter 5, Let's Make Text*
▸ The *Using shape masks* recipe of this chapter

Creating an advanced logo effect with shapes and masks

When you duplicate layers and combine masks, you can create some pretty cool animations and effects. Let's take a look at how we can animate a glow across a logo while it scales up over time.

Getting ready

Under the exercise folder of this chapter, double-click on the `06_10` project file. The project consists of two logo groups; `Logo glow` and `Logo`. The image used was an Illustrator file. In order, to scale it up without distortion, we went to the **Media** tab of the **Inspector** and turned off **Fixed Resolution**. If you look inside the **Logo Glow** group, you should see several copies of the logo each containing a glow filter. To create this dynamic glow, duplicating the logo, as well as changing the blend mode between the layers, was needed. The **Logo** group only contains the **Illustrator** layer and no glow. Our goal is to create a mask around the **Logo Glow** group and animate it so that it's only seen for a few seconds.

How to do it...

Let's create a mask to animate one of our logo layers.

1. Zoom out on the Canvas by pressing *Command + -*. Select the **Logo Glow** group. From the toolbar, select the **Bezier Mask** tool underneath the **Rectangle Mask** tool. Click to create control points of your choosing off to the side. Make sure the length of the shape you create is enough to cover the logo. Click on the first point to close the shape. The glow disappears. It's still there but the mask we created does not encompass that group.

2. Press the *F7* key to bring up the HUD. Increase the **Feather** of the mask to **100**. Press the *F4* key to go to the **Mask** tab of the **Inspector** and increase the **Roundness** to **20** and the **Falloff** to **-30**.

3. With the mask still selected and the playhead at the beginning of the project, press the *A* key to activate **Record Keyframes**. Click on the mask and nudge it to force a keyframe. Move to 3 seconds. Drag the mask up and offscreen to the right. Press the *A* key to deactivate **Record Keyframes** and play back the project. Adjust the mask points to taste by selecting the mask, *Ctrl* + clicking on the *Canvas*, and choosing **Edit Points**.

4. Select both logo groups in the **Layers** tab and navigate to **Object | Group**. With the new group selected, go to the gear icon in the toolbar and choose **Grow/Shrink** from under **Basic Motion**. Change the behavior in the HUD as desired.

See also

- ▶ *Applying a Glow filter to a layer* in *Chapter 1, Getting Around the Interface*
- ▶ The *Applying a Fade in/ Fade Out and Grow/Shrink behavior to a still* recipe of *Chapter 3, Making It Move with Behaviors*
- ▶ The *Keyframing a group* recipe in *Chapter 4, Making It Move with Keyframes*
- ▶ The *Using shape masks* recipe in this chapter

7
Let's Make Particles

In this chapter, we will cover:

- ▸ Making particles and changing values in the HUD
- ▸ Tweaking particle parameters in the Inspector
- ▸ Adding randomness values
- ▸ Working with particle behaviors
- ▸ Working with particle presets
- ▸ Working with particle presets in 3D
- ▸ Using an image sequence in a particle emitter
- ▸ Working with and manipulating multiple cells
- ▸ Creating a tunnel through the frame effect
- ▸ Creating your own Bokeh

Introduction

The particle systems in Motion 5 are a powerful engine by which we can take nearly any object, image, layer, or group and animate it using the parameters available to us in the HUD and Inspector. A particle system consists of two items—the emitter and the cell. The cell is referenced by the emitter and the emitter creates the animation over a lifespan specified by you. Let's say we had a PNG layer of an orange. If we created particles out of it, that orange would be put into a cell that is referenced by the emitter. You could use the emitter's parameters to duplicate that orange multiple times per second and have it animate in a particular direction until you decide it should end or die. On top of the ability to turn nearly anything your heart desires into particles, in Motion's library there are pre-animated particle emitters available to incorporate in all of your animations.

Making particles and changing values in the HUD

Let's take a look at how we can create a particle system using a shape from Motion's library and tweak a few of its parameters using the HUD.

Getting ready

From this chapter's exercise files, double-click the `07_01` project. There is the **Shape** layer in the **Layers** tab, whose scale has been animated to repeat for the duration of the project. Our goal is to place the heart in a particle system so that we can have hundreds rain down onto the Canvas.

How to do it...

The following steps will take you through creating your first particle system:

1. Make sure your playhead is at the beginning of your project. Select the **Pink Heart** layer and press *E*, or from the toolbar choose **Create a particle emitter** (the icon with the three bubbles rising up, as shown in the following screenshot):

2. Play back the project. Several things just happened after you pressed that button. In the **Layers** tab, notice that the **Pink Heart** layer has been turned off. A cell and emitter have been created just above it. The cell holds information about the heart while the emitter is creating all the duplicate copies of the heart that are shooting out in a 360-degree circle across the screen at the same speed. You can see a screenshot of this next. Press *F7* to bring up the HUD and see some of these parameters in more detail:

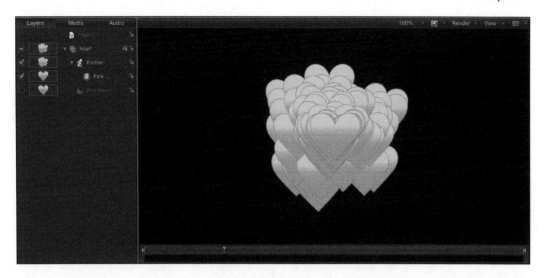

3. Right now, thirty hearts are being born every second and live for a duration of five seconds where they pop off the screen. All the duplicate hearts also hold the original scale of the heart being referenced. Change the **Birth Rate** value to **5** and **Life** to **10**. Bring down the **Scale** parameter to **50**, as shown in the following screenshot:

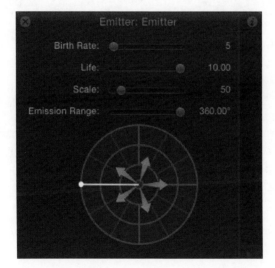

4. Instead of having the hearts come from the center of the screen, let's have them rain down from the top of the Canvas. Decrease the size of your Canvas by clicking on it and pressing *Command + -* a few times. Select the particle emitter and drag it up and offscreen. Use the *Shift* key to constrain the movement. Change the **Emission Range** slider from 360 to 180 and make sure the arrows point down. Play back the animation and tweak the **Birth Rate** and **Scale** sliders as desired. See the following screenshot for reference:

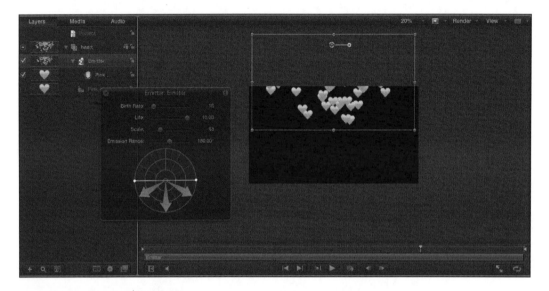

There's more...

If you're finding the HUD limited in terms of the options available to you for the emitter, don't worry, the Inspector has several additional parameters, including the option to add random values to your emitter that will add more realism to it! Take a peak at the following screenshot:

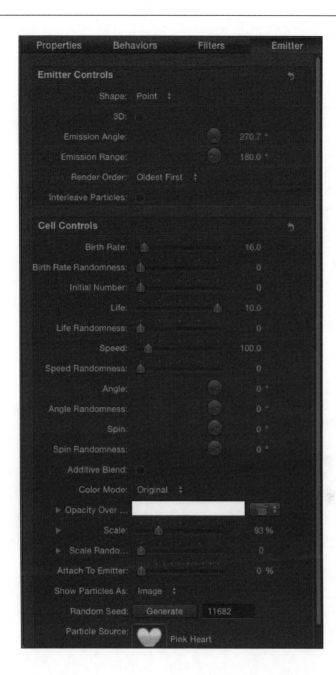

Tweaking particle parameters in the Inspector

In the previous recipe, we switched a few parameters in the HUD for our particle system of hearts, but if we're looking to fine-tune our animation, we need to go to the Inspector. Let's take a look at the several additional parameters available.

Getting ready

From this chapter's exercise files, double-click the 07_02 project. Play back the project. There is a particle system in the center of the Canvas being emitted in the form of a rectangle. Currently, thirty hearts are being born every second and live for five seconds. We're going to tweak our particle system to change the flow of the animation so that our hearts emit out in a circle and away from the screen.

How to do it...

By following these steps, we'll gain a better understanding of how we can control the particle system:

1. Select the Emitter in the **Layers** tab. Press *F4* to open the **Emitter** tab of the Inspector. Change the **Shape** menu's option from rectangle to circle and the **Arrangement** option to **Random Fill**. Set the radius to 500.

2. Increase **Birth Rate** to 200 and set **Speed** in **Cell Controls** to 0. If you play back the project, you'll see the hearts trying to form the shape of a circle. Since there is no speed value, the hearts stay put in the shape they originate from, as shown in this screenshot:

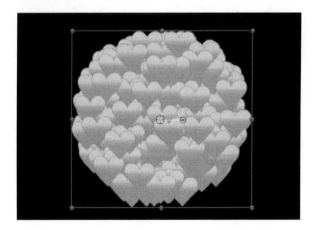

3. Set **Angle Value** to 15 and **Spin** to 30.

4. Rather than having the particles pop onscreen when they're born and pop offscreen when they die, we're going to add some tags to the **Opacity Over Life** parameter. The trick is to click the white line where we want to add a tag above it. Click the line once close to the beginning and twice close to the end. Use the following screenshot for reference:

5. Click on the first tag and under the line, drag the **Opacity** slider to 0 (indicated in this screenshot). Repeat this step for the last slider. Now the hearts fade in at birth and fade out at death:

6. As a final step, we're going to keyframe the speed of the particle system to start at 100 percent and eventually go down to 0 to reveal the shape of the circle we created. Go to the beginning of the Timeline and click the diamond icon next to **Speed** to add a keyframe. Change its value to 100. Move to three seconds and add another keyframe by clicking the diamond icon next to **Speed** again. Move to three seconds and set **Speed** to 0. Play back the animation and compare it to the following screenshot:

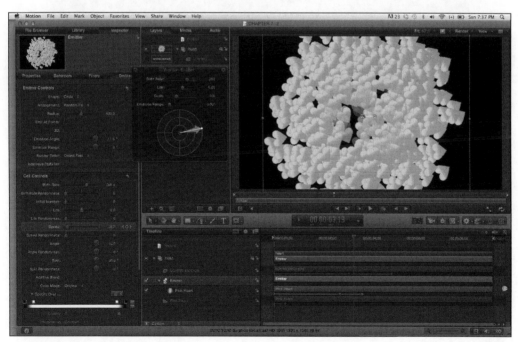

There's more...

You can create some amazing animations by changing the type of shape used to emit particles. For instance, if you change the shape of your particles to **Image** and use text as the source, the particles will spell out the word as long there is a substantial number of hearts being born and the **Arrangement** option is set to **Random Fill**. We'll see an example of this in a later exercise, but the following screenshot gives you a sneak peak on the end results you can get:

Adding randomness values

To give your particle systems just a little more, we're going to add a little randomness to some of the parameters. This randomness will help give your animations a more organic feel.

Getting ready

From this chapter's exercise files, double-click the 07_03 project. Play back the project. The particle system consists of little demograms that rain down from a line. The **Angle** and **Spin** values cause the demograms to rotate while moving, and the **Opacity Over Life** parameter allows each particle to fade in and out during its lifespan. The particles also change color over their life as reflected in the **Color Mode** menu and the gradient outlining the cycle. We're going to add randomness values to tweak the animation. Whenever we add a randomness value, it's going to look at the original value above it and add and subtract to it randomly every second based on the number you specify. For example, say the **Scale** value is set to 50. If you add a **Scale** randomness of 10, every second the demograms will be somewhere between a scale of 40 and 60.

How to do it...

Let's start to randomize different values in this recipe:

1. Select the emitter in the **Layers** tab and press *F4*. In the **Emitter** tab of the Inspector, change the **Birth Rate Randomness** slider's value to 10. Now, every second, somewhere between 10 and 30 objects are born.

2. Now, set **Life Randomness** to 3, **Angle Randomness** to 40, **Spin Randomness** to 50, and **Scale Randomness** to 80. Play back the project. Now we have our demograms growing at different sizes, being born at different angles and spinning at different rates! The following screenshot shows the Inspector with all of the mentioned changes and also a **Color Over Life** change (see the previous recipe to learn how to do it).

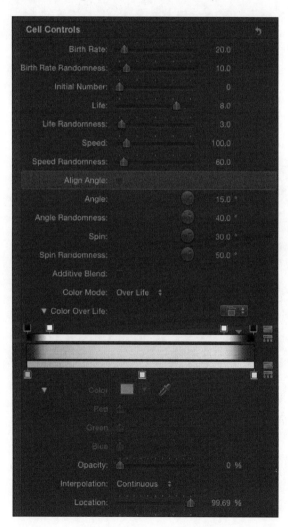

The following is a screenshot showing a frame of the particle animation in the Canvas with random values applied:

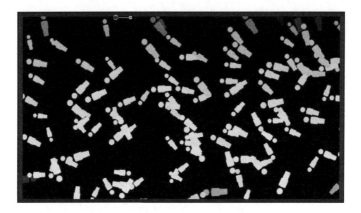

3. While playing back, click the **Generate** button next to **Random Seed**. You'll notice that your animation changes and a new number is created next to **Generate**. **Random Seed** takes all the random parameters and creates the animation based on this number. Change this number and change the randomness of the animation, as shown here:

See also

▶ The *Making particles and changing values in the HUD* recipe.

▶ The *Tweaking particle parameters in the Inspector* recipe.

Working with particle behaviors

While there are already a ton of parameters you can animate by keyframing their values in the particle and cell emitters, Motion offers you a few particle behaviors worth taking a look at from the library as well.

Getting ready

From this chapter's exercise files, double-click the 07_04 project. Play back the project. The animation consists of a bouncing alarm clock from Motion's library in the foreground and a particle system referencing that alarm clock in the background. Unlike the other particle systems we've worked with in the previous recipes, the source of the particle system has been turned back on to preserve it. Our goal is to add two particle behaviors to have the clocks scale down and spin over its life cycle. By adjusting the speed and direction of our emitter, we will also have the clocks look like they're being pulled off into the distance. Also note, the anchor point of the clock was adjusted in advance in order to have the particles spin around the center of the clock.

How to do it...

1. Open the **Particle** group and select **Emitter**. Press *Command + 2* to go to the **Library** tab. Under **Behaviors**, choose **Particles | Spin Over Life**. Click **Apply**.

2. Press *F7* to open the HUD. Set **Increment Type** to **Birth and Death Values**. Set **Birth** to 360 and **Death** to 0. If you're having trouble, try changing the values in the **Behaviors** tab of the Inspector. Now, play back the animation.

3. Now, let's have the clocks in the particle system scale over life. Select the **Emitter** again. Press *Command + 2* to go to the **Library**. Under **Behaviors**, choose **Particles | Scale Over Life**. Click **Apply**.

4. In the HUD, set **Increment Type** to **Birth and Death Values**. Set **Scale at Birth** to 100 and **Scale at Death** to 0. If you're having trouble, try changing the values in the **Behaviors** tab of the Inspector. Play back the animation. The clocks now scale down gradually until they die, as shown in the following screenshot:

5. Press *F4* to go to the **Emitter** tab of the Inspector. Change the **Emission Longitude** value to **180** and **Speed** to **2000**, as shown in the following screenshot. Change the other parameters as desired.

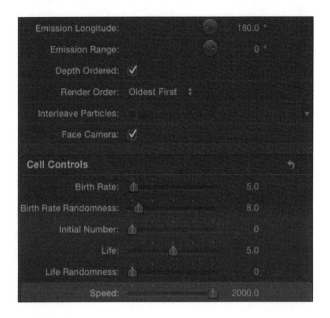

There's more...

When you start building complex particle animations, keep in mind that you can save them to the **Library** as well as any of the behaviors you tweak. All particle presets can be found in the **Library** under **Particle Emitters** in a dedicated theme folder you create. The more time you spend automating your work, the more time you can dedicate to the creative process!

See also

▶ The *Making particles and changing values in the HUD* recipe.

▶ The *Tweaking particle parameters in the Inspector* recipe.

Working with particle presets

So far, we've created our own particle systems by selecting objects to place into cells referenced by the emitter. Motion ships with over 200 presets! One of the best ways to learn Motion is to dissect how some of the particle presets were created. Let's take a look at what it has to offer!

Getting ready

From this chapter's exercise folder, double-click on the `07_05` project. There are two particle presets in this project but one has been turned off. Play back the project and familiarize yourself with the **Magic Dust** preset. Stop the playback. Turn off the **Magic Dust** group and turn on the **Buskerit** group. Play back the project again. In this recipe, we'll take a look at each of these presets and change a few parameters to look at how the animations were created.

How to do it...

Let's now tweak these parameters of our presets in more detail:

1. Reveal the content of the **Buskerit** group by clicking the disclosure triangle next to it. It contains a group called **busker** and seven still images that have been turned off. The images are being referenced by the emitter.

2. Click the disclosure triangle next to the **Busker** group. It contains the content of the **Busker** emitter and the seven cells that hold information from those layers that have been shot off. The Emitter also has a **Scale Over Life** behavior in it. While the object continually changes scale over the animation, the **Scale Over Life** behavior was used to animate the "pop-up" intro of the instruments, whereas keyframes were used to change the scale over the project.

3. Select the **Scale Over Life** behavior and press *F2* to go to the **Behaviors** tab of the Inspector. Notice the **Increment Type** parameter set to **Custom**. Click the disclosure triangle next to **Custom Scale** to see the graph, as shown in the following screenshot:

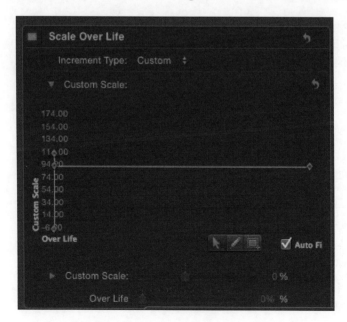

4. Select the Emitter in the **Layers** tab and press *Command + 8* to open the **Keyframe Editor**. Notice that both the scale and rotation of the emitter are keyframed periodically throughout the entire animation, as shown in the following screenshot. In the **Keyframe Editor**, press *Shift + K* to move forward between keyframes. Change the **Rotation** and **Scale** values by double-clicking the values while on an existing keyframe. You'll know you're on one because the diamond shape will appear highlighted!

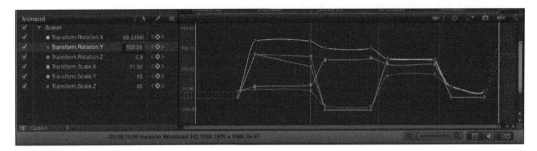

5. Click the disclosure triangle to close the **Buskerit** group, turn it off, and turn on the **Magic Dust** group. Click the disclosure triangle to open it. A still image of a spark was used as the source for the Emitter. Several behaviors were used to animate the sparks.

6. With the emitter selected, press *F4* to go to the **Emitter** tab of the Inspector. Set **Emission Range** to **45**, **Birth Rate** to **200**, and **Speed** to **1000**. Play back the project to see the effect it has and compare it to the following:

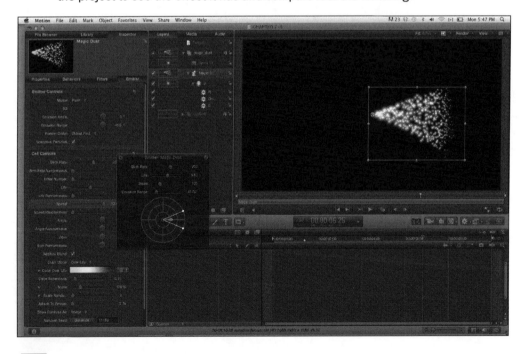

7. Select the **Magic Dust** group and go to the gear icon under the mini-Timeline. Choose **Basic Motion | Motion Path**. Tweak the path as desired. Play back the animation.

There's more...

Learning how particle presets work is a great way to get used to Motion.

Particle presets are the best way to learn Motion!

Looking at the library and seeing how something was created is the best way to get under the hood of the application and start creating your own animations. Don't be afraid to explore.

See also

▶ The *Making particles and changing values in the HUD* recipe.

▶ The *Tweaking particle parameters in the Inspector* recipe.

Working with particle presets in 3D

Particle presets are already powerful on their own but turn them into 3D and you'll find that a few of them will actually look like they have been extruded. Let's take a look!

Getting ready

From this chapter's exercise folder, double-click on the 07_06 project. Play back the project. There is a particle system of thin water being projected across the screen. Go to the **Properties** tab in the Inspector and click the rotation disclosure triangle to see the object rotate 90 degrees on its y axis. The water becomes invisible because it's flat the minute you change perspective. If we promote a particle system to 3D, we can get rid of this problem and have a few additional options available to us in terms of the way we emit the water.

How to do it...

Let's get rid of the flatness of our particle system by making it 3D:

1. Select the **Particle Emitter** category and press *F4* to go to the Inspector. Click on the **3D** checkbox. As soon as you press the button, more options become available to you in the **Emitter Controls** section, including **Emission Latitude** and **Emission Longitude**, as seen here:

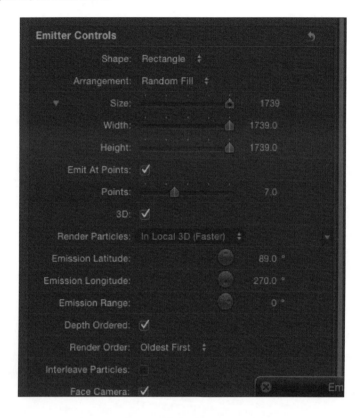

2. Two additional selections—**Box** and **Sphere**—also became available under the **Shape** drop-down. Click on the word **Rectangle** and choose **Box**.

3. Press *F1* to go to the **Properties** tab of the Inspector. Click the disclosure triangle next to **Scale** and increase **Scale Z** to **200**.

4. Rotate the water **90** degrees on the **Y** axis and notice it's no longer flat. Use the following screenshot of the **Properties** tab for reference:

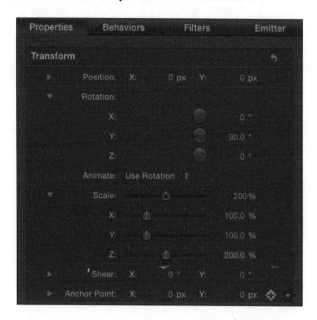

5. Go to the beginning of the Timeline and bring back **Rotation Y** to 0. Click the diamond shape next to **Rotation Y** to add a keyframe. Move to the end of the Timeline; and change the parameter to 720. Play back the project and see that, no matter what angle it is, the particle system never goes flat, as shown here:

Using an image sequence in a particle emitter

So far, all the content we've used for our particle emitters has been through selecting presets or using content through Motion's library. In this recipe, we're going to find a collection of photos on our drive to bring into Motion and use them as the source for our particle system.

Getting ready

Locate a collection of around 20 photos on your hard drive. It's best if these photos aren't extremely large in size, because we will be displaying several of them onscreen at once. Feel free to use your favorite photo-editing application to scale them down. We want Motion to see these photos as an image sequence; to do that, we'll need to give them the same name followed by a numerical number. The numbers assigned should be sequential. For example, if you have a set of photos with buildings, you'll call the first photo `building_1`, the second `building_2`, and so on. Once this is finished, launch Motion and choose a project with **Duration** set to `10` seconds, **Preset** set to `720p`, and **Frame Rate** set to `30`. When we go to the **File Browser** and find the image sequence, Motion will display only a single file containing all the photos as long as the **Collapsed Image Sequence** button is active. See the following screenshot for reference:

How to do it...

Let's take our image sequence and apply it to a particle system:

1. Make sure you are on the first frame of your project. Press *Command + 1* to go to the **File Browser**. Find the image sequence, click on it and choose **Import**. Play back the project. The duration of the image sequence will be determined by the number of photos you have imported. Each photo plays for one frame in the order they were named.

2. Stop the playback and go back to the beginning of the project. With the image sequence selected, go to the **Object** menu and choose **Make Particles**, as shown here:

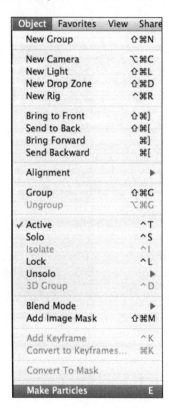

3. Press *F7* to show the HUD. Set **Birth Rate** to **5**, **Life** to **10**, and **Scale** to **50**. Change the **Emission Range** slider's value as desired. Play back the animation. The following screenshot is an example of what you could end up with:

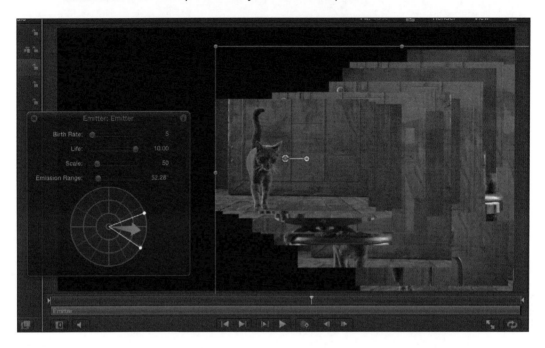

4. Currently, the particle emitter is playing each photo in the image sequence. We want each photo born to be random, but not play through the entire image sequence. Press *F4* to go to the **Emitter** tab of the Inspector. Uncheck **Play Frames**.

5. Click the disclosure triangle over **Opacity Over Life** and add three tags to create a fade-in effect and a fade-out effect over the image. Let's have our pictures form in the shape of some text.

6. Type a two or three letter word of your choice on screen. Make the size big and choose a thick font. Turn off the **Text** layer.

7. Select the Emitter. In the Inspector, Set **Shape** to **Image** and **Arrangement** to **Random**. Drop the **Text** layer into the image source well in the Inspector.

8. Bring down the **Speed** slider to 0, increase the **Birth Rate** value to 1200, set **Scale** to 3, and set **Scale Randomness** to 2. the following is how your output should look:

How it works

When we brought the image sequence into our project, we turned it into a particle system. By changing some of the particle parameters in the Inspector, we were able to tell the emitter to randomly display each photo.

See also

▶ *Changing the text format* in Chapter 5, *Let's Make Text*.

▶ *Changing the text style* in Chapter 5, *Let's Make Text*.

▶ The *Making particles and changing values in the HUD* recipe.

▶ The *Tweaking particle parameters in the Inspector* recipe.

Working with and manipulating multiple cells

In an earlier recipe, where we looked at particle presets in detail, we saw that an emitter can reference multiple cells. Let's take a look at how we can add additional cells to our project.

Getting ready

From this chapter's exercise files, double-click the 07_08 project. Play back the project. There is a particle system in the project with one cell that's referencing the **Atomic Cluster** layer. By changing the values in the Inspector, I was able to change the color of the atoms over its life, have them fade in and out, and emit straight towards us. A gravity simulation behavior was added, so the particles appear to be falling too. In the **Layers** tab there is a group called **Atom 02**. We want this group to move with our particle system. We'll duplicate the existing cell and change the source. We'll also change the **Random Seed** value so that the objects don't occupy the same space.

How to do it...

1. Select the **Atom Cluster** cell and press *Command + D* to duplicate it. Drag the **Atom 02** group onto the duplicate cell layer to change its source.

2. If you play back the project, the cells are on top of each other. Select the duplicate cell and press *F4* to open the **Particle Cell** tab of the Inspector. Click on the **Generate** button next to **Random Seed** to change the random parameters of the animation and play back the project.

3. Change the other values of the cell in the Inspector as desired and compare them to the following screenshot:

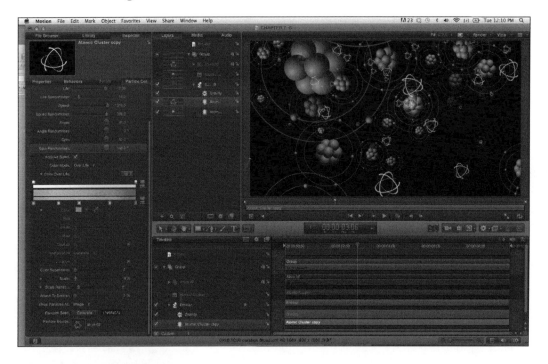

See also

▸ The *Making particles and changing values in the HUD* recipe.

▸ The *Tweaking particle parameters in the Inspector* recipe.

Creating a tunnel through the frame effect

It's time to put our knowledge of particle systems to use and create a full system from scratch.

Getting ready

Launch Motion and choose a project with **Duration** set to 10 seconds, **Preset** set to 720p, and **Frame Rate** set to 30. Click **Open**. Go to the **Library** and, under **Content**, select **Big Frame**. Make sure you are on the first frame of the project and click **Import**. We're going to take this frame and place it into a particle system with **Line** as our chosen shape. We're going to make that line 3D and position it in 3D space. We'll then add a camera to our project and move across that line while frames are being born across it.

How to do it

1. Select the **Big Frame** layer and press *E* to turn it into a particle system. Select the Emitter and press *F4* to go to the **Emitter** tab.

2. Change the **Shape** value of the Emitter to **Line** and click the **3D** checkbox. Reveal the start and end points. Change both **X** positions to **0**. Change the **Z** start point to **-10000** and the **Z** end point to **10000**, as shown here:

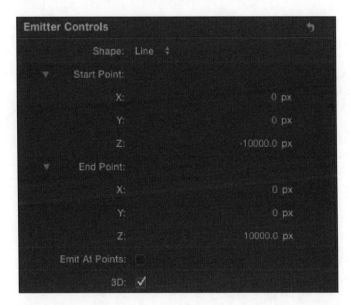

3. Set **Emission Longitude** to 270 and **Emission Range** to 360. Change the **Birth Rate** value to 13 and the **Initial Number** value to 50. Set **Speed** to 0. Set **Angle Randomness** to 360, **Spin** to 41, and **Spin Randomness** to 26.

4. Change **Color Mode** to **Color Over Life**. Change the color to a style preset or a color of your liking. Add the appropriate opacity tags to have each of the particles fade in and out. Use the following screenshot for your reference:

5. Move to six seconds. Add a keyframe to **Birth Rate**, **Initial Number**, and **Life**. Move to nine seconds and make all the values shown here 0:

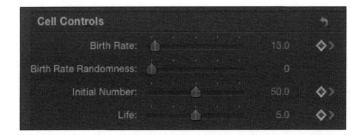

6. Add a camera to the scene by going to the **Object** menu and choosing **New Camera**. Switch all your groups to 3D by clicking **Yes**. This will allow groups to interact with your camera. Make sure you are at the beginning of the project. With your camera selected, press *F1* to go to the **Properties** tab. Twirl down the position properties and add a keyframe for **Scale**. Change its value to -8000. Move to the end of the Timeline and change the **Position** value to 6000. A keyframe is added automatically. Play back the animation to get the following result:

There's more...

Some of the particle emitters are referencing very abstract still images. Take a look for yourself to see how the particle emitters were created and how you can use them in your own layers.

See also

▸ The *Making particles and changing values in the HUD* recipe.

▸ The *Tweaking particle parameters in the Inspector* recipe.

▸ The *Adding randomness values* recipe.

▸ *Making it 3D* in *Chapter 10, Intro to 3D*.

▸ *Moving a camera versus moving a layer* in *Chapter 10, Intro to 3D*.

Creating your own Bokeh

You may have noticed an image called **Bokeh** in the Content or the **Particle Emitter** section of the **Library**. It creates a series of randomly blurred circles with bright highlights used to mimic a similar effect seen in photographs, usually on the background of the image. We're going to learn how we can create our own Bokeh from scratch.

Getting ready

Double-click the **07_10** project file from this chapter's exercise folder. The project consists of a group that has been turned off to act as the foreground of the project when we've done our Bokeh. Right now in the empty group, we're going to create a circle, add some filters, and throw it into a particle system. We will adjust the parameters and add some simulation behaviors to have it float offscreen left.

How to do it...

1. Select the **Bokeh** group and go to the toolbar to select the **Circle** tool underneath the **Rectangle** tool. *Shift* + drag your mouse in the Canvas to create a small circle on the screen. Press the *Esc* key to move back to the selection tool.

2. Press *Command + 2* to go to the **Library** and select **Filters | Blur | Prism**. Drag that over to your **Circle** layer. Press *F3* to go to the **Filters** tab and change the **Amount** value to **15** and the **Mix** value to **75**, as shown in the following screenshot:

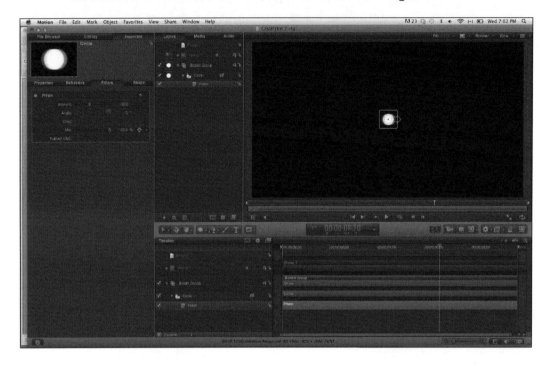

3. Press *Command + 2* to go to the **Library** tab and select **Filters | Glow | Glow**. Drag that over to your **Circle** layer to add it. Press *F3* to go to the **Filters** tab and increase the **Radius** value to 40 and the **Threshold** value to .01.

4. Make sure you are at the beginning of the project. Select the **Circle** layer and press *E* to create particles.

5. Select the emitter and press *F4* to go to the **Emitter** tab of the Inspector. Set **Shape** to **Rectangle**. Set **Arrangement** to **Random Fill**. Increase **Size** to 1000. Click the **3D** checkbox.

6. Set **Birth Rate** to 4, **Life** to 10, and **Speed** to 0. Under **Opacity Over Life**, add three more tags to create a fade in and fade out effect. Set **Scale Randomness** to 66.

7. Press *Command + 2* to go to the **Library** tab and select **Behaviors | Simulations | Gravity**. Drag that over to your **Circle** layer to add it. Press *F7* to bring up the HUD and drag the arrow to the left.

8. Press *Command + 2* to go to the **Library** tab again and select **Behaviors | Simulations | Random Motion**. Drag that over to your **Circle** layer to add it. In the HUD, set **Amount** to 25. Drag the emitter over to the right on the Canvas. Turn on the group that is currently turned off in the **Layers** tab and play back the project. Use the following screenshot for reference:

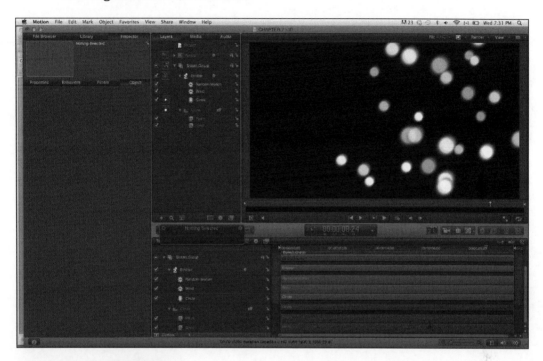

See also

▸ The *Making particles and changing values in the HUD* recipe.

▸ The *Tweaking particle parameters in the Inspector* recipe.

▸ *Using image masks* in *Chapter 6, Paint and Masks*.

8
Replicators – It's No Fun By Yourself

In this chapter, we will cover the following:

- ▶ Creating a replicator and changing parameters in the HUD
- ▶ Tweaking replicator parameters in the Inspector
- ▶ Working with the Sequence Replicator behavior
- ▶ Keyframing the replicator's parameters
- ▶ Working with replicator presets
- ▶ Making it 3D! Looking at 3D options for replicators
- ▶ Adding a camera to interact with your replicator
- ▶ Creating your own video wall
- ▶ Faking 3D Extrusion with shapes

Introduction

Whether you look at motion graphics on television or printed on a billboard, the images that we see are made and organized into patterns. Replicators in Motion 5 make the process of creating patterns and repeating designs extremely simple. We can even animate these replicator systems using behaviors and keyframes so that they move together as if they were in sync.

Replicators share similarities to particles, in that, when you create a replicator, the element you use is brought into a cell referenced by it. Unlike particles, replicators do not have life spans. They remain fixed on the screen from where you chose to create them. In Motion, almost any item (a group, video file, Photoshop still, or even a vector illustration) can be used as a source inside a replicator. The following cookbook recipes will introduce you to the fundamentals of using the replicator in Motion along with the main parameters, functions, and behavior parameters you should be familiar with in your replicating journey!

Creating a replicator and changing parameters in the HUD

Let's take a look at how we can create a replicator using a shape from Motion's Library and tweak a few of its parameters using the HUD!

Getting ready

Under the exercise files of this chapter, double-click on the 08_01 project. There is a **Shape** layer in the **Layers** tab whose rotation has been animated to repeat for the duration of the project. Our goal is to place the star in a replicator so that we can have a pattern in our Canvas.

How to do it...

1. Make sure your playhead is at the beginning of your project. Select the **Star** layer and press **L**; alternatively, from the toolbar choose **Create a replicator** (the icon with a grid of squares, as shown in the following screenshot).

2. Play back the project. Several things just happened after you pressed that button. In the **Layers** tab, notice the **Star** layer has been turned off. A cell and replicator have been created just above it. The cell holds information about the star while the emitter is creating all the duplicate copies of the star that remain stagnant on the screen in a rectangle pattern. The problem is that the rectangle is too small. Drag the square bound box handles in the Canvas to increase the size of the replicator shape. Keep increasing the size till it is evenly spread out across the Canvas. Press the *F7* key to bring up the HUD and see some of these parameters in more detail.

3. Right now there are approximately 25 stars spread out in five columns and five rows in the shape of a rectangle. Unlike an emitter, the replicator stays static on the screen without a life span. The reason it's rotating is because the original star was keyframed. Let's change the value of **Shape** to **Circle**.

4. In the HUD, change the value of **Arrangement** from **Tile Fill** to **Outline**. Increase the value of **Points** to **9**. In the Canvas, drag the circle handles to increase the size of the **Radius** until you can see all the stars as shown in the following screenshot. Play back the project.

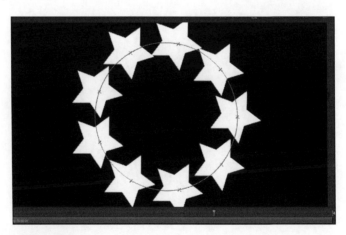

There's more...

Where are all the options for my replicator?

Finding the HUD limited?

If you're finding the HUD limited in terms of the options available to you for the replicator, don't worry. The **Inspector** has several additional parameters for the replicator that we can't see in the HUD. They're hidden, but not because the parameters are used less often; they simply won't fit because there are so many of them. The following screenshot shows the available parameters in the **Inspector**:

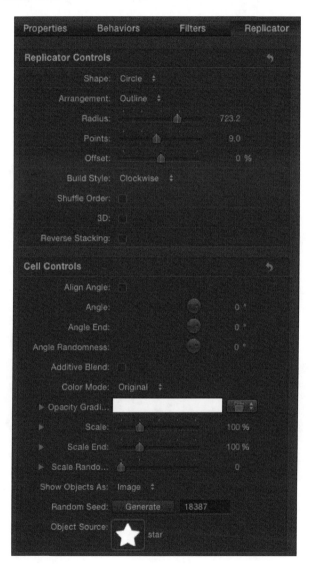

See also

▸ The *Making particles and changing values in the HUD* recipe of *Chapter 7, Let's Make Particles*

▸ The *Tweaking replicator parameters in the Inspector* recipe of this chapter

Tweaking replicator parameters in the Inspector

In the last recipe, we switched a few parameters in the HUD for our replicator of stars; however, if we're looking to fine-tune the replicator, we need to go to the Inspector. Let's take a look at the additional parameters available.

Getting ready

In the exercise folder of this chapter, double-click on the 08_02 project. Play back the project. If you've worked on the previous exercise, you'll see it's where we finished tweaking our replicator in the HUD.

How to do it...

1. Select **Replicator** in the **Layers** tab. Press the *F4* key to open the **Emitter** tab of the **Inspector**. In the **Cell Controls** add an **Angle Randomness** value of 90. Each star now starts from a different angle position.

2. Change the value of **Color Mode** to **Over Pattern**.

3. Under the **Gradient Presets** menu to the right-hand side of **Color Gradient**, change it to **Rainbow** as indicated in the following screenshot:

4. Change the value of **Color Repetitions** to **20** and the **Scale End** to **20**. Notice how the gradient wraps around the stars and how the stars start at **100** and get smaller as you move clockwise around the circle.

5. As a final step, change the value of **Build Style** to **Counter Clockwise** and scrub the offset value to see how you can change the position of where the first star begins. When you're done, change the value of **Offset** to **80%**.

There's more...

Like emitters, you can use your own custom shape as a source to spread out the image you're replicating in that pattern. For example, if you change the shape of your replicators to **Image** and use **Text** as the source, the replicator will spell out the word if a substantial amount of points are made, the stars are small enough, and the value of **Arrangement** is set to **Random Fill**. See the following screenshot for reference:

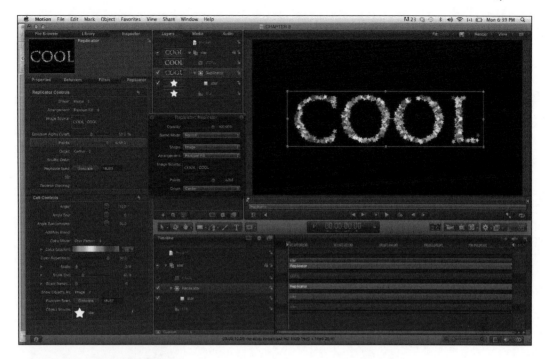

▶ The *Creating a replicator and changing parameters in the HUD* recipe of this chapter

▶ The *Customizing a gradient generator* recipe of *Chapter 2, Looking at Motion's Library*

Working with the Sequence Replicator behavior

Just as we customized text animation using a Sequence Text behavior, we can animate replicators using a Sequence Replicator behavior.

Getting ready

From the exercise files of this chapter, double-click on the 08_03 project. The project consists of a bokeh.png file from Motion's **Library** that has been replicated on a line. We're going to add a Sequence Replicator behavior to animate the circles onscreen.

How to do it...

1. Select the replicator and press *Command + 2* to go to the **Library**. Under **Behaviors** navigate to **Replicator | Sequence Replicator**, as shown in the following screenshot. Choose **Apply**. If you play back the project, you'll notice that nothing has changed. We'll need to add properties in the **Behaviors** tab of the **Inspector** to animate it.

2. Press the *F2* key to move to the **Behaviors** tab of the **Inspector**. Add the **Scale** and **Rotation** parameters. Change the value of **Scale** to **0** and **Rotation** to **360**. Play back the project. The circles start at their original size value and scale down to 0 while rotating 360 degrees over the length of the project.

3. Change the value of **Sequencing** from **From** to **To**, the **Traversal** to **Ease In/Out**, and the **Spread** to **20**.

4. Select **Sequence Replicator** in the **Layers** tab and move to 5 seconds in the Timeline. Press the *O* key to trim the behavior's out-point to 5 seconds. Press *Command + Option + O* to trim the play range as well. Play back your project.

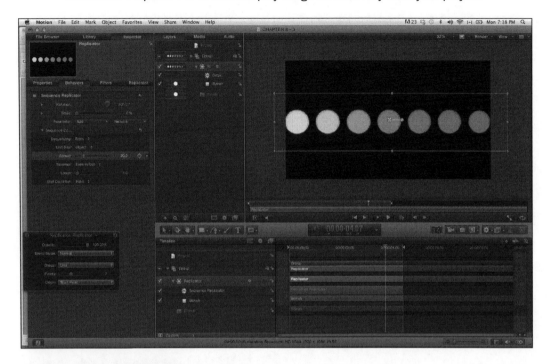

See also

▶ The *Sequence Text* recipe in *Chapter 5, Let's Make Text*

▶ The *Creating a replicator and changing parameters in the HUD* recipe

▶ The *Tweaking replicator parameters in the Inspector* recipe

Keyframing the replicator's parameters

As we've seen in earlier chapters, we can do some pretty amazing things combining keyframes and behaviors. Let's see how we can combine both keyframes and behaviors when working with replicators.

Getting ready

From the exercise files of this chapter, double-click on the 08_04 project. Play back the project. The animation consists of a series of books that animate from offscreen to onscreen. If you select the replicator and go to the **Replicator** tab of the **Inspector**, you can see that they are being replicated along the shape of a line; however, because the line is so small, the books are overlapping. If you click on the **Behaviors** tab, you'll see a **Sequence Replicator** added. Three parameters have been added: **Rotation**, **Color**, and **Position**. Over the span of 2 seconds, the books go from the parameter values set in the **Sequence Replicator** to values established in the **Replicator** tab.

How to do it...

We're going to keyframe the line's length in the **Inspector** so that it grows out while the books animate.

1. Select the replicator and press the *F4* key to go to the **Replicator** tab of the **Inspector**. Move to the 1 second point in the mini-Timeline and add a keyframe to **Start Point** and **End Point** as shown in the following screenshot:

2. Move to 2 seconds. Change the **X** value of **Start Point** to 600 and the X value **End Point** to -600. Play back the project and compare it with the following screenshot. The books now fall onto a line that grows from 1 to 2 seconds. Let's also have the books change scale over time.

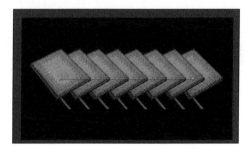

3. Move to 1 second and in the **Replicator** tab under **Replicator Controls** add a keyframe next to **Scale**. Move to 2 seconds and change the value of **Scale** to **60%**.

4. On the lower-right corner of the Timeline, click on the **Show Keyframe Editor** icon. Make sure that the **Animated** keyframes are displayed and the replicator is selected as shown in the following screenshot. Drag a marquee around all the keyframes in the graph. _Ctrl_ + click any one of them and choose **Ease Both**. Play back the project and notice the change to the books' **Scale** from 1 to 2 seconds.

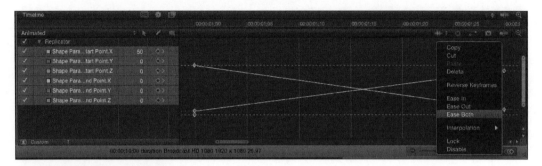

There's more...

When you start building complex replicator animations, keep in mind that you can save them, as well as any of the behaviors you tweak, to the **Library**. The more time you spend automating your work, the more time you can dedicate to the creative process!

See also

▸ The _Creating a replicator and changing parameters in the HUD_ recipe

▸ The _Tweaking replicator parameters in the Inspector_ recipe

▸ _Working with multiple parameters in the Keyframe Editor_ in Chapter 4, _Making It Move with Keyframes_

▸ _Combining keyframes and behaviors – animating a Photoshop file_ in Chapter 4, _Making It Move with Keyframes_

Working with replicator presets

So far, we've created our own replicators by selecting objects to place into cells referenced by the replicator. Motion ships with over 200 replicator presets! One of the best ways to learn Motion is to dissect how some of the replicators were created. Some of the elements can be even used to create transitions between elements. Let's take a look at what it has to offer!

Getting ready

From the exercise files of this chapter, double-click on the 08_05 project. There are two replicator presets in this project but one has been turned off. Play back the project and familiarize yourself with the animation and then stop the playback. If you select the replicator in the **Squares** group and look in the **Replicator** tab of the **Inspector**, notice that a series of rounded orange rectangles replicate in a rectangle shape. By changing the cell controls, the rounded replicated rectangles all have different scales. The blinking was made possible from the **Sequence Replicator** behavior that we can view in the **Behaviors** tab.

How to do it...

We're going to change a few of the parameters to see how we can customize this preset. If you haven't already done so, click on the disclosure triangle for the **Squares** group and select the **Blink** group.

1. Press the *F4* key to go to the **Replicator** tab of the **Inspector**. Under the **Cell Controls**, change the value of **Angle** to **45** and the **Angle Randomness** to **90**.

2. Go to the **Behaviors** tab and, under the **Sequence Replicator**, change the value of **Spread** to **12**, the **Traversal** to **Ease In / Ease Out**, and the **Loops** to **40**. Play back the project and compare it with the following screenshot. Notice how many more squares are being affected because of the spread increase and how often the blinks occur now.

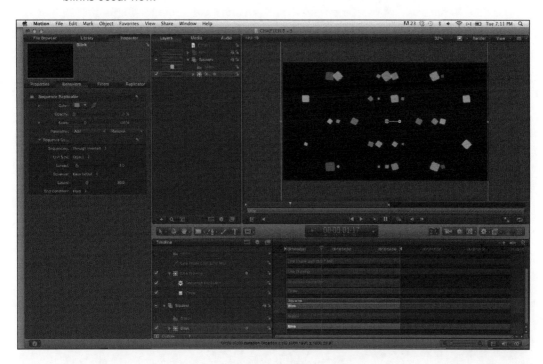

3. Let's focus our attention on the other preset that's been turned off in this project. Turn off the **Squares** group and turn on the **Lines** group in the **Layers** tab. Play back the animation and notice it's a graph being written onscreen. Believe it or not, those are circles that are being replicated across a custom geometric shape whose animation is being controlled by the **Sequence Replicator**. Open the group and select the **Replicator**. Move your playhead to 3 seconds. Go to the **Inspector** and look at the various parameter settings under the replicator. Decrease the value of **Points** under **Replicator Controls** to **15** to see the circles being generated as shown in the following screenshot. Play back the project.

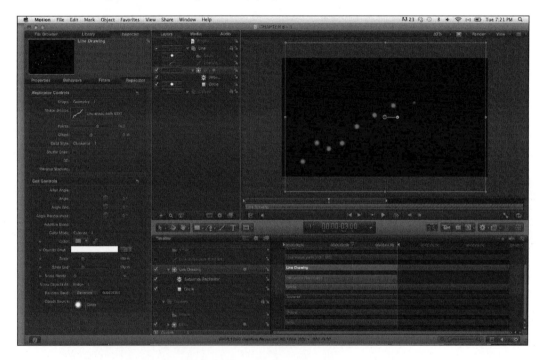

4. Increase the value of **Points** back to **200**. Under **Cell Controls**, change the value of **Scale End** to **50**.

5. Click on the **Behaviors** tab. Change the value of **Scale** to **3000** and of **Spread** to **3**. Play back the project. Compare your results with the following screenshot:

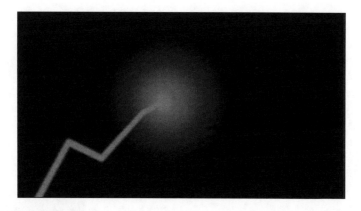

There's more...

Looking at the Library and seeing how something was created is the best way to get under the hood of the application and start creating your own animations. Don't be afraid to explore.

See also

▸ The *Creating a replicator and changing parameters in the HUD* recipe of this chapter

▸ The *Tweaking particle parameters in the Inspector* recipe in *Chapter 7, Let's Make Particles*

Making it 3D! Looking at 3D options for replicators

Replicators are already powerful on their own but turn them into 3D and you'll find options for a few new shapes as well as parameters. Let's take a look!

Getting ready

Under the exercise files of this chapter, double-click on the 08_06 project. Play back the project. Inside the project, there is a Replicator of leaves being animated onscreen in the shape of a rectangle. Go to the **Replicator** tab in the **Inspector** to see that the value **Origin** is set to **Lower Left** and of the **Build Style** is set to **By Column**. These two parameters control the way the sequence replicator animates onscreen. Click on the **Behaviors** tab and then click on the disclosure triangle next to **Position**. Notice that the **Z** value is set to **-4000**. In previous recipes, it was mentioned that **Z** refers to depth in a project. Let's see how this is affected the instant we make our replicator 3D.

How to do it...

1. Select the **Replicator** in the **Layers** tab and press the *F4* key to go to the **Replicator** tab of the **Inspector**. Click on the **3D** checkbox and play back the animation as shown in the following screenshot. The leaves now animate to their resting position from further back in Z space.

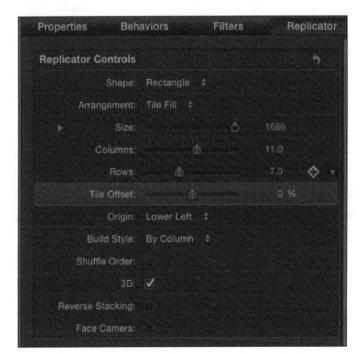

2. Two additional selections also became available under the **Shape** dropdown: **Box** and **Sphere**. Under the **Shape** menu, choose **Box**.

3. Reduce the value of **Column, Rows**, and of the new parameter **Ranks** to **5**.

4. Press the *F1* key to go to the **Properties** tab of the **Inspector**. Click on the disclosure triangle next to **Rotation** and change **Y Rotation** to **25**.

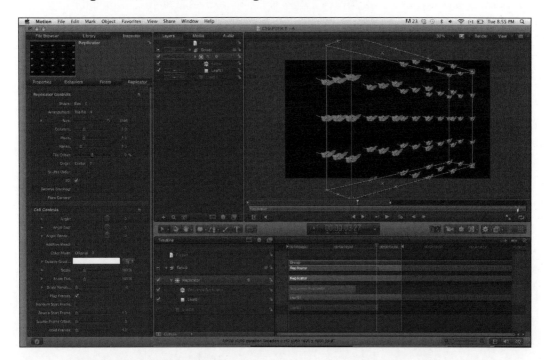

5. Move to the first frame of the Timeline and add a keyframe next to **Y Rotation**. Move forward 3 seconds and change the **Y Rotation** value to **-25**. Adjust the keyframe interpolation in the Keyframe Editor as desired. Play back the animation.

See also

▶ The *Keyframing a group* recipe in *Chapter 4, Making It Move with Keyframes*

▶ The *Working with particle presets in 3D* recipe in *Chapter 7, Let's Make Particles*

▶ The *Creating a replicator and changing parameters in the HUD* recipe

▶ The *Tweaking replicator parameters in the Inspector* recipe

Adding a camera to interact with your replicator

Adding a camera to our project and having it interact with a replicator adds even more creative possibilities in Motion. Let's take a look at how we can make replicators and cameras play nicely with each other by adding our own camera to a project.

Getting ready

From the exercise files of this chapter, double-click on the 08_07 project. Play back the project. You should see a grid of animated rounded rectangles that changes size, color, and scale over time because of the sequence replicator. We're going to add a camera to the scene and a behavior to that camera to have it interact with our replicator.

How to do it...

Let's begin by adding a camera to the scene.

1. Make sure you are on the first frame of your project. Go to the **Object** menu and choose **New Camera**. A dialogue box will appear asking if you want to keep the groups as 2D or switch them to 3D. Choose **Switch to 3D** as shown in the following screenshot:

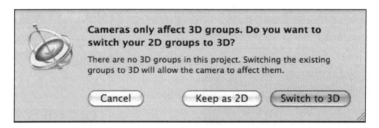

2. We're going to add a behavior to the camera to have it rotate around the **Loft Replicator**. Press *Command + 2* to go to the **Library**. Under **Behaviors**, go to **Camera | Sweep**. Select the **Sweep** behavior and drag it onto the **Camera** in the **Layers** tab. By default, the behavior matches the length of your camera, which is the length of the project. Move to 5 seconds and trim the behavior's out-point by selecting it and pressing **O** in the mini-Timeline.

3. Press the *F7* key to show the HUD. Change the value of **Start** of the **Sweep Behavior** to **-180** and the end to **180**. Set the value of **Speed** to **Ease Out**. Play back the animation.

4. The **Camera** rotates around the rectangles but we can clearly see they are flat. We're going to change that by having them always face the camera. Select the replicator and press the *F4* key. Under the **Replicator** tab in the **Inspector** click on the **3D** checkbox and the **Face Camera** checkbox as shown in the following screenshot. Play back the animation. The squares always turn to face the camera.

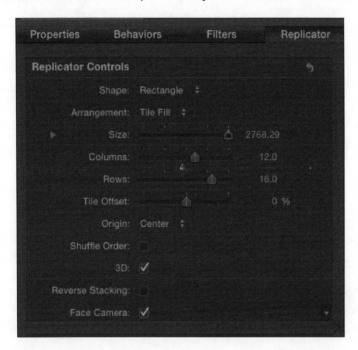

5. Now that we've turned our replicator to 3D, we can also take advantage of two new shapes. Under **Shapes**, choose **Box** and set the value of **Ranks** to **4**. Play back the animation again and refer to the following screenshot:

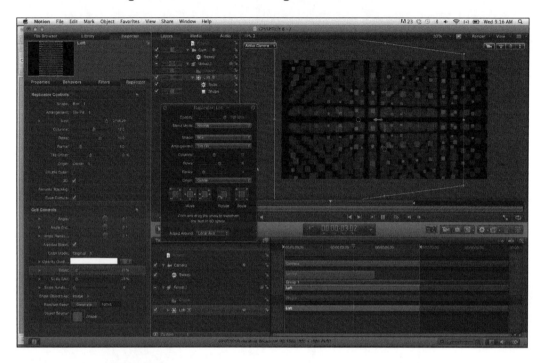

See also

▶ The *Creating a replicator and changing parameters in the HUD* recipe

▶ The *Tweaking replicator parameters in the Inspector* recipe

Creating your own video wall

It's time to put our knowledge of replicators to use and create an awesome video wall from floor to ceiling.

Getting ready

Locate a collection of around 80 to 100 photos on your hard drive or locate a few video clips. If you choose photos, it's best if these photos aren't extremely large in size because we will be displaying several of them on the screen at once. For optimum results, make sure every photo is 320 by 180 pixels. Feel free to use your favorite photo-editing application to scale them down. We want Motion to see these photos as an image sequence, and to do that, we'll need to give them the same name followed by a numerical number. The numbers assigned should be sequential. For example, if you have a set of photos with buildings, you'll call the first photo as building_1, the second as building_2, and so on.

Alternatively, if you have video clips, create a Motion project and lay the clips out sequentially in the Timeline. Export it out of Motion via the **Share** menu and choose **Image Sequence**.

Once you are finished, launch Motion and choose a project with a **Duration** of 7 seconds, a **Preset** of **720p**, and a **Frame Rate** of **30 fps**. When we go to the **File Browser** and find the image sequence, Motion will display only one file containing all the photos as long as the **Collapsed Image Sequence** option is active. For this project, it's best that you set the resolution to a quarter and the quality to draft until final export.

How to do it...

1. Make sure you are on the first frame of your project. Press *Command + 1* to go to the **File Browser**. Find your image sequence, click on it, and choose **Import**. Play back the project. The number of photos in your image sequence will determine how long it should be. Each photo plays for one frame in the order they were named.

2. Stop the playback and go back to the beginning of the project. With the image sequence selected, go to the **Object** menu and choose **Replicate**.

3. Press the *F4* key to go to the **Replicator** tab. Adjust the size of the shape in the **Replicator Controls**. Increase the value of **Columns** to **20** and of **Rows** to **10**. Increase the **Size** of the shape under **Replicator Controls** until the photos don't overlap. Decrease the size of the individual photos under **Cell Controls**.

4. Click on the empty box next to **Random Start Frame** to turn it on and turn off **Play Frames**.

5. Change the name of the replicator to `center` by double-clicking on the name in the **Layers** tab. Go to the **Properties** tab and click on the disclosure triangle next to **Position**. Change the **Z** value to **-2200**. Look at the following screenshot for reference:

6. Select the **center** replicator and duplicate it 4 times by pressing *Command + D*. Name them **top**, **bottom**, **left**, and **right** as shown in the following screenshot. This will represent the five walls for our video wall once we move them to different locations.

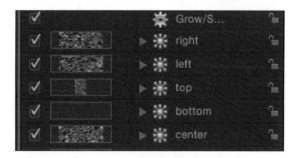

7. You're going to need to go to the **Properties** tab of the **Inspector** and click on the disclosure triangles to reveal the **Position** and **Rotation** co-ordinates for each duplicated replicator. Enter values as indicated in the following chart:

	Pos X	Pos Y	Pos Z	Rot X	Rot Y	Rot Z
Top	0	900	-500	-107	0	90
Bottom	0	-900	-500	107	0	90
Left	-1200	0	0	0	-77	0
Right	1200	0	0	0	77	0

8. Press *Command + 2* to go to the **Library**. Navigate to **Behaviors | Basic Motion | Grow/Shrink**. Select the behavior and drag it to the group in which all the behaviors are present. Press the *F7* key to show the HUD display and increase the value of **Grow/Shrink** as desired. Use the following screenshot for reference:

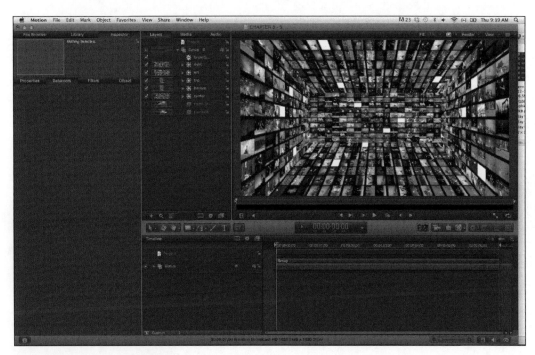

There's more...

If you like, try turning on **Play Frames** in the **Replicator** tab for the **center** replicator.

See also

- ▸ The *Keyframing a group* recipe in *Chapter 4, Making It Move with Keyframes*
- ▸ The *Creating a replicator and changing parameters in the HUD* recipe
- ▸ The *Tweaking replicator parameters in the Inspector* recipe
- ▸ The *Working with the Sequence Replicator behavior* recipe

Faking 3D extrusion with shapes

Motion 5 doesn't make 3D objects. For that, you would need to go to a dedicated 3D application such as Cinema 4D and Maya. What Motion *does* allow is for us to fake 3D. As we saw when working with particles and even replicators, a number of camera tricks can be employed so that our object never appears flat.

Getting ready

From the exercise folder of this chapter, double-click on the 08_09 project file. The project consists of a diamond. We're going to replicate it and spread it out in a line on the Z axis, making it seem that, when we rotate around it, the object has depth.

How to do it...

1. Select the diamond and navigate to **Object | Replicate**.
2. Press the *F4* key to go to the **Replicator** tab of the **Inspector**. Change the value of **Shape** from **Rectangle** to **Line**.
3. The diamonds overlap on a line spread out from left to right. We want it to spread out in Z space and for the diamonds to be close together. Click on the **3D** checkbox.

4. Click on the disclosure triangle for the start and end point of the line. Change the **X** values to 0. Under **Start Point** change the **Z** position to 30. Under **End Point** alter the **Z** position to -30.

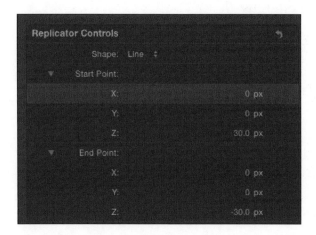

5. Change the value of **Points** under **Replicator Controls** to **60**.

6. Under **Color Mode** change the value to **Over Pattern**.

7. Go to the **Properties** tab of the **Inspector** and click on the disclosure triangle next to **Rotation**. Change **Y Rotation** to **-50**.

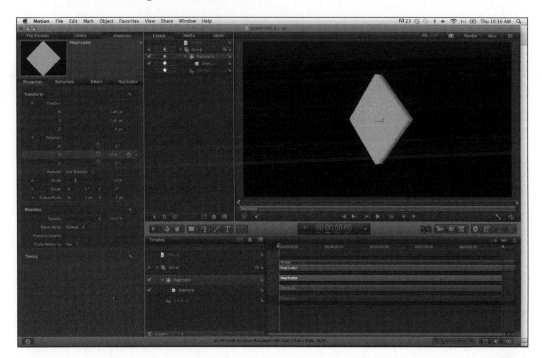

8. Go to the beginning of the Timeline and click on the diamond icon next to **Y Rotation** to add a keyframe. Change the value to 0. Jump to the end of the Timeline and change the **Y Rotation** value to 360. Play back the project. The shape rotates over time and looks as if it's 3D!

See also

▸ The *Keyframing a group* recipe in *Chapter 4, Making It Move with Keyframes*

▸ The *Creating a replicator and changing parameters in the HUD* recipe

▸ The *Tweaking replicator parameters in the Inspector* recipe

9
Motion Tracking and Keying

In this chapter, we will cover:

- ▶ Stabilizing a clip
- ▶ Analyze and Match Move
- ▶ Offset tracking
- ▶ Match Move Four Corner
- ▶ Luma-keying a logo
- ▶ Keying a green screen
- ▶ Advanced green screen techniques
- ▶ The Pleasantville effect

Introduction

Motion 5 has the ability to help us analyze the Motion in a clip using a series of behaviors located in the motion tracking category. We may need to use motion tracking behaviors for a variety of reasons, such as when stabilizing a shaky shot. You may also want to use the data from an analysis so that you can apply it to another layer in your project and make it seem as if it was filmed at the same time. It could be a sign you want to replace from a billboard or text that you want to mimic the movement of someone walking. Whatever reason you need to use it, the motion tracker can help us perform difficult tasks without the need to rotoscope.

In addition to having the ability to track single or multiple points, Motion 5 has a powerful keyer that we can use for green screen shots. The keyer is shared with FCP X and has an array of automated and manual correction parameters that make it ideal for most green screen footage. Using both the motion tracker and keyer together puts a vey powerful workflow at your fingertips.

Stabilizing a clip

Sometimes in the fast-paced world, production of pivotal shots may suffer a bit of shakiness that you want to smooth out in order to show it in your final work. The **Stabilize** behavior is all you need to make that happen.

Getting ready

Find a piece of footage that has a relative amount of shakiness in it. While Motion 5 can also work with clips with extreme amounts of shakiness, part of its solution is to scale up your clip to compensate. The more shaken the clip, the more scaling will take place. Create a new project based on the Frame Size, Frame Rate, and length of your clip. Import the clip into Motion using the File Browser or **File | Import** command.

How to do it...

Let's add the **Stabilize** behavior to our clip.

1. Make sure your playhead is at the beginning of your project. Select the clip in the **Layers** tab. Press *Command + 2* to go to the Library. Go to **Behaviors | Motion Tracking | Stabilize** as shown in the following screenshot. Click on **Apply** at the top of the Library. The behavior is added to the clip.

2. Make sure the **Stabilize** behavior is selected and press *F7* to bring up the HUD. Notice that the **Source** currently shows the clip you added the behavior to. We need to choose what we want the **Stabilize** behavior to adjust; **Position** is currently selected. Click on **Scale Smooth** and **Rotation Smooth** and notice that they turn blue, indicating they're active as shown in the following screenshot:

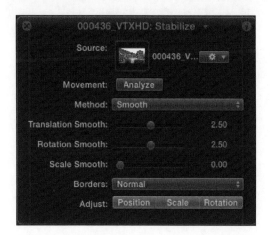

3. If you're trying to preserve the motion in your selected clip, change the value of **Method** from **Stabilize** to **Smooth**. If you're trying to lock down a shot, keep it at **Stabilize**. Click on **Analyze**. Motion will analyze all the movements in your shot based on the settings you entered, as indicated in the following screenshot:

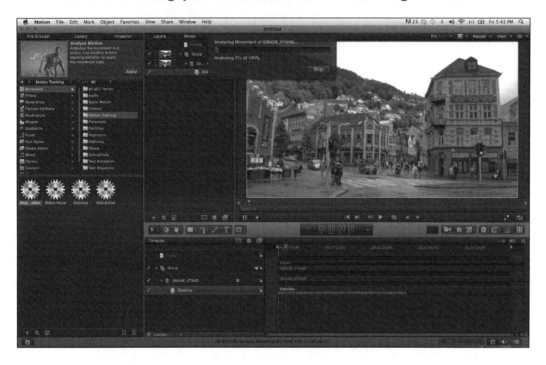

4. Once Motion has finished analyzing, playback the project. You should see that your shot is smoother but you may see the borders of your clip showing. This is because Motion has adjusted your clip's rotation and position frame-by-frame to stabilize it. To compensate, we need to zoom in on the image. For this, change the value of **Borders** from **Normal** to **Zoom**.

There's more...

Stabilization is usually your first line of defense before you perform a match move, as we'll see in an upcoming recipe. Motion tracking is easier to accomplish when the footage you are tracking has been stabilized.

▸ The *Analyze and Match Move* recipe

▸ The *Match Move Four Corner* recipe

Analyze and Match Move

In the last recipe, Motion analyzed the clip for us and decided on the best method to stabilize a clip based on the properties we wanted to adjust. With the Analyze behavior, we choose our own point or points to track and Motion attempts to follow them through the duration of the project. We'll then take the information from our tracking points and apply the data to a match move behavior that's attached to a text element, so that it mimics the movement of the point we tracked.

Getting ready

Under the `Chapter 9` exercise files double-click the `09_02` project. Playback the project. It's a series of balls that fall from the sky and bounce on the table in slow motion. We're going to analyze a few of the balls' movement as they fall and bounce on the ground.

How to do it...

Let's add a behavior to our clip to analyze the movement.

1. Select the video clip. Press *Command + 2* to go to the **Library**. Go to **Behaviors | Motion Tracking | Analyze Motion**. Click on **Apply** at the top of the **Library**. The behavior is added to the clip.

2. Make sure the behavior is selected in the **Layers** tab and press *F7* to bring up the HUD. Go to the beginning of your project. By default, the **Analyze Motion** behavior gives us one tracking point. Grab the point and drag it across the screen and attach it to the lower part of the green ball on its right edge. Notice that, when you drag, the track point zooms in on the location you're under so you can clearly see where you're adding the point.

Click on **Analyze** in the HUD as shown in the following screenshot:

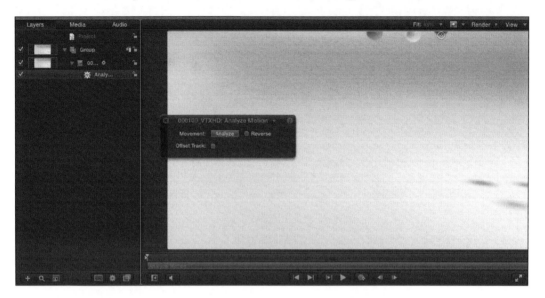

3. Use the left and right arrow keys to move frame-by-frame throughout the project and follow the points with your eye. If the analysis was successful, you should see a series of dots connected by a red line showing you the balls' movement as displayed in the following screenshot. If it wasn't successful, Motion may showcase to you a red X. If this is the case, go back to the beginning of the project. Drag the tracker to a new point and click on **Analyze** again.

4. Let's apply the tracking data to some text. Press *T* to select the text tool and type Green in the Canvas. Press the *Esc* key to exit text entry mode. Choose a green color of your liking. Go to the **Library** and then to **Behaviors | Motion Tracking | Match Move**. Click on **Apply** at the top of the **Library**. The behavior is added to the text.

5. Select the **Analyze Motion** behavior on the clip and drag it over the **Match Move** behavior on the text. Wait for the hooked arrow and release the mouse.

6. Select the **Match Move** behavior and in the HUD add **Scale** and **Rotation** to the **Adjust** field by clicking on them. The boxes will turn blue. Playback the project to see how the text now follows the ball.

7. Reposition the text to where you'd like it on the screen. Use the following screenshot for reference:

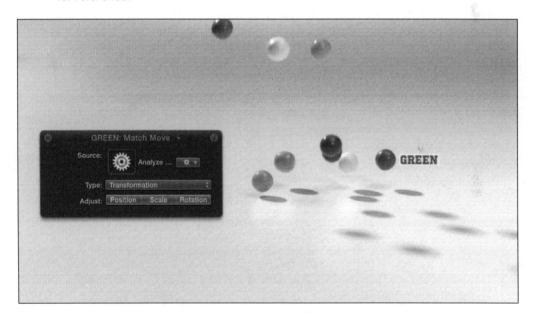

There's more...

If you *Option* + click when you drag your tracker, Motion tries to give you a series of points it thinks would be good to track. Simply align your tracker with the recommended point and let Motion analyze as shown in the following screenshot. Keep in mind, though, that its tracking recommendations are based on that frame only!

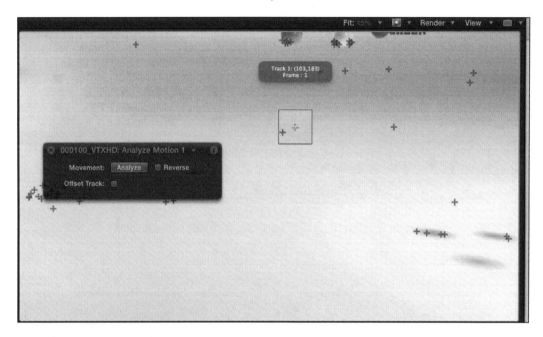

See also

- ▸ The *Stabilizing a clip* recipe
- ▸ The *Offset tracking* recipe
- ▸ The *Creating the text format* recipe in *Chapter 5, Let's Make Text*

Offset tracking

Unlike the last recipe, sometimes the point you want to track isn't so easy. In fact, the point you need might become obscured by an object in the foreground for a series of frames or even end up going offscreen. For this, the **Analyze Motion** behavior gives us an option to offset our tracker with the click of a button.

Getting ready

Under the exercise files relating to this chapter, double-click on the `09_03` project. Playback the project and notice it's where we left off in the last recipe. Now we would like to analyze another ball's movement in the clip and attach some text to it as well.

How to do it...

We'll begin this recipe by analyzing some motion in our image first.

1. Select the video clip in the **Layers** tab. Press *Command + 2* to go to the **Library**. Go to **Behaviors | Motion Tracking | Analyze Motion**. Click on **Apply** at the top of the **Library**. The behavior is added to the clip.

2. Rename the new behavior `orange analyze`. Rename the other to `green analyze`.

3. Make sure the **Analyze Motion** behavior is selected and press *F7* to bring up the HUD. Go to frame 19 of your project. Grab the point and drag it across the screen. Attach it to the lower part of the orange ball on the top-middle edge of the screen. It's best to try and find a point of high contrast. The specular on the upper-right side seems like a good candidate. Use the following screenshot for reference. Click on **Analyze** in the HUD once you've found your point.

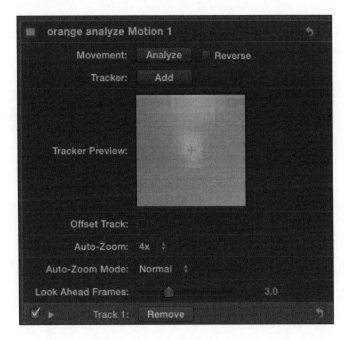

4. You may notice an **X** icon appear, indicating that at some point Motion lost the tracking point as shown in the following screenshot. We need to find the frame with the last good tracking point. Press the left arrow key to move back in your project frame-by frame. You'll notice after just 3 seconds that a white ball obscures the tracking point. Move to 3 seconds and 9 frames just before this occurs.

5. In the HUD, click on the square next to **Offset Track** to add a checkmark as shown in the following screenshot. Move the tracker to a point on the left side of the ball where it won't get obscured by the white ball (try the upper-left side of the other specular). Click on **Analyze**.

6. Motion writes over the previous points. Select the **GREEN** text and press *Command + D* to duplicate it. Change the duplicate text onscreen to orange and move it close to the orange ball.

7. Select the **orange analyze** motion behavior on the clip and drag it over the **Match Move** behavior on the *Orange* text. Wait for the hooked arrow and release the mouse. Playback the project and reposition the text as necessary. Use the following screenshot for reference:

See also

▶ The *Analyze and Match Move* recipe

Match Move Four Corner

Replacing a billboard is a common task in motion tracking. Let's see how we can use the **Match Move** behavior to track the four points of a sign and replace it with another element.

Getting ready

Under this chapter's exercise files, double-click the `09_04` project. Playback the project. The animation consists of a family walking to a *For Sale* sign. We want to replace this with a *For Rent* sign (this is a still image layer that's been temporarily turned off in the project). To achieve this, we'll apply a **Math Move** behavior to the still image and select the **Four Corner** tracking as the type.

How to do it...

To attach *For Rent* to the sign, follow these steps:

1. Turn on the *For Rent* layer by clicking the empty box to the left in the **Layers** tab.

2. Select the video clip. Press *Command + 2* to go to the **Library**. Go to **Behaviors | Motion Tracking | Match Move**. Click on **Apply** at the top of the **Library**. The behavior is added to the *For Rent* layer.

3. Make sure you're at the beginning of the project. Press *F7* to reveal the HUD. With the **Match Move** behavior selected in the **Layers** tab, change the value of **Track Type** from **Transformation** to **Four Corners**. Four points are displayed in the Canvas.

4. Drag each point in the Canvas to its closest corner, as shown in the following screenshot. Try to find a point that's high in contrast. Once you've set all the points click on the **Analyze** button.

5. Motion attempts to analyze the footage and fails along the way. Move back to the 1 second mark. In the HUD, click on the **Offset Tracking** square and move the tracking points to the white marks on the frame of the sign. Click on the **Analyze** button again. Repeat these steps until you are satisfied with the track.

There's more...

Perfecting motion tracking can be a lengthy process. It's always good to attempt several different points until you get your desired result. Keep trying different points and offsets until you are satisfied!

See also

▶ The *Analyze and Match Move* recipe
▶ The *Offset tracking* recipe

Luma-keying a logo

Sometimes you may receive a logo from a client that has a white or black background embedded in it. What you would like to do is remove the background so that the logo appears as a lower third bug on your footage without a rectangular white/black box around it. Rather than going back to your client for a new logo, you may be able to extract the background using the **Luma Key** filter in Motion.

Getting ready

Find a piece of footage you would like to place a logo over. Launch Motion and create a new project based on your clip settings. Make sure your playhead is at the beginning of the project. Go to the **File Browser**, locate your clip and import it into the project. Find the LIFT_EXERCISE9_5_LOGO in this chapter's exercise folder. Notice, from the info panel at the top of the **File Browser**, that the logo is a JPEG that does not contain an alpha channel. We'll need to key this out with the Luma Keyer.

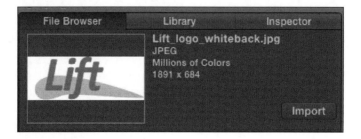

How to do it...

Let's add a Luma key to the logo:

1. With the logo selected in the **File Browser**, click on **Import** to bring it into the project. With the logo selected, press *Command + 2* to go to the **Library** and choose **Filters | Keying | Luma Keyer**. Click on the **Apply** button.

2. Right now, **Luma Keyer** is trying to key-out the darker part of the image. Press *F3* to go to the **Filters** tab and click on the empty box next to **Invert**. The filter now is trying to key-out the white part of the image.

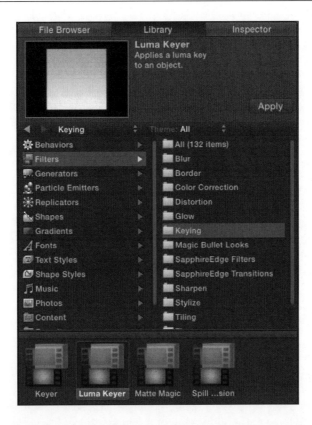

3. Flip through the different types of views available including the **Matte** view to make sure you're not removing any of the logo. If you are, play with **Luma Rolloff** to adjust the key. Reveal the **Matte** and **Light Wrap** tools to see how you can manipulate the key.

See also

▶ The *Keying a green screen* recipe

▶ The *Advanced green screen techniques* recipe

Keying a green screen

It sounds simple in theory; place a subject in front of a green screen and, when you bring it into post with the click of a button, all the green is removed from the image. You can now place any background you want behind it. Unfortunately, rarely are green screens that simple. The color space of your camera, wrinkles in the screen, uneven lighting, and improper space between the subject and screen can all lead to problematic keys where several passes may be necessary in order to remove the color. Whether you have an amazing green screen or a bit of a puzzle to solve, Motion is here to help. It shares its Keyer with FCP X.

Getting ready

Find a piece of green screen footage on your system. Launch Motion and create a new project based on your clip settings. Make sure your playhead is at the beginning of the project. Go to the **File Browser** and find your footage. Click on the **Import** button to bring it into your project.

How to do it...

Let's add a filter to key out the green.

1. Select the green screen clip in the **Layers** tab and press *Command + 2* to go to the **Library**.

2. Go to **Filters | Keying | Keyer**. Drag the **Keyer** to the green screen clip in your **Layers** tab. Press *F3* to go to the **Filters** tab of the **Inspector**.

3. Just like **Luma Keyer**, there are different ways we can view our selection. Click on the middle button in the **View** area (the white button) to reveal the **Matte**, as shown in the following screenshot. In this Canvas, white represents what you want to keep and black represents what you want to remove. Motion has attempted to apply some default settings to key-out the green. If they seem to work well, you can leave them as is and look at refining the **Matte**.

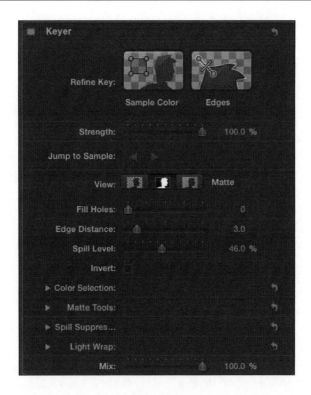

4. Still in **Matte** mode, drag up the **Fill Holes** parameter if your subject has areas of soft transparency (that is, any area that's semi-grey or even black that you want to appear). Stop when the area is white.

5. Click on the disclosure triangle next to **Matte Tools**. Play with the **Shrink/Expand**, **Soften**, and **Erode Effects** to see what they do.

6. If you have a magenta hue around the edges of your subject, play with the **Spill Suppression** parameters to neutralize the color.

How it works...

Working with color in Motion and most graphic applications is an additive process. This means we add colors to end up at white. When we key a green screen, the system works so hard to key out green that sometimes it introduces its complementary color, magenta. To get rid of this spill suppression, we reintroduce a bit of green into the image in order to neutralize it. The Mac OS color wheel is a great way to see how color is laid out. This works great on color casts too.

See also

▸ The *Advanced green screen techniques* recipe

▸ The *Luma-keying a logo* recipe

Advanced green screen techniques

In the last recipe, Motion did a lot of the initial work for us. In this recipe, we'll select our own key color to remove the green and fine-tune the edges in the image. From there, we'll refine the key and look at some additional ways we can add, take away, and refine our selection.

Getting ready

Find a piece of green screen footage on your system as well as a file that you'd like to use as a background. Launch Motion and create a new project based on your clip settings. Make sure your playhead is at the beginning of the project. Go to the **File Browser** and find your footage. Click on the **Import** button to bring both files into your project.

How to do it...

Let's start by adding a **Keyer** to our clip like the last recipe.

1. Select the green screen clip in the **Layers** tab and press *Command + 2* to go to the **Library**.

2. Go to **Filters | Keying | Keyer**. Drag the **Keyer** to the green screen clip in your **Layers** tab. Press *F3* to go to the **Filters** tab of the **Inspector**.

3. The **Strength** slider is what controls the initial green selected from the **Keyer**. To make your own selection, set the **Strength** amount to 0 as shown in the following screenshot. All the green returns to the image.

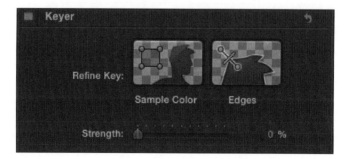

4. Switch the **View** to **Matte**. Click on the **Sample Color** button. In your Canvas, drag out a rectangle around a small section of the green screen area. In you're unsure of where to start, try somewhere close to the subject. If you need to sample more green colors, hold down the *Shift* key and draw out another rectangular selection in the Canvas. Use the following screenshot for reference.

5. Click on the **Edges** button. Draw a line extending from you subject's hairline to the black area that's now transparent. What you're trying to do is define the area of semi transparency. Drag the middle line back and forth to adjust the selections.

6. Change the value of **View** back to **Composite**. Play with the **Fill Holes, Edge Distance**, and **Spill Suppression** parameters as required.

7. Open the **Color Selection** settings by clicking on the disclosure triangle. You have two options here: **Scrub Boxes** and **Manual**. If you wanted to, you could bypass the **Refine Key** section and select your chrominance and edge values. In the **Scrub Boxes** tab, the adjustments we make here affect our edge selection. Play with the Chroma wheel and the other parameters to see the effect it has on the edges of your selection. Click back and forth between **Matte** and **Composite** mode to get a sense for the changes from both views.

8. Click the disclosure triangle next to **Matte Tools** and **Light Wrap**. These settings allow you to adjust your selection even further. Play with the parameters under **Matte Tools** and notice the effect it has on your image. Do the same with **Light Wrap**, paying close attention to how the edges try to blend in with the background image.

There's more...

If your subject stays near the center of the image, you may want to create a mask around your image to remove unwanted areas and focus on the green closer to your main subject. This will create less work for you at the end and is commonly referred to as **creating a garbage matte**.

See also

- ▶ The *Keying a green screen* recipe
- ▶ The *Luma-keying a logo* recipe

The Pleasantville effect

The use of color can have a strong impact on your audience. Some films such as Schindler's List and Pleasantville use the impact of color in stylistic ways. The effect is focused on having only one color within the image while everything else becomes desaturated. As in our previous keying recipes, to accomplish this we'll need to make a selection in our image based on color. By using masks and filters, we'll create one selection for everything we want to turn black and white, and another for the colors we want to keep.

Getting ready

Locate a video clip on your computer, preferably one with a strong vivid/saturated color you want to keep and to which you want to draw the viewer's attention. Launch Motion and create a new project based on your clip settings. Make sure your playhead is at the beginning of the project. Go to the **File Browser** and find your footage. Click the **Import** button to bring the file into your project

How to do it...

Let's add a **Keyer** to our clip like the last recipe.

1. Select the clip in the **Layers** tab and press *Command + 2* to go to the **Library**.
2. Go to **Filters | Keying | Keyer**. Drag the **Keyer** to the clip in your **Layers** tab. Press *F3* to go to the **Filters** tab of the **Inspector**.
3. The **Strength** slider controls the initial green selected from the **Keyer**. To make your own selection, set the **Strength** amount to 0.
4. Switch the **View** to **Matte**. Click on the **Sample Color** button. In your Canvas, drag out a rectangle around the color you want to keep. If you need to sample more of the same color, hold down the *Shift* key and draw out another rectangular selection in the Canvas.

5. Click the **Invert Selection** button. This reverses the selection so that we affect everything but the color we want to keep.

6. Change the value of **View** back to **Composite**. Play with the **Fill Holes**, **Edge Distance**, and **Spill Suppression** parameters as required.

7. With the clip selected, press *Command + D* to duplicate it. Select the **Keyer** filter on the original clip and delete it.

8. Press *Command + 2* to go to the **Library**. Go to **Filters | Color Correction | Hue/Saturation**. Drag it to the original clip. Press *F3* to go to the **Filters** tab in the **Inspector**. Drag the **Saturation** amount down to -1. Playback your project and notice the only selection that remains is the color you chose. Use the following screenshot for reference:

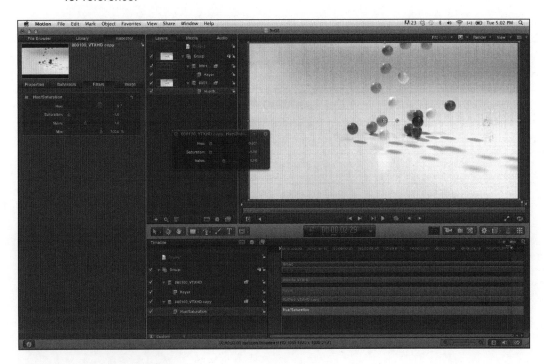

See also

▶ The *Keying a green screen* recipe

▶ The *Advanced green screen techniques* recipe

▶ The *Luma-keying a logo* recipe

10
Intro to 3D

In this chapter, we will cover:

- ▸ Making it 3D
- ▸ Moving a camera versus moving a layer
- ▸ Where am I again? Controlling the view of your world using viewports
- ▸ Adjust Around
- ▸ Integrating 3D and 2D
- ▸ Using the Framing camera behavior
- ▸ Let's add some light
- ▸ Creating reflections
- ▸ Turning on Depth of Field

Introduction

A videographer would never be able to capture his incredible footage without the aid of a camera and the same is true with Motion. If you think you've seen a lot with Motion so far, think again because we've just scratched the surface. By making our projects 3D, we're about to bring an extraordinary dimension to our fingertips. This dimension will give us the ability to add cameras and lights to our scenes that will interact with any 3D object. Through this chapter, we'll begin to explore the basics so that we become more comfortable navigating around our 3D world. From there, we'll begin to animate our scenes by using behaviors and keyframes along with exploring some new effects that become possible only in 3D, such as Reflection and Depth of Field. Let's take a plunge into the abyss!

Making it 3D

Making a layer or group 3D is literally done with the click of a button. Seeing all the options that become available once you click that button requires a bit of trial and error. Let's hop on the fast track to turn our layers into 3D with a camera.

Getting ready

From this chapter's exercise files, double-click the `10_01` project. The project consists of two groups and a light. One group contains a rectangle that has been rotated and acts as our floor. The other group contains four rounded rectangles that are positioned in x and z space, so that one appears closer than the other while slightly overlapping. Click the checkmark next to the light to see that it has no effect on our groups. In order for it to interact with our projects, the groups need to be 3D. Click on the **Render** menu above the Canvas to see that both **Reflections** and **Shadows** are currently turned on; once again, though, it doesn't appear as if there are any effects of it showing in the scene.

How to do it...

Let's add a camera to our project:

1. Under the **Object** menu, choose **New Camera**. You'll be presented with a dialog box that asks you if you'd like to turn your 2D groups to 3D, as shown in the following screenshot. Choose **Switch to 3D**:

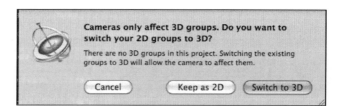

2. Wow! A lot of stuff just happened. The minute you chose to switch your groups to 3D, your floor started to reflect the rounded rectangles and the overall luminance of the scene went down since a light (spotlight) is now controlling it. On top of this, an icon on the two groups in the **Layers** tab changed and a series of camera controls appeared in the Canvas. On the **Floor_1** group in the **Layers** tab, click the icon that looks like a stack of three rectangles, as shown in the following screenshot. Notice how it flattens. Once it does, the reflections go away and the group doesn't interact with the spotlight. That's because you made it 2D. This brings us to one of the most important rules when we work in 3D. 2D groups *do not* interact with cameras and lights. Only 3D groups do. Click the icon again to change it to 3D.

3. Select the **Light** layer in the **Layers** tab and press *F4* or *Fn + F4* to go to the **Light** properties in the Inspector. Increase the **Intensity** property of **Light** to 600. Currently, the light is set to spotlight, much as you'd see in a theatrical show. That spotlight has been placed above our layers. We'll see in some of the later recipes how we'll be able to see the light from a different type of view.

4. To the upper-right of the Canvas, click and select the first camera control called **Pan Camera**. Notice how, when you hold down your mouse and scroll, you pan across your scene left, right, up, and down. Once you're done panning, double-click the control to reset it.

5. Click and select the second control. Notice that, when you scroll, it allows you to rotate around the scene. Once you're done, double-click the control to reset it.

6. Click, select, and scroll the third control called **Dolly Camera** and notice how it allows you to move in and out on the scene. Once again, double-click the control to reset your camera.

7. Select the **Camera** layer in the **Layers** tab and press *F1* to go to the **Properties** tab of the Inspector. Click the disclosure triangle next to **Position** and **Rotation** to see the individual x, y, and z coordinates. Select each of the camera controls again and notice how the values of our camera change in the Inspector. You should see the following:

   ❑ Pan Camera affects the **X** and **Y** position.

   ❑ Orbit Camera affects the **X**, **Y**, and **Z** rotation

   ❑ Dolly Camera affects the **Z** position

How it works

We explored rotation in earlier chapters but it's worth explaining further how rotation works because it's the foundation of how we'll orbit in 3D space.

X Rotation

First of all, what is the X Position in Motion? X Position is left and right. Now how would you you rotate around this? Picture a pizza roller that's used to flatten dough. The pizza roller rotates along the x axis.

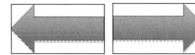

Y Rotation

The Y Position in Motion is up and down. Now picture a cowboy with his rope as he twirls it in the air. Much as with a flag on a pole, the rope rotates on the y axis.

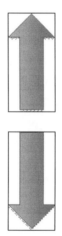

Z Rotation

You may be unfamiliar with the Z Position if you come from a background having experience in an editing application such as FCP X. The Z Position refers to depth in your project. If I were to show you arrows, they would appear as a dot because it would be pointing away from us. Now picture holding a TV converter straight out in front of you with your arm fully extended. If you were to rotate it along the z axis, you may be surprised to find it's very familiar to how the hands of a clock rotate; in a circular type fashion. This is the one and only rotation available to us in FCP X.

See also

▸ The *Moving a camera versus moving a layer* recipe.

▸ The *Where am I again? Controlling the view of your world using viewports* recipe.

▸ The *Adjust Around* recipe.

Moving a camera versus moving a layer

In the last recipe, we learned how to make a group 3D with a camera. We also looked at how we could move our camera in 3D space using our camera controls situated above the Canvas. In this recipe, we're going to explore moving our camera and our layers in the HUD.

Getting ready

While this book is designed as a cookbook where you can start up from any recipe, if you are new to 3D I highly recommend breezing over the last recipe to help build up your knowledge. From this chapter's exercise files, double-click the 10_02 project. It's the same project we left off with from the previous recipe. It consists of a floor and four rounded rectangles above the floor, casting reflections based on the render settings. There is also a light and a camera in our scene. We're going to move around our camera using the HUD controls and also see how we can move our layers in the same way.

How to do it...

Let's start by moving our camera in the HUD:

1. Select **Camera** from the **Layers** tab. Press *F7* to show the HUD. Press *F1* to open the **Properties** tab of the Inspector. The reason we are displaying both the **Properties** tab and the HUD is to see what happens to our **Position** and **Rotation** values once we play around with the camera icons at the bottom of the HUD.

2. Notice that the **Camera** value is currently set to **Framing**. Think of **Framing** as a camera that wants to stay fixated on your scene. Right now, the camera is framing the floor and rectangles. So, rather than the camera rotating around its own body, it will rotate around the scene you're currently looking at. To visualize this even further, think of yourself as the cameraman framing these layers. If these rectangles and floor were the main attraction, you would never move you camera off the action no matter where you yourself moved. Also, there is a set of camera controls at the bottom of the HUD, as shown in the following screenshot. Select the first **Move** control on the left and scrub your mouse forward and backward. Notice how you dolly forward and backward in your scene. See how the **Z** position in the **Properties** tab of the Inspector becomes affected every time you scrub. Release your mouse and press *Command + Z* a few times until your camera's **Position** is set to **[0,0,0]**.

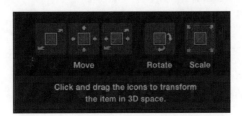

3. Select the second **Move** control and notice how you pan around the scene, moving your camera's position along the x and y axis. Repeat this step for the third **Move** control and notice how it affects both the **X** and **Z** position. Rather than use *Command + Z*, click the hooked arrow at the top of the window to reset all the parameters of the camera, as shown in the following screenshot:

4. To rotate our camera, we're going to use the **Properties** tab instead of the HUD. The reason for doing so is that this will allow us to rotate our camera along each axis separately. Under **X Rotation**, click and scrub the value until you reach **-8**. Press *Command + Z* to undo. Under **Y Rotation**, scrub the value until **-10**. Undo the change. For **Z Rotation**, scrub the value till **20**, as shown in the following screenshot:

5. Click the disclosure triangle for the **Rectangles** group in the **Layers** tab. Select the **Green** rectangle. Notice how the Canvas updates to show you the layer is selected with a set of arrows in the center of it, as shown in the following screenshot. Unlike cameras in our current view, we can move layers directly on screen. The arrows displayed are red, green, and blue, which represent position coordinates **X**, **Y**, and **Z** respectively.

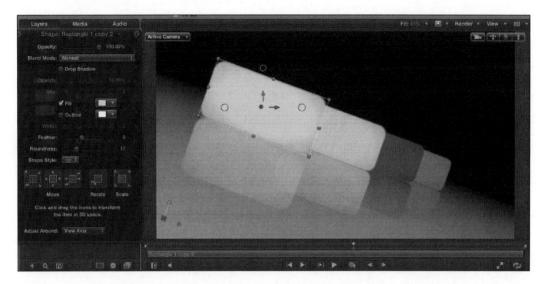

6. You'll also see three circles. When you click on a circle, it will correspond to a type of rotation. Position your mouse over the circle to your right and notice whether clicking and dragging the circle affects its Z Rotation, as shown in the following screenshot. Press *Command* + *Z* to undo your change. Similar to position, the colors displayed (red, green, and blue) represent rotation coordinates **X**, **Y**, and **Z** respectively:

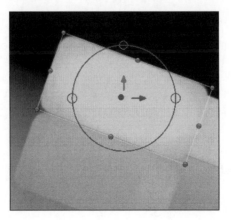

7. Click and select a few move controls in the HUD to experiment with changing the selected layer. Undo any changes you make by pressing *Command + Z*. Unlike the camera controls above the Canvas we used in the first recipe of this chapter, the HUD constantly changes what we affect based on what is selected in the **Layers** tab. The camera controls above the Canvas *only* affect the camera.

There's more...

We can also constrain the movement of our controls in the HUD. If you *Command* + click a camera control icon, you can minimize the movement or rotation to the direction you drag If you *Shift* + click while dragging a rotation handle in the Canvas, you will constrain your movement to 45-degree increments.

See also

▸ The *Make it 3D* recipe.

▸ The *Where am I again? Controlling the view of your world using viewports* recipe.

Where am I again? Controlling the view of your world using viewports

Motion 5 offers a lot of ways for you to navigate throughout a 3D environment using the different viewports available. With our viewports, we're able to see our world from a series of different perspectives. This allows us to better orient ourselves within the 3D space.

Getting ready

From this chapter's exercise files, double-click the 10_03 project. It appears to be the same exercise from the last recipe, but with a few additions. There are two groups within the project. One contains the floor, a light, and the rectangles we're currently looking at. The other group contains the floor, a light, and the circles that are 4000 pixels to the left of our location. We can't see this other group because our camera is currently pointing at the first group. Click on the **Scene 2** group and, in the **Properties** tab of the Inspector, verify its **Position X**. Click on **Scene 1** and the **Camera** to verify their **Position** coordinates.

How to do it...

Let's see how we can get an overall better sense of this project by looking at our project in different viewports:

1. At the upper-right of the Canvas is a rectangle icon next to the **View** menu. Click it and choose the third icon from the top (**View | Horizontal**), as shown here:

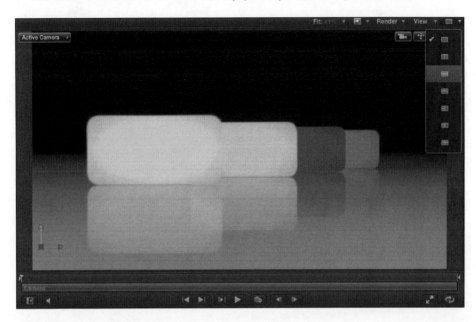

2. Your screen splits into two views. The top view currently displays the **Active Camera** view while the bottom view displays a different view of your world. Make sure the menu on the left-hand side of that view reads **Top**, as shown in the next screenshot.

Once you make the change, notice the view being selected, which is indicated by a yellow box outlining it.

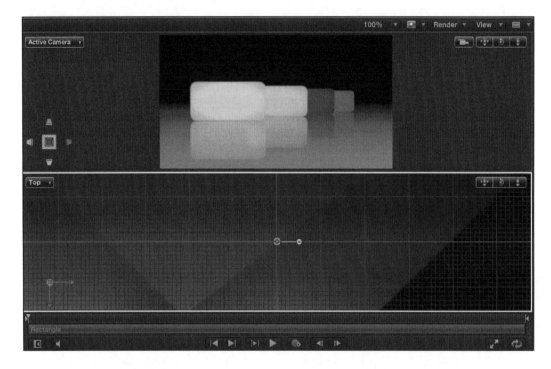

3. The **Top** view is one of several orthographic views. These views look directly down an axis, in this case y, to give us a set of different eyes on the scene. Open the content of the **Scene 1** group and select the **Rectangles** layer. You should see it selected as a line in the **Top** view. If you don't see it, use the dolly camera and pan around controls in the active viewport to frame the group, as shown in the following screenshot. Notice how this has no effect on the **Active Camera** view.

4. There is a compass on the lower-left hand side of the viewports. Click the red button to jump into the **Right** view. Select **Camera** in the **Layers** tab and notice how you're looking at it from the right-hand side, directly down the x axis, as indicated in the following screenshot. Once again, there is no change to the **Active Camera** view.

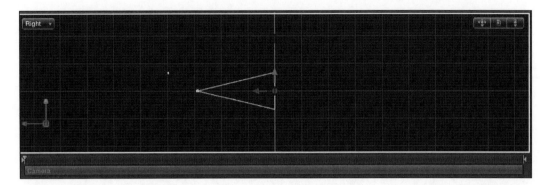

5. From the drop-down menu that currently has **Right** selected, choose **Perspective**. Unlike orthographic views that look down the x, y and z axis, **Perspective** view offers you a new set of eyes by also introducing some orientation. As a challenge, use the camera controls in the viewport to dolly out until you can see the second group. Use the pan camera tool as well, if you need to. Use the following screenshot for reference. Select **Camera** from the **Layers** tab to see where it's positioned:

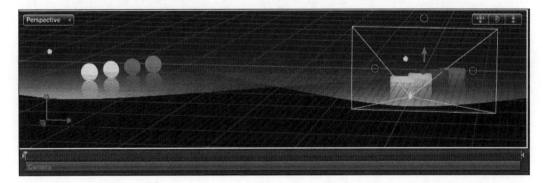

6. With **Camera** still selected in the **Layers** tab, press *F1* to go to the **Properties** tab. Scrub the **X Position** value to the left and watch both viewports update. You should see the camera moving towards the next scene. Stop scrubbing and enter -4000 for **X**. Use the following screenshot for reference:

How it works

If you ever select a view where your layers or groups are not well framed within the viewport, you can always try to frame or fit your object in the view by selecting it from the **Camera View** menu, as shown in the following screenshot. Just make sure the objects you want to frame are selected in the **Layers** tab!

See also

▶ The *Making it 3D* recipe.

▶ The *Moving a camera versus moving a layer* recipe.

▶ The *Adjust Around* recipe.

Adjust Around

Adjust Around allows us to move objects from different perspectives. Let's say I tell you to walk left. You may come back and ask me: "Well, my left or your left?". With Motion, my left translates to the **View** access while your left would be **Local** access. Not to forget that we also both exist in a world with directions (that is, North, South, East, and West). Let's see how this can help our process as we move objects in 3D.

Getting ready

From this chapter's exercise files, double-click the 10_04 project. The project consists of a group with some text, four circles, a floor, and a spotlight. The Canvas shows three viewports—our **Active Camera** view and two orthographic views from the **Top** and **Right** view. We're going to reposition each of our circles and text so that they are slightly angled toward the camera.

How to do it...

While we make the above changes, we'll also use our **Adjust Around** pop-up menu to move the objects in different ways.

1. Reveal the content of the **Circles** group. Click the **Text** layer to select it in the **Layers** tab and *Command* + click each of the **Circle** layers to select it and see where they appear in the different viewports. Go to the **Properties** tab of the Inspector and single-click each object to see where it's located in 3D space. Use the following image for reference:

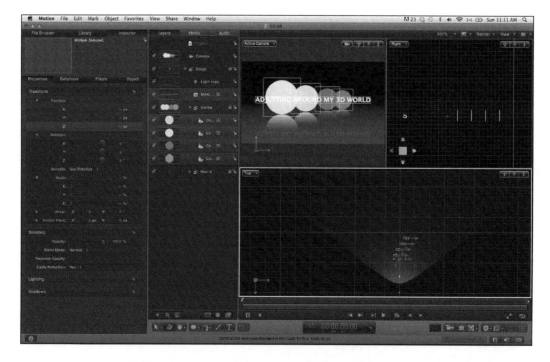

2. Select the **Text** layer again and press *F1* to go to the **Properties** tab of the Inspector if it's not already showing. Reveal the individual rotation properties and, for **Rotation Y**, type 45. Select **Circle 4** in the Inspector and, for **Rotation Y**, type -45. For the remaining circles, type in the following co-ordinates:

    □ **Circle 3**: Set **Rotation Y** to 45

    □ **Circle 2**: Set **Rotation Y** to -45

    □ **Circle 1**: Set **Rotation Y** to 45

3. Select the **Text** layer and press *F7* to bring up the HUD. At the very bottom of the HUD, make sure **Adjust Around** is set to **Local Axis**, as shown in the following screenshot. In the **Top** view, you should see a red and blue line attached to the floor (red = x and blue = z. Note that we can't see a green line because y is up and down and won't show on a floor). This is known as the 3D grid and is one of several 3D overlays that have been automatically turned on for you. This can be toggled on and off from the **View** menu above the Canvas.

4. Flip between **Local Axis**, **World Axis**, and **View Axis** and notice the following results in your **Top** view:

   ▫ In **Local Axis**, the blue arrow points in front of the object

   ▫ In **World Axis**, the blue arrow stays aligned with the blue line on the 3D grid

   ▫ In **View Axis**, the blue arrow points straight at you

5. Drag the blue arrow in each of the **Adjust Around** axes and see what happens in the **Active Camera** view. Once you finish, press *Command + Z* to undo.

6. Try to use different **Adjust Around** options to reposition the order of the circles and see how they are spread out.

There's more...

The **Adjust Around** drop-down menu takes a little getting used to: Take your time when moving objects in 3D space. The more time you spend now, the less you'll have to worry about later on!

See also

▶ The *Making it 3D* recipe.

▶ The *Moving a camera versus moving a layer* recipe.

▶ The *Where am I? Controlling the view of your world using viewports* recipe.

Integrating 3D and 2D

When working in 3D, sometimes you don't want elements to be affected by cameras so that the layer or group remains constant throughout your project. For example, you may want a background to remain the same for the duration of your project. One way to achieve that is by making your background 2D.

Getting ready

From this chapter's exercise files, double-click the `10_05` project. The project consists of a gradient background and a PSD file with several layers. Click the disclosure triangle next to the **Casa Loma** group to reveal its content. There are several groups that have different z-axis positions. You can confirm this by selecting the groups and pressing *F1* to reveal the **Properties** tab of the Inspector. Look at the **Z Position** co-ordinate and notice how each group has a different number. The reason for this is to ensure that, if we add any type of camera move, it will appear that there is some depth between each of the buildings as we move through the group. The goal of this recipe is to start with the gradient background and slowly dolly through the scene revealing each of the buildings. Press *F6* to hide your Timeline. A camera has already been added to the scene.

How to do it...

Let's add a behavior to the camera and have it move through each of the buildings:

1. Press *Command + 2* to go to the **Library** tab. Go to **Behaviors | Camera | Dolly**. Select the **Dolly** behavior and drag it to the camera in the **Layers** tab.

2. We want the camera to start in front of the buildings and slowly reveal them. To help us move the camera, above the Canvas on the upper-right select the rectangle icon and choose the third icon from the top to change to two up-horizontal views. Make sure the bottom view is set to **Top** and is selected. If you need to, zoom out to see the whole scene.

Select the background, the **Casa Loma** group in the Layers tab, and the camera to see them in **Top** view, as shown in the following screenshot:

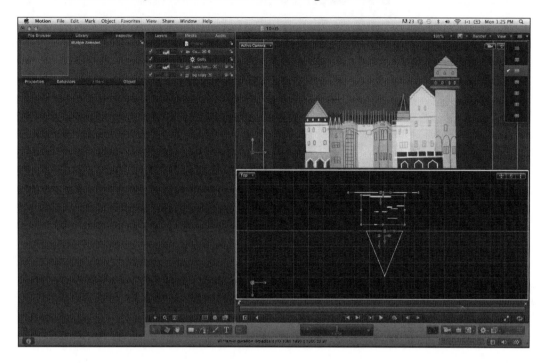

3. Make sure only the camera is selected in the **Layers** tab. Use the blue arrow in the **Top** view to push your camera back until you can no longer see the entire background in the **Active Camera** view. Now click the icon to the right of the **Background** group to make it 2D, as shown in the following screenshot. Now the camera has no effect on it; it will be seen at all times.

4. With the camera still selected, press *F4* to reveal the **Camera** tab of the Inspector. We want to fade in on each of the layers as we dolly through them. Set **Near Plane** to 400 and **Near Fade** to 600. Press *F1* to go to the **Properties** tab of the Inspector. Make sure you're at the beginning of your project and change your camera's **Z Position** to -3700.

5. Press *F2* to go to the **Behaviors** tab of the Inspector. Type in -3700 for the **Distance** field and set **Speed** to **Ease Both**.

6. Select the **Active Camera** view and press the Space bar to play back the animation.

There's more...

If you hold down the *Command* and *Option* keys while using the **Move Z** icon in the HUD, it will scale and reposition the layer. This will ensure the layer will appear the same to the camera, although now there will be **Z Space** between the various layers.

See also

▸ The *Making it 3D* recipe.

▸ The *Moving a camera versus moving a layer* recipe.

▸ The *Where am I? Controlling the view of your world using viewports* recipe.

▸ The *Adjust Around* recipe.

Using the Framing camera behavior

The **Framing** camera behavior is one of the strong indications where traditional keyframing would seem tedious in retrospect once you use it. All the **Framing** behavior needs is a source; the source can be a group or a layer. Once it has a source, the **Framing** behavior will fly to the source's position and frame it in the center of the screen. Let's see how we can use it to our advantage.

Getting ready

From this chapter's exercise files, double-click the 10_06 project. Press the Space bar to play back the project. It consists of a clock where the hour and minute hands have been animated using **Parameter** behaviors. If you open up the content of the **Full Clock** group, notice how each of the groups contained within it has been spread out and scaled in **Z Space**. Notice how the content of the clock group have also been repositioned and scaled.

How to do it...

We're going to use a series of **Framing** behaviors to zoom in and out of our clock.

1. If your Timeline is open, press *F6* to close it. With the camera selected, go to the gear icon underneath the Canvas and choose **Camera | Framing**, as shown in the following screenshot. The behavior is now applied.

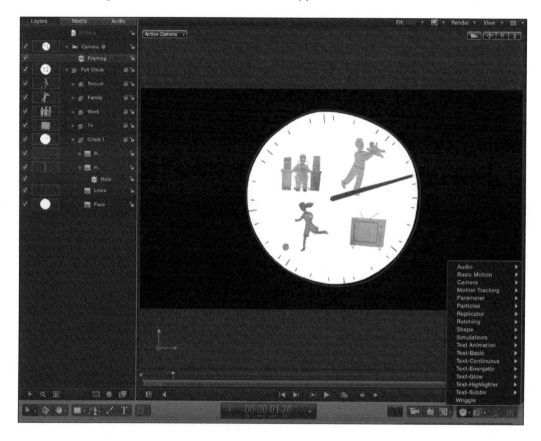

2. By default, the behavior is applied to the entire length of the camera. With **Framing** selected, move to the one-second mark in the mini-Timeline. Press *I* to trim the in-point to your playhead. Move to the three-second mark on the mini-Timeline and press *O* to trim the out-point to your playhead, as shown here:

3. Let's say you want to fly to the **TV** group. Select the **TV** group and drag it over the **Framing** behavior in the **Layers** tab and, when you see the hooked arrow, release, your mouse. Select the behavior and press *F7* to bring up the HUD. Set **Transition** to **Ease Both**. Play back the project. From one to three seconds, the camera flies into the TV, as shown in the in the following screenshot:

4. Let's say we want to zoom back up at the five-second mark. Move to 5 seconds. Select the **Framing** behavior and press *Command + D* to duplicate it. Press *Shift + [* to move the in-point of the behavior to your playhead. Rename the first **Framing** behavior as `Frame TV` and the duplicate as `Frame Full Clock`. Drag the **Full Clock** group into the source well of the **Frame Full Clock** behavior. Play back the project.

5. Move to the nine-second mark. Select one of the **Framing** behaviors and press *Command + D* to duplicate it. Rename the duplicate `Frame Work`. Press *Shift + [* to move the in-point of the behavior to your playhead. Drag the **Work** group into the source well of the **Frame Work** behavior. Play back the project.

How it works

You can change the way your camera travels by playing with the **Framing** behavior parameters. Try playing with some of the parameters under the **Framing** behavior to change the path and framing of the groups you want your camera to travel to.

- ▸ The *Making it 3D* recipe.
- ▸ The *Moving a camera versus moving a layer* recipe.
- ▸ The *Where am I? Controlling the view of your world using viewports* recipe.
- ▸ The *Adjust Around* recipe
- ▸ The *Integrating 3D and 2D* recipe.

Let's add some light

Lighting in Motion in any project can make all the difference. Use and animate lights to create complex animations for all your clients. Let's see a few of the light types available to use once we've made our groups 3D.

Getting ready

From this chapter's exercise folder, double-click the 10_07 project. Press the Space bar to play back the project. It's the same project from the last recipe including the **Framing** behavior moves we made. Make sure you have two horizontal viewports displayed. Set the upper view to **Active Camera** and the bottom view to **Front**. Reposition the scene as necessary in the **Front** view using the camera controls. We're going to change the lighting in our scene a bit. We're going to add three lights: an ambient light to illuminate the overall scene and two spotlights that we'll animate to turn on when we move in on the clock. Select the camera and each of its behaviors to familiarize yourself with the timing.

How to do it...

1. From the **Object** menu, choose **New Light**. A light is added to the scene that interacts with all the 3D groups and layers in your group. When you added the light, all the ambient light in the scene was turned off. We want to replace that with our own ambient light that is positioned back in **Z Space** so that we create a silhouette-type effect.

2. Select the light and press *F7* to show the HUD. The default light type is **Point**. We can place it anywhere we want by changing its **Position** value and we control its brightness by adjusting the **Intensity** value. In the HUD, set **Intensity** to 45 and **Falloff** to 9. Press *F1* to go to the **Properties** tab of the Inspector and set the light's **Z Position** to -500. Use the following screenshot as a reference. The silhouette effect was made possible by separating the characters in **Z Space** from the back of the clock.

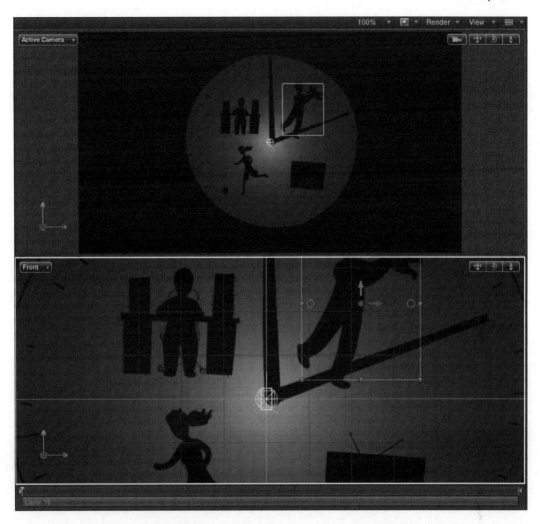

3. Let's add two additional lights to our scene. From the **Object** menu, select **New Light**. In the HUD, set **Light Type** to **Spotlight**. Rename the light as Spot TV. With the light selected, press *Command + D* to duplicate it. Name the duplicate Spot Work.

4. Select **Spot TV** and press *F1* to go to the **Properties** tab of the Inspector. Enter 200, -125, -125 for its **X**, **Y**, and **Z** position respectively. For **Rotation X**, enter -10. Go to the **Light** tab in the Inspector and set **Intensity** to **80**, **Falloff** to **2.5**, and **Soft Edge** to **11**, as shown in the following screenshot. For the time being, turn off the **Spot Work** light by clicking the checkmark next to it in the **Layers** tab.

5. We're going to keyframe the **Intensity** value of the **TV** light so that it turns on as we zoom into the TV. Press *F6* to show the Timeline. Move to the two-second mark. In the **Light** tab of the Inspector, click the diamond shape next to **Intensity**. Move to one second and change the **Intensity** value to 0. A keyframe is added automatically. Move to five seconds and click the diamond shape next to **Intensity** to lock the value at 80. Move to six seconds and change the **Intensity** value back to 0. Play back the animation. The light now fades in as the camera zooms on the TV and fades out when it leaves.

Use the following screenshot for reference:

6. Turn back on the **TV Work** light and see if you can reposition the light where the camera zooms in the second time. Repeat the steps from the last number to try to animate the light to turn on and off as the camera zooms in and out.

There's more...

When you make your objects 3D, your objects have full interactivity with lights, including the option to cast and receive shadows. As long as you have **Shadows** enabled under the **Render** menu from the **Properties** tab, you can choose how shadows for the selected layer interact in your 3D project.

See also

▸ *Autokeyframing multiple parameters on a shape* in *Chapter 4, Making It Move with Keyframes.*

▸ The *Making it 3D* recipe.

▸ The *Moving a camera versus moving a layer* recipe.

▸ The *Where am I? Controlling the view of your world using viewports* recipe.

- ▶ The *Adjust Around* recipe.
- ▶ The *Integrating 2D and 3D* recipe.
- ▶ The *Using the camera Framing behavior* recipe.

Creating reflections

In the last few recipes, you may have recognized that some of the objects had reflections turned on. Let's see how we can turn reflections on manually.

Getting ready

From this chapter's exercise files, double-click the 10_08 project. Press the Space bar to play back the project. You may notice the project does not play in real time. You can try to adjust the quality and resolution temporarily to allow the project to play back faster. The project consists of a camera and a few lights interacting with a floor, background, and a text layer. One of the lights has been animated using a **Parameter** behavior to wriggle the **Intensity** value of the light. The text has been animated using a **Sequence Text** behavior that has been set to rotate each character along the y axis. We want to reflect our text on the floor. Before we enable text on the **Floor** layer, select the **Reflection** text and under the **Properties** tab of the Inspector make sure **Casts Reflection** is set to **Yes**. Also, check the **Render** menu to make sure there is a checkmark next to **Reflections**, as shown here:

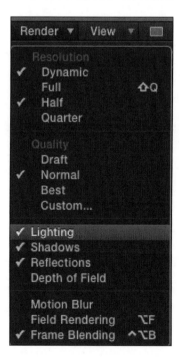

How to do it...

Now we are ready to add a reflection to the floor:

1. Select the **Floor** layer in the **Floor** and **Background** group. Press *F1* to go to the **Properties** tab. Click the empty square next to **Reflection** to activate it, as shown in the next screenshot. If needed, click on the word **Show** next to **Reflection** to see each of the parameters.

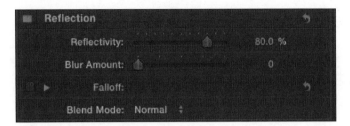

2. Set **Reflectivity** to 50 and **Blur Amount** to 6.

3. For a more fine-tuned adjustment, click the empty square next to **Falloff**. Click the disclosure triangle to reveal its properties.

4. Set **Begin Distance** to **100**, **End Distance** to **350**, and **Exponent** to **2**. Use the following screenshot for reference:

See also

▸ *Sequence Text* in *Chapter 5, Let's Make Text*.

▸ The *Making it 3D* recipe.

▸ The *Moving a camera versus moving a layer* recipe.

▸ The *Where am I? Controlling the view of your world using viewports* recipe.

▸ The *Adjust Around* recipe.

▸ The *Integrating 3D and 2D* recipe.

Turning on Depth of Field

Motion allows us to create some very realistic camera effects by enabling a property called **Depth of Field**. With it, we can choose an object we want to focus on by using its **Z Position** to guide us, in turn blurring other layers around it. Let's see how we can use it.

Getting ready

From this chapter's exercise files, double-click the `10_09` project. Press the Space bar to play back the project. You may notice the project does not play in real time. You can try to adjust the quality and resolution temporarily to allow the project to play back faster. The project consists of a camera and a few lights interacting with a floor and two text layers. Select each text layer and pay attention to its **Z Position** value in the **Properties** tab of the Inspector. We want to enable **Depth of Field** for our project, so that only the text in the foreground is in focus. We will then animate the focus by keyframing the **Offset** value.

How to do it...

Let's make sure our project is set up properly:

1. Under the **Render** menu, click the word **Depth of Field** to enable it for the project. You should notice that both the text layers have gone out of focus.

2. Select your camera and press *F4* to go to the **Camera** tab of the Inspector. Twirl down the **Depth of Field** parameters by clicking the **Show** button, as shown here:

3. Set **DOF Blur Amount** to `80` and **Near Focus** to `1700`.

4. Move to the one-second mark and add a keyframe next to **Focus Offset** by clicking the diamond icon. Move to the two-second and change the **Focus Offset** value to `1700`. A keyframe is added automatically as shown here:

5. As a final step, set **Filter** from **Gaussian** to **Defocus**. It creates a more realistic blur. Keep in mind, it's render intensive!

See also

- ▶ *Sequence Text* in *Chapter 5, Let's Make Text*.
- ▶ The *Making it 3D* recipe.
- ▶ The *Moving a camera versus moving a layer* recipe.
- ▶ The *Where am I? Controlling the view of your world using viewports* recipe.
- ▶ The *Adjust Around* recipe.
- ▶ The *Integrating 3D and 2D* recipe.
- ▶ The *Creating reflections* recipe.

11
Publishing Your Work to FCP X

In this chapter, we will cover the following:

- ▶ Opening and changing text from FCP X in Motion
- ▶ Publishing a Motion 5 generator and its parameters to FCP X
- ▶ Creating an effect for FCP X
- ▶ Creating a transition for FCP X
- ▶ Publishing parameters versus publishing rigs 101 – part 1
- ▶ Publishing parameters versus publishing rigs 101 – part 2
- ▶ Combining a slider, checkbox, and pop-up rig – part 1
- ▶ Combining a slider, checkbox, and pop-up rig – part 2
- ▶ Combining a slider, checkbox, and pop-up rig – part 3

Introduction

Motion 5 has made incredible leaps and bounds with its round-tripping process with FCP X. In previous versions of Final Cut Studio, users had the ability to send files to Motion and have any saved changes appear embedded in the Final Cut Pro Timeline. Users also had the ability to save templates that users could tweak directly in Final Cut Pro. The problem was that the changes you could make were limited, such as text, font, size, color, and drop zones. In Motion 5, users can create text, transitions, effects, and generators to be stored in the FCP X **Media Browser**. Also, not only does the user have the ability to create templates for the user to have access to, but also you have control over sending those parameters *you* choose to be available in Final Cut Pro X. It's like bringing in parts of Motion's architecture directly in to FCP X. This can help users automate their workflows in a variety of different project settings. Let's get deep under the hood of Final Cut X and Motion to gain a stronger understanding of how both applications play together.

Opening and changing text from FCP X in Motion

If you have FCP X and Motion running on your MAC, you may have noticed certain similarities between the two applications and their interfaces. When exploring FCP X, you might have right-clicked on a text file from the **Media Browser** and noticed an option to open it in Motion. Let's now walk through what happens when we do.

Getting ready

Go into your application folder and double-click on the **Final Cut Pro** icon to launch it. Press *Command + 0* to go to the **Project Library** and from the **File** menu choose **New Project**. Name the project Text to Motion, associate it with any event you'd like, and click on **OK**.

How to do it...

1. From the **Window** menu, navigate to **Media Browser | Titles** as shown in the following screenshot. The **Media Browser** opens to the right-hand side of the Timeline showing all of the available text presets. We're going to find one and send a copy of it over to Motion.

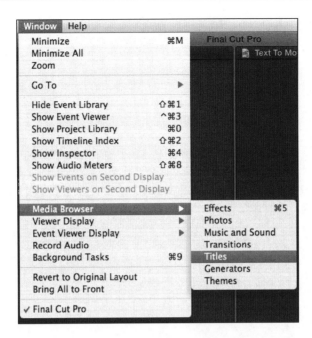

2. Under **All Category**, scrub over the **Drifting** text by hovering over it with your mouse. A preview of the text animation is displayed. Let's say you pretty much like the animation but would prefer to animate the text in the opposite direction. *Ctrl* + click the text and choose **Open a copy in Motion**. Motion launches and opens up a project entitled **Drift Copy**.

3. Press *Command+ -* to zoom out on your Canvas window a few times until it reads **25%**. Open up the group in the **Layers** tab by clicking on the disclosure triangle and select each of the text layers, paying attention to where keyframes lie along their Motion paths. Make sure your playhead is at the beginning of the project.

4. With the **Title** layer selected, press the *F1* key to go to the **Properties** tab of the **Inspector** and change the **Position X** value to **1482**.

5. Press *Shift + K* to move to the next keyframe and set the **Position X** value to **74**. Press *Shift + K* again and change the **Position X** value to **-74**. Press *Shift + K* again and change the **Position X** value to **-1482**. You should have now made changes to the four existing keyframes. Play back the animation. Notice how both text layers move in the same direction. Use the following screenshot for reference.

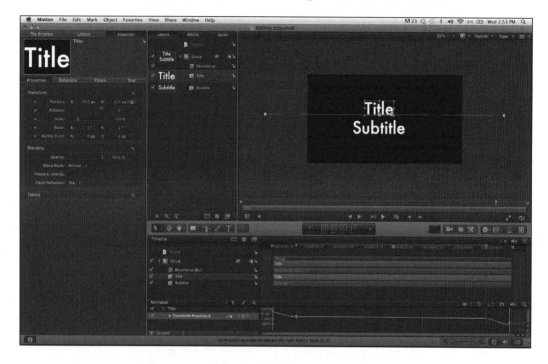

6. Select the **Subtitle** layer and move to the beginning of the project. In the **Properties** tab of the **Inspector**, enter **-1586** for **Position X**.

7. Press *Shift + K* to move to the next keyframe. Set the **Position X** value to **-74**. Press *Shift + K* again and change the **Position X** value to **74**. Press *Shift + K* again and change the **Position X** value to **1586**. Play back the animation.

8. We're now ready to send the text back over to Motion. Press *Command + S* to save the file. Press *Command + Tab* to go back over to FCP X on the dock. In the **Media Browser**, you should notice a new text template in the **Media Browser** called **Drift Copy**. Drag it into the Timeline, as shown in the following screenshot. Press *Shift + Z* to fit the text to your Timeline window and the Space bar to play back the animation. Notice how your changes have been carried over!

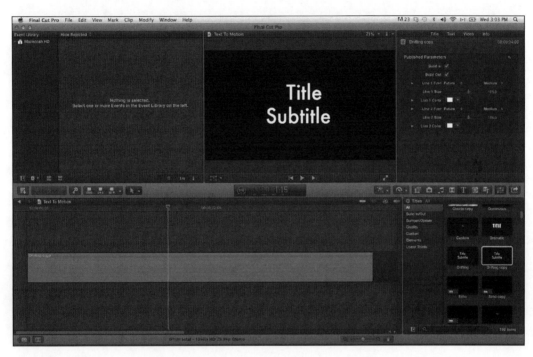

How it works...

You can choose to allow the user control over certain parameters from Motion in Final Cut. In FCP X, select the **Drift Copy** in your Timeline and press *Command + 4* to go to the **Inspector**. Every parameter you see in the **Title** tab, someone chose to publish it over from Motion giving the FCP X user control of it. For instance, the **Build In**, **Build Out** checkboxes control the animation of your text at the beginning and the end. They were set up using a special type of marker in Motion, allowing the user an option to turn the animation on or off.

You should note that, when you create a title project in Motion, it gets added to FCP X's **Media Browser** automatically once you save.

There's more...

When you create an FCP title project in Motion and save it, it gets added to the **Media Browser** in FCP X under the **Titles** section. On top of this, you get a **Text** tab containing a majority of the options you have for working with text in Motion. See the following screenshot for reference:

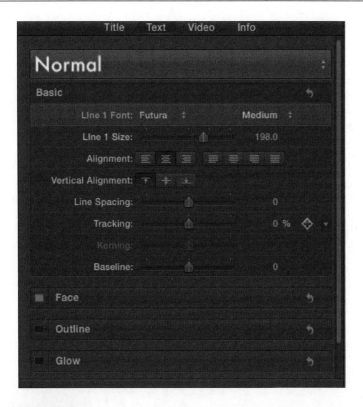

See also

The following recipes in *Chapter 5, Let's Make Text*:

- ▶ *Creating a lower third for FCP X in Chapter 5, Let's Make Text*
- ▶ *Changing the text format in Chapter 5, Let's Make Text*
- ▶ *Changing the text style in Chapter 5, Let's Make Text*
- ▶ *Keyframing a group in Chapter 4, Making It Move with Keyframes*

Publishing a Motion 5 generator and its parameters to FCP X

If you've worked with some of the earlier chapters, you'll know that there are several generators available to you in Motion's Library. Some of them aren't available in FCP X. Let's add a generator and its parameters to FCP X by saving our project as a Final Cut Pro generator.

Getting ready

Launch Motion. From the welcome screen, select a Final Cut generator project. Choose a project with a **Preset** of **Broadcast HD 1080**, a **Frame Rate** of **29.97**, and a **Duration** of 10 seconds. Click on **Open**. Motion's interface launches.

How to do it...

From here we'll add a generator to our Timeline and use the **Inspector** to choose the parameters we wish to publish.

1. Press *Command + 2* to go to the **Library**. Navigate to **Generators | Spirals**. With **Spirals** selected and your playhead at the beginning of the project, click on **Apply**.

2. With the Canvas selected, press *Shift + Z* to fit it to the window. Select **Spirals** from the **Layers** tab and press the *F4* key to go to the **Generators** tab of the **Inspector**.

3. The trick to publishing parameters to FCP X is to find them in the **Inspector**. Once you do, it's a matter of *Ctrl* + clicking on the appropriate word to publish. *Ctrl* + click on the word **Width** in the **Generator** tab and choose **Publish** as shown in the following screenshot:

4. Click on the **Project** layer in the **Layers** tab. In the **Project** tab of the **Inspector**, you should see that **Width** appears under **Published Parameters** as shown in the following screenshot. Select the **Spirals** layer again in the **Layers** tab. In the **Generator** tab of the **Inspector**, *Ctrl* + click on the word **Height** and choose **Publish**.

5. Repeat the last step for every remaining parameter. When you get to **Scale**, you'll notice that the parameter is grayed out. **Scale** is associated with the **Modern (linear)** type of spiral. To publish it, select **Modern (linear)** from the **Type** menu and then publish it as with the other parameters.

6. Select the **Project** layer again and double-check that all the parameters are published in the **Project** tab of the **Inspector**. The **Published Parameters** section also represents the order in which the FCP X user will see each parameter, as shown in the following screenshot:

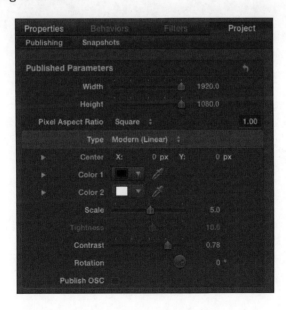

7. To get this over into Final Cut, navigate to the **File** menu and choose **Save**. We'll call the template `Spirals`.

8. You need to create a new category and theme in order to see this in FCP X. Under the **Category** menu choose **New Category**. Name it `Generators`.

9. Under **Theme**, choose **New Theme** and call it `Motion 5 Generators`. Make sure **Make Preview Movie** is selected and press **Publish**. Motion begins to save the file to FCP X as shown in the following screenshot:

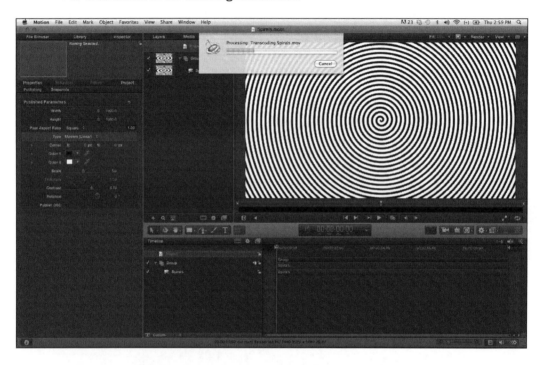

10. When the process is complete, launch Final Cut. Create a new project and event if necessary. Navigate to **Window | Media Browser | Generators**. Find the **Generators** category on your left-hand side and notice the theme the **Spirals** generator is in. Drag **Spirals** to bring it into the project. Select it and press *Command + 4* to bring up the **Inspector**. Verify that all the parameters you published are present. Use the following screenshot for reference:

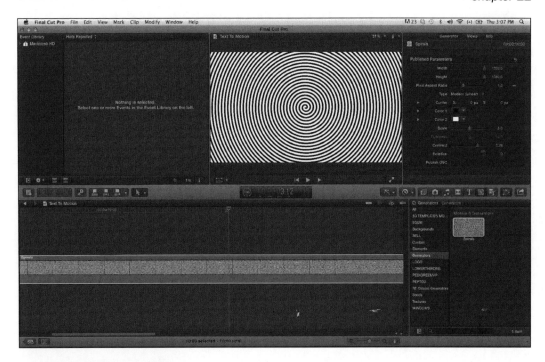

There's more...

It's easy to change the order of the published parameters.

Changing the order of published parameters

In Motion, if you click on the word of any published parameter and hold your mouse, you can drag that parameter up or down to change its order and verify how it will be seen in FCP X.

If you ever need to transfer Motion files for FCP X to another computer, everything is contained in the **Movies** folder.

Finding Titles, Effects, Transitions, and Generators at the system level

Under your user **Movies** folder, there is a folder called **Motion Templates** that contains all the **Effects**, **Generators**, **Titles**, and **Transitions** that you publish over to Final Cut. If you want to install them on another system, find the category your items are in and copy that folder over to another system. Use the following screenshot for reference:

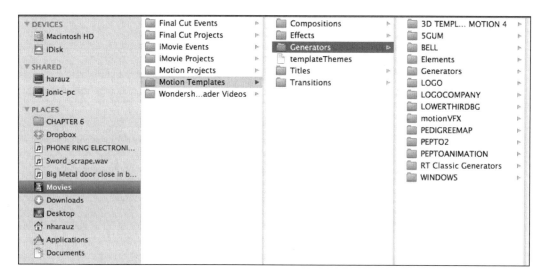

See also

▶ The *Creating a lower third for FCP X* in *Chapter 5, Let's Make Text*

Creating an effect for FCP X

Almost all the effects in the FCP X library come from Motion 5. Let's create our own effect in Motion and bring it to FCP X with some parameters that we can tweak.

Getting ready

Locate some video footage on your computer that you'd like to add an effect to and that is about 10 seconds in length. Launch Motion. From the welcome screen, select a Final Cut Effect project. From the **Preset**, choose a **Broadcast HD 1080** project with a **Frame Rate** of **29.97** and a **Duration** of 10 seconds. Click on **Open**. Motion's interface launches. Make sure you are at the beginning of your project. Drag the footage from your **File Browser** over to the **Effect Source** well. When you see a hooked arrow, release the mouse. The placeholder now gets updated with your footage. Select the Canvas and press *Shift + Z* to fit the video to the window.

How to do it...

1. We're going to add three effects to this clip and then choose to publish the parameters we want the FCP X user to have access to. While the effects we will be using already exist in FCP, think of Motion allowing you the ability to save a preset where several effects in a row easily get added to the clips helping to automate your workflow in FCP X. Press *Command + 2* to go to the **Library** and navigate to **Filters | Distortion | Flop**. Click-and-drag it over to the **Effect Source** well in the **Layers** tab.

2. Under the **Library** in **Filters**, navigate to **Stylize | Halftone**. Click-and-drag it over the **Effect Source** well in the **Layers** tab. With **Effect Source** selected, press the *F3* key to go to the **Filters** tab of the **Inspector**. Change the value of **Scale** to 8 and the **Contrast** to 0.7.

3. Press *Command + 2* to go back over to the **Library**. Under **Filters** navigate to **Border | Simple Border**. Click-and-drag it over to the **Effect Source** well in the **Layers** tab. Press the *F3* key to jump back to the **Filters** tab and select a blue color and a width of your liking.

4. At this point, we could send the effect over to FCP X. The problem is, none of the parameters on the effects would be copied over. The user would only have the option to turn the effect on or off. To fix this, we'll publish each parameter. Start off by *Ctrl* + clicking on the word **Width** in the **Filters** tab and, from the menu that appears, choose **Publish**. Continue *Ctrl* + clicking on every parameter name until you've published every parameter.

5. Click on the **Project** layer in the **Layers** tab. In the **Project** tab of the **Inspector**, you should see that the all the parameters appear under **Published Parameters**. Rename **Width**, **Color**, and **Mix** to `Border Width`, `Border Color`, and `Border Mix`. You can rename by double-clicking on the parameter you wish to rename. Double-check and make sure the mix value you rename is attached to the border.

6. For all the parameters associated with **Halftone**, add the letter H in front of them. Add the word Flop in front of the **Flop** parameters as shown in the following screenshot:

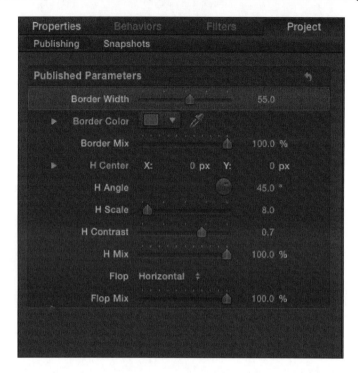

7. After you've verified that all the parameters work. Go to the **File** menu and choose **Save**. Call the template Border, Halftone, and Flop. Create a new theme and a new category of your liking. Click on **Publish** when finished. The next time you launch Final Cut, the effect will be within the **Media Browser** under **Effects**. You can add it to any clip on your Timeline.

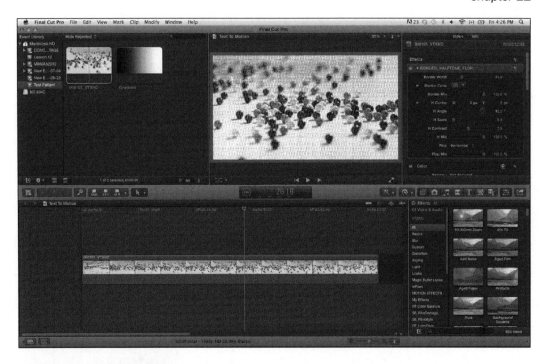

There's more...

Unlike effects and transition projects, Final Cut generators can be saved from a Motion project. You can choose to create a generator project when you launch Motion or create a generator from any Motion project by navigating to **File | Publish Template** and then clicking on **Publish as Final Cut Generator**, as shown in the following screenshot:

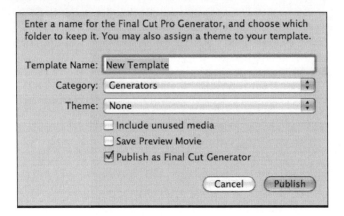

See also

▶ The *Creating a lower third for FCP X* recipe of *Chapter 5, Let's Make Text*

▶ The *Publishing a Motion 5 generator and its parameters to FCP X* recipe

Creating a transition for FCP X

Just as we can create effects to use in Final Cut Pro X, we can also create custom transitions. Transitions can be created using overlaying graphics and also by animating placeholders that will appear as soon as you launch a Motion transition project.

Getting ready

Locate two still images on your computer that you'd like to a transition between. Launch Motion. From the welcome screen, select a Final Cut transition project.

1. From the **Preset**, choose a **Broadcast HD 1080** project with a **Frame Rate** of **29.97**, and a **Duration** of 1 second. This represents how long we want the transition to be.

2. Click on **Open**. Motion's interface launches. Make sure you are at the beginning of your project. There are two transition sources in the project; **Transition A** and **Transition B**.

3. Drag your first still image to **Transition A**. When you see a hooked arrow, release the mouse. The **Transition A** placeholder now gets updated with your footage.

4. Repeat this for the second video clip and **Transition B**. Select the Canvas and press *Shift + Z* to fit the video to the window. Before we create our transition, there are two essential rules we need to know. First, **Transition A** should always be full-frame on the first frame of our project. Second, on the last frame, **Transition B** should be full-frame. Your animation will begin and end between these two points that we'll identify so that we can stretch out the duration of the transition in FCP X later on.

How to do it...

What we'd like to do is start with **Transition A** and move to **Transition B**, which is going to come onscreen from the right-hand side. To do this, we'll reposition the **Transition B** layer offscreen on the right-hand side and then we'll keyframe the group to move between the transitions.

1. Press *Command + -* to zoom out on the Canvas and select **Transition B**. *Shift* + drag the layer in the Canvas until it is offscreen to the right-hand side, as shown in the following screenshot:

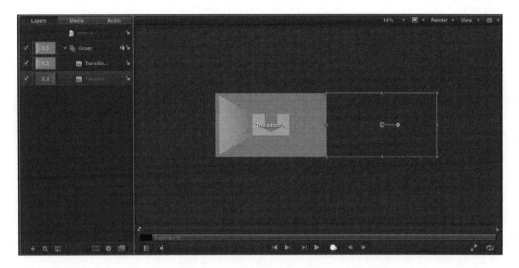

2. Move to first frame 1 of the project. With **Transition B** still selected, press the *I* key to extend its in-point to frame 1. Select **Transition B** and move to frame 28. Press the *O* key to trim its out-point.

3. Move back to frame 1. Select the **Group** and press the *F1* key to go to the **Properties** tab of the **Inspector**. Click on the diamond shape next to **Position** to add a keyframe. Move to the frame 28 and enter -1920 for the **X** value. A keyframe is added automatically. Use the following screenshot for reference:

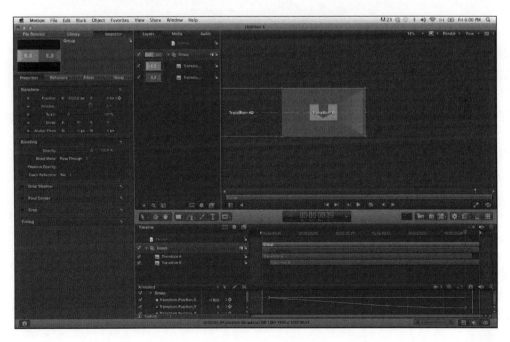

4. Press *Command + 8* to bring up the Keyframe Editor. Select the last two keyframes in the graph and *Ctrl +* click either one. From the menu, choose **Ease In**. Play back the animation.

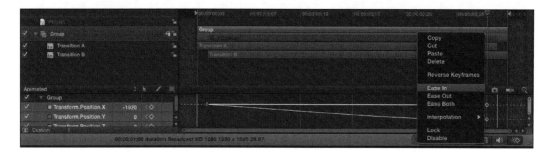

5. Press *Command + S* to save the transition to Final Cut. Call the transition `Left to Right`. Create a new category called `My Transitions` and choose a new theme of your liking as shown in the following screenshot. Make sure **Save Preview Movie** is selected and choose **Publish**.

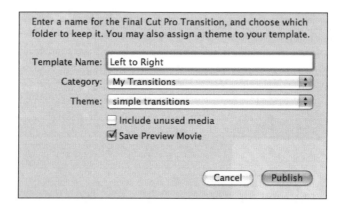

6. Launch Final Cut and, from the **Window** menu, go to **Media Browser | Transitions**. Verify that the transition is there and apply it to the edit point over any two clips or stills in your Timeline by clicking and dragging from the **Media Browser** to the edit point. Play around the transition point.

How it works...

In FCP X's preferences, all transitions have a default length of 1 second. If you create a transition longer than the FCP X default length in Motion, you need to go into your **Project Properties** and click on the **Override FCP** option. With this option, if you had a 3-second transition, it would appear as 3 seconds in Final Cut and cannot be sped up to 1 second.

See also

▶ The *Working with multiple parameters in the Keyframe Editor* recipe in *Chapter 4, Making It Move with Keyframes*

▶ The *Creating a lower third for FCP X* recipe in *Chapter 5, Let's Make Text*

▶ The *Publishing a Motion 5 generator and its parameters to FCP X* recipe

▶ The *Creating a transition for FCP X* recipe

Publishing parameters versus publishing rigs 101 – part 1

While publishing parameters to FCP X gives us a lot of flexibility, publishing rigs gives us even more. A **rig** allows us to have control over several parameters at once while, at the same time, helping us to create a more simplified user interface for the FCP user. In this exercise, we'll explore some of the similarities and differences between publishing and rigging.

Getting ready

From the exercise files of this chapter, double-click on the 11_05 project. Play back the project. The project consists of four animated arrows that are interacting with lights and have a **Colorize** filter placed on the group they're in. If you look directly under the **Project** layer, you'll see a rig has already been created called **Arrow Color**. In the end, this rig is going to allow the FCP X user to choose between four colors for his arrows. Before we can do that, we'll have to add one additional snapshot to our rig and publish it over to Final Cut.

How to do it...

1. Select the **Arrow Color** layer directly under **Rig** in the **Layers** tab and press the *F4* key to reveal the **Widget** tab of the **Inspector**. The type of rig that has been added to this project is a **pop up**. It allows the FCP X user to choose different settings from a pop-up menu; in this case, the color. Change the value of **Arrow Color** from **Red** to **Green** as shown in the following screenshot:

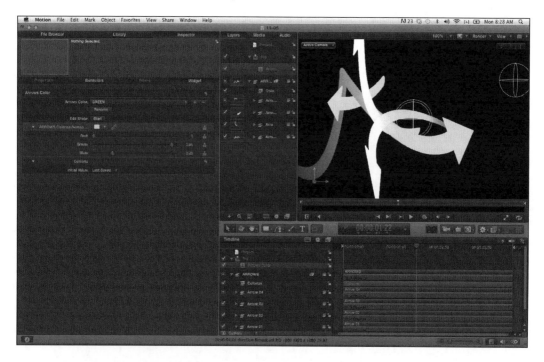

2. Click-and-drag in between the **Inspector** and **Layers** tab until you can clearly see the name of the parameter with the color well set to green. This parameter is from the **Colorize** filter. We've told Motion that, when the pop-up menu displays green, the remap white parameter is set to green. Change the value of **Arrow Color** from **Green** to **Purple**. Notice how the color well changes to purple. We want to have access to one more color option in Final Cut before we publish our rig over.

3. Next to the **Arrow Color** pop-up menu, click on the plus icon to add a snapshot. Rename the snapshot as `blue`. *Ctrl* + click on the **Color** well and set it to a blue color. Flip between each of the different colors again to make sure each color is displayed appropriately.

4. While the pop-up widget appears to be working fine, we need to publish the rig in order for the FCP X user to have access to it. *Ctrl* + click on the word **Arrows Color** and choose **Publish**. Select the **Project** layer and notice how the rig has been published over. Set the value of **Arrows Color** to **Red**. This will be the first color the user sees in FCP X.

5. We need to save this project as a template to have access to it in FCP X. From the **File** menu, choose **Publish Template**. Name the template Colored Arrows and click on the **Publish as Final Cut Generator** box. Create a new category and theme of your choice and select **Publish**. Use the following screenshot for reference:

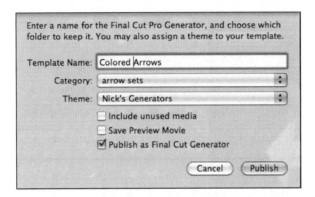

6. Launch Final Cut Pro. Search your **Media Browser** under **Generators** and bring **Color Arrows** into a project. Look in the **Inspector** to see the pop-up widget. In the next exercise, we'll add another widget to our rig in order to control the amount of arrows we see.

How it works...

Please note, you can't publish a parameter that's controlled by a rig. In the last exercise, the **Colorize** filter's remap white parameter was controlled by the rig. It's important to note that rigged parameters can't be published. Essentially, when a parameter is being controlled by a rig, publishing that parameter will have no effect.

See also

▶ The *Creating a lower third for FCP X* recipe in *Chapter 5, Let's Make Text*

▶ The *Publishing a Motion 5 generator and its parameters to FCP X* recipe

▶ The *Creating a transition for FCP X* recipe

▶ The *Creating an effect for FCP X* recipe

Publishing parameters versus publishing rigs 101 – part 2

In this exercise, we'll build on our exploration of rigging by creating our own rig and selecting parameters we want associated with it to control which arrows we see. We'll then publish that rig over to our existing **Color Arrows** Final Cut Pro generator.

Getting ready

From the exercise files of this chapter, double-click on the 11_06 project. Press the Space bar to play back the project. It consists of the same animated arrows from the past exercise. We'll create a new pop-up rig so that we only see one arrow appear at a time rather then all of them at once.

How to do it...

1. Select the **Arrow 1** layer. In order to control the visibility of arrows in Final Cut, we can use the opacity parameter. Press the *F1* key to go to the **Properties** tab of the **Inspector**. *Ctrl* + click on the word **Opacity** and navigate to **Add to Rig | Rig | Add to New Pop-Up**, as shown in the following screenshot:

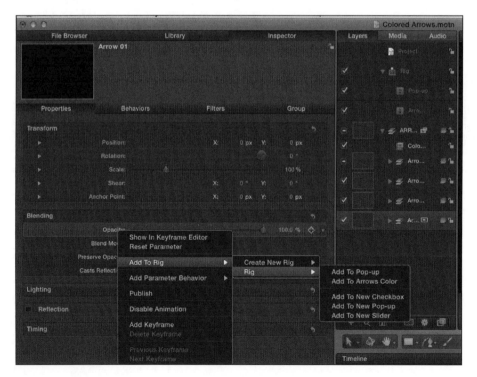

2. In the **Layers** tab, a new pop up is added under the existing rig. In the **Layers** tab, rename the pop up to `Arrow Choice`. Select **Arrow Choice** and press the *F4* key to go to the **Widget** tab of the **Inspector**.

3. We're going to add the opacity parameters of the remaining arrows and then link them to the appropriate snapshots. Select **Arrow 2** and, if needed, press the *F1* key to go to the **Properties** tab in the **Inspector**. *Ctrl* + click on the word **Opacity** and navigate to **Add to Rig | Rig | Add to Arrow Choice**.

4. Repeat the preceding step for **Arrow 3** and **Arrow 4**.

5. Select **Arrow Choice** in the **Layers** tab and notice in the **Widget** tab that all four arrows' opacities appear. We must link them to the appropriate snapshots. Click on the **Rename** button under **Snapshot 1**. Rename the snapshot as `Arrow 1`. Drag down the opacity sliders to 0 for **Arrow 2** to **Arrow 4** (Watch out! They're in reverse order).

6. Set the value of **Arrow Choice** to **Snapshot 2**. Click on the **Rename** button and type `Arrow 2`. Drag down the opacity slider to 0 for **Arrow 1**, **Arrow 3**, and **Arrow 4**. Use the following screenshot for reference:

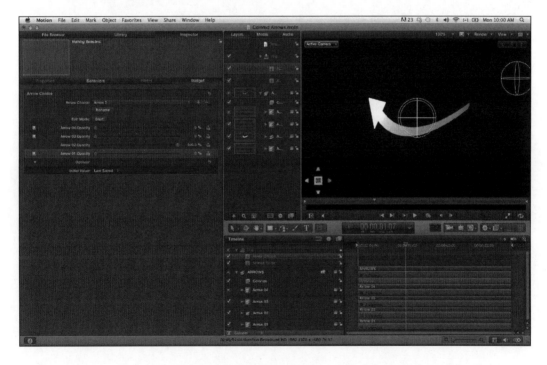

7. Set the value of **Arrow Choice** to **Snapshot 3**. Click on the **Rename** button and type `Arrow 3`. Drag down the opacity slider to 0 for **Arrow 1**, **Arrow 2**, and **Arrow 4**.

8. Click on the plus icon to the right-hand side of the **Arrow Choice** pop up. Rename it as `Arrow 4`. Drag down the opacity slider to 0 for **Arrow 1**, **Arrow 2**, and **Arrow 3**.

9. *Ctrl* + click on the words **Arrow State** and from the menu choose **Publish**. Click on the **Project** layer and in the **Project** tab of the **Inspector**, verify the different pop-up states and that they correspond with the correct arrows' opacity.

10. Since this generator is already published to FCP X, press *Command* + S to save it. The file will be updated in Final cut.

11. Launch Final Cut Pro. Search in **Media Browser** under **Generators** and bring the **Colored Arrows** into a project. Look in the **Inspector**. The new pop-up widget **Arrow State** has been published over, as shown in the following screenshot:

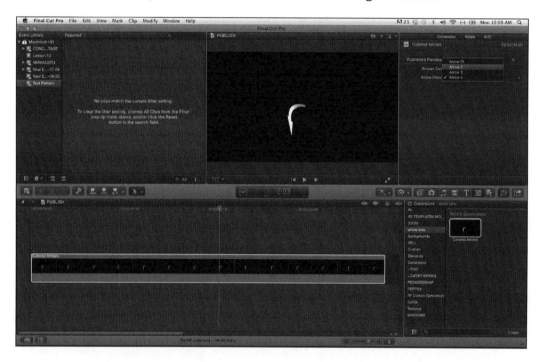

There's more...

When we update generators for FCP X, they're updated in the **Generators** section of the **Media Browser** only. If you have updated a generator in Motion that is embedded in a FCP X project, the project version of the generator does not get updated. Simply replace the generator in your project with the generator from the **Media Browser**.

See also

▶ The *Creating a lower third for FCP X* recipe in *Chapter 5, Let's Make Text*

▶ The *Publishing a Motion 5 generator and its parameters to FCP X* recipe

▶ The *Creating a transition for FCP X* recipe

▶ The *Creating an effect for FCP X* recipe

▶ The *Publishing parameters versus publishing rigs 101 – part 1* recipe

Combining a slider, checkbox, and pop-up rig – part 1

In the next exercise, we'll begin to create a complex rig that allows the FCP X user choices over a simulated lighting effect.

Getting ready

From the exercise files of this chapter, locate the `11_07` project folder. Drag the content of the folder to the **Effects** folder by navigating to **Movies | Motion templates** from under your user on the computer. Double-click on the `.moef` project from this location. Press the Space bar to play back the project. It consists of a still photo that has a light interacting with it. Two properties of the light have parameter behaviors applied to them; **Intensity** and **Position**. Turn each behavior on the **Light** on and off to see its effect. We want to link a few parameters from each of these behaviors to a slider so the FCP X user can control how much the light changes intensity and moves simultaneously.

How to do it...

Let's add some of our behavior parameters to a rig.

1. Select the **Light** in the **Layers** tab and press the *F2* key to go to the **Behaviors** tab of the **Inspector**. You'll see two parameter behaviors; **Light Movement** and **Light Flick**. We're going to link the amount and frequency parameters from each behavior so the FCP X user will have control over them. *Ctrl* + click on the word **Amount** from the **Light Movement** behavior and navigate to **Add to Rig | Add to New Rig | Create New Slider** as shown in the following screenshot. A new rig and slider are created in the **Layers** tab. Name the rig `Lighting Controls` and the slider `Light Animation Intensity`.

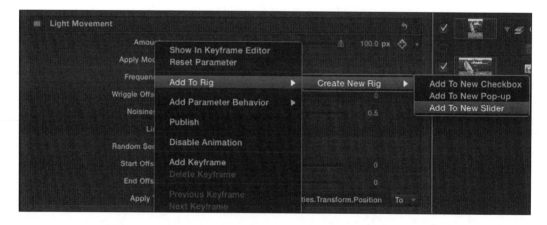

2. Select **Light** and press the *F2* key to go back to the **Behaviors** tab of the **Inspector**. Under **Light Movement**, *Ctrl* + click on the word **Frequency** and select **Add to Rig | Lighting Controls | Add to Lighting Animation Intensity**.

3. Repeat the preceding step for the **Amount** and **Frequency** controls for **Light Flick**. Select **Rig** in the **Layers** tab and verify each parameter has been added in the **Rig** tab of the **Inspector**.

4. If you use FCP X or Motion often, the slider will look very familiar. The only difference for us Motion users is that it now controls several individual parameters. Think about it as one master control to rule them all! We need to set the states for the slider. In the **Rig** tab of the **Inspector**, move the **Light Animation Intensity** slider down to 0 and set all the parameter states underneath to 0, as shown in the following screenshot. Play back the project and notice that no flicker or movement of the light occurs.

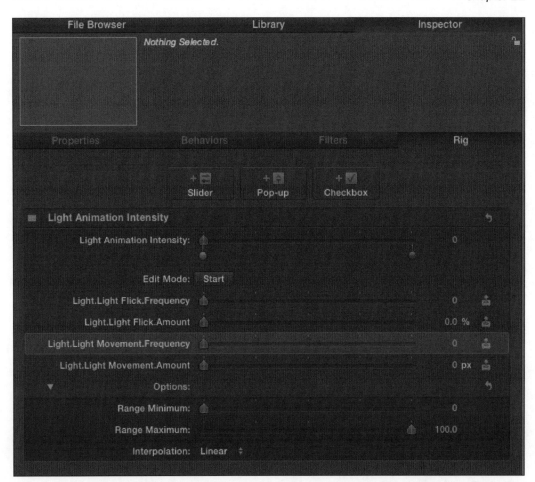

5. In the **Rig** tab of the **Inspector**, drag the **Light Animation Intensity** up to 100. Set the **Light Flick Frequency** to 1, the **Light Intensity** to 150, the **Light Movement Frequency** to 2, and the **Light Movement** amount to 150. Play back the project and notice the light settings when the slider is set to 100. Drag the **Light Animation Intensity** slider up and down to move between the two states.

6. *Ctrl* + click on the word **Lighting Animation Intensity** in the **Rig** tab and from the menu that appears choose **Publish**. Select the **Project** layer and verify in the **Project** tab of the **Inspector** that the slider has been published. Set the slider to 50.

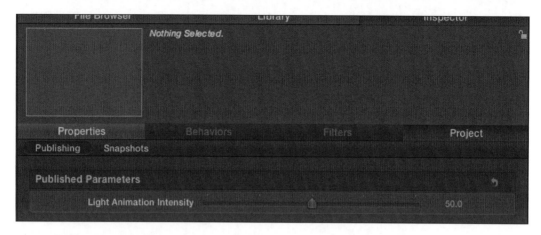

7. Since the project has been saved already, press *Command* + *S* to update the template.

8. Launch Final Cut Pro. Search in your **Media Browser** under **Effects** and bring the **Lighting Effects** into a project. Look in the **Inspector** and verify the content there.

There's more...

As a bonus step in Motion, there is a **Bad TV** filter that's been placed on the **Effect Source**, temporarily turned off. Select a few parameters from the **Effect** to add and control from the existing slider.

See also

▸ The *Creating a lower third for FCP X* recipe of *Chapter 5, Let's Make Text*

▸ The *Publishing a Motion 5 generator and its parameters to FCP X* recipe

▸ The *Creating a transition for FCP X* recipe

▸ The *Creating an effect for FCP X* recipe

▸ The *Publishing parameters versus publishing rigs 101 – part 1* recipe

▸ The *Publishing parameters versus publishing rigs 101 – part 2* recipe

Combining a slider, checkbox, and pop-up rig – part 2

Let's continue with where we left of in the last exercise and add a checkbox rig to our effect.

Getting ready

From the exercise files of this chapter, locate the `11_08` project folder. Drag it to the **Effects** folder by navigating to **Movies | Motion Templates** under your user on the computer. Double-click on the `.moef` project from this location that is in the folder. Press the Space bar to play back the project. It's the same project as the last exercise and contains the slider rig we created and published over to FCP X. We want to give the user in Final Cut an option to turn on and off the **Vignette** effect created by our spotlight. We can do this by creating a checkbox rig and linking it to the different light types. We'll also give access to control the size of a vignette by publishing one parameter.

How to do it...

1. Select **Light**, and in the **Light** tab of the **Inspector**, *Ctrl* + click on the word **Light Type** and navigate to **Add to Rig | Lighting Controls | Add To New Checkbox**.

2. The checkbox rig is the most simple of the three rigs available. We simply decide what happens when the FCP X user checks the box. Select the checkbox rig in the **Layers** tab and rename it as `Vignette`. In the **Widget** tab of the **Inspector**, with the box blank, change the value of **Light Type** to **Ambient**, as shown in the following screenshot:

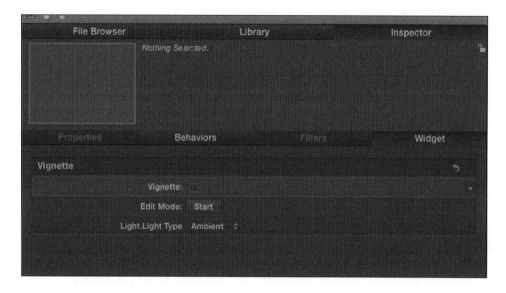

3. Click the box next to **Vignette**. Make sure the **Light** type is set to **Point**. Play back the project while turning on and off the **Vignette**.

4. *Ctrl* + click on the word **Vignette** and from the menu choose **Publish**. Select the **Project** layer and in the **Project** tab verify the **Vignette** checkbox is there beneath **Light Animation Intensity** from the previous exercise. Set it to on.

5. Select **Light** and, under the **Light** tab in the **Inspector**, *Ctrl* + click on the word **Falloff** and choose **Publish**.

6. With the **Project** selected in the **Layers** tab, in the **Project** tab rename **Falloff** to `Vignette Size`. Set the value to `8` as shown in the following screenshot:

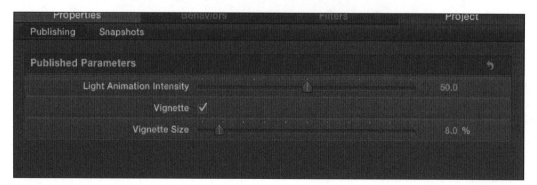

7. Press *Command + S* to save it to Final Cut.

8. Launch Final Cut Pro. Search in your **Media Browser** under **Effects** and bring the **Lighting Effects** into a project. Look in the **Inspector** and see that the new **Checkbox** widget has been published over.

There's more...

Your project settings *do* matter.

Be careful of your project settings

When dealing with effects, you should always be aware of your project settings. For one reason: if we apply an effect to a 5-second project that's animated, in Final Cut it will be a 5-second effect. So let's say you apply apply a filter to a clip with a longer duration. The effect's speed will be adjusted to fit the clips duration. To avoid this scaling, we need to add a specific marker to our project to have the animation loop. Under the **Mark** menu, add a new marker to the project and, in the marker settings, make it a **Project Loop End** marker.

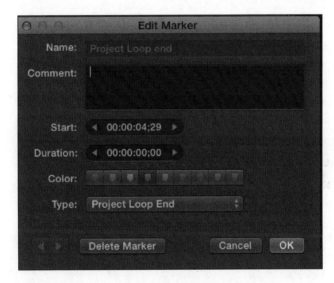

We should also be concerned with the aspect ratio of our project

Project snapshots and DARS

So far, every effect we created is meant for a 16:9 project. We can verify this by going to the **Project** tab of the **Inspector** and looking under the **Snapshots** pane. If we wanted our project to be ready for 4:3 or even 3:2 projects, we could add a new snapshot by clicking on the plus icon and fixing the template so that it is properly scaled for the correct display aspect ratio.

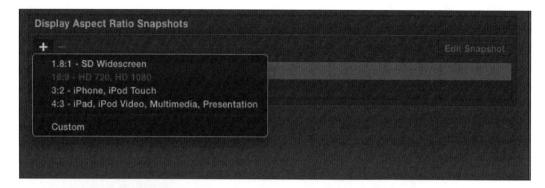

See also

- ▸ The *Creating a lower third for FCP X* recipe of *Chapter 5, Let's Make Text*
- ▸ The *Publishing a Motion 5 generator and its parameters to FCP X* recipe
- ▸ The *Creating a transition for FCP X* recipe
- ▸ The *Creating an effect for FCP X* recipe
- ▸ The *Publishing parameters versus publishing rigs 101 – part 1* recipe
- ▸ The *Publishing parameters versus publishing rigs 101 – part 2* recipe
- ▸ The *Combining a slider, checkbox, and pop-up rig – part 1* recipe

Combining a slider, checkbox, and pop-up rig – part 3

In the last few exercises, we created two rigs, a checkbox, and slider. We're going to add a pop-up rig to our effect and publish it over to FCP X.

Getting ready

From the exercise files, locate the `11_09` project folder. Drag it to the **Effects** folder by navigating to **Movies | Motion templates** under your user on the computer. Double-click on the `.moef` project from this location. Press the Space bar to play back the project. It's the same project from the last exercise and contains the slider and checkbox rig we created and published over to FCP X. We want to give our user in Final Cut the option to have different light colors available from a pop-up menu.

How to do it...

1. Select **Light,** and in the **Light** tab of the **Inspector,** *Ctrl* + click on the word **Color** and navigate to **Add To Rig | Lighting Controls | Add To New Pop-up**.

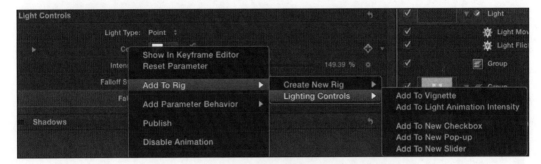

2. Select the pop-up rig in the **Layers** tab and rename it as `Light color`.

3. In the **Widget** tab of the **Inspector**, rename the three snapshots to three colors of your choice. Change the color well to match the color of the selected snapshot. It's best practice to add only a bit of color, rather than highly saturated values, so the light remains close to white. Use the following screenshot for reference:

4. Click on the plus icon next to the pop-up widget to add a fourth color. Name it as White. Change the **Color** well to white. Go through each of the states to make sure they're correctly set.

5. *Ctrl* + click on the word **Color** and choose **Publish** from the menu. Verify the rig has been published over to the project by going into the **Project** tab. Set the default pop up to **White**.

6. Press *Command + S* to save it to Final Cut.

7. Launch Final Cut Pro. Search in your **Media Browser** under **Effects** and bring the **Lighting Effects** into a project. Look in the **Inspector** and see that the new pop-up rig widget has been published over. Use the following screenshot for reference:

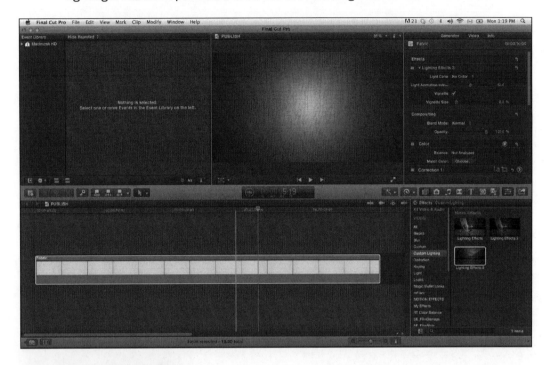

See also

▶ The *Creating a lower third for FCP X* recipe of *Chapter 5, Let's Make Text*

▶ The *Publishing a Motion 5 generator and its parameters to FCP X* recipe

▶ The *Creating a transition for FCP X* recipe

▶ The *Creating an effect for FCP X* recipe

▶ The *Publishing parameters versus publishing rigs 101 – part 1* recipe

▶ The *Publishing parameters versus publishing rigs 101 – part 2* recipe

▶ The *Combining a slider, checkbox, and pop-up rig – part 1* recipe

▶ The *Combining a slider, checkbox, and pop-up rig – part 2* recipe

12
Customization and Exporting

In this chapter, we will cover the following:

- ▶ Changing your background, color, and safe zones
- ▶ Creating your own project presets
- ▶ Exporting a full-resolution copy of your project
- ▶ Exporting to DVD
- ▶ Exporting a still image and image sequence
- ▶ Exporting an alpha channel and video separately
- ▶ Exporting using Compressor
- ▶ Saving a template

Introduction

While learning how to create complex motion graphics can be fun, a lot of times this process can be wasted if you don't know the fundamentals of how Motion operates. Some of these fundamentals involve customizing Motion to work for you while others involve knowing how to correctly export your video to a variety of different platforms and sharing your projects with your intended audience. This chapter explores creating some of your own project preferences and presets. It also looks at the variety of different export options made available to you in Motion as well, through a standalone complimentary application called **Compressor**.

Changing your background, color, and safe zones

Motion allows you to customize your project and interface through options available in the **Preferences** menu. Some of those options allow you to make sure your text will be seen on a television correctly while others allow you to change the background. Let's explore by heading to the **Project Properties** and **Preferences** menu.

Getting ready

Launch Motion. From the welcome screen, select a Motion project. From the Presets, choose a **Broadcast HD 1080** project with a **Frame Rate** of **29.97**, and a **Duration** of 10 seconds. Click on **Open**. Motion's interface launches. Make sure you are at the beginning of your project. Select the Text tool by pressing the *T* key. Type in any word of your choice close to the center of the screen and press the *Esc* key to exit the text entry mode. Press the *F7* key to reveal the HUD and make the text black, as shown in the following screenshot. You can't see it any more. This is one occasion where we want to be able to see our text and also ensure it's within safe boundaries. In the future, the project will also be exported to DVD and we need to make sure the background is a solid color rather than a transparent one.

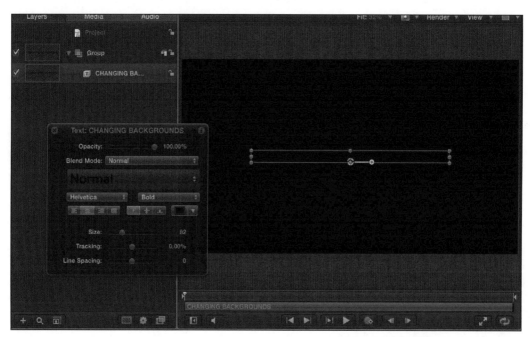

1. From the **Edit** menu choose **Project Properties**; it opens in the **Properties** tab of the **Inspector**. *Ctrl* + click on the **Color** well to change the background from black to white as shown in the following screenshot:

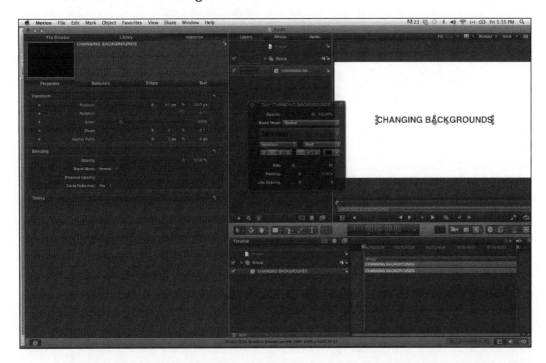

2. While the background may look white, it's actually transparent. You can see this displayed from the **Background Color** parameter in **Project Properties**. Change this from **Transparent** to **Solid** as shown in the following screenshot. Now the solid background will render out.

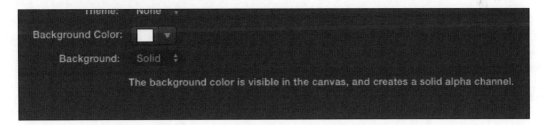

3. As a final step, we want to ensure our text is within safe boundaries. Not all TV screens are made alike and we want to ensure that our text won't be cut off by a TV. To activate safe zones, go to the **View** menu on the top-right corner of the Canvas and choose **Safe Zones**. The inner rectangle is for title safe and the outer box representing 90 percent of the screen is for action safe, as indicated in the following screenshot:

There's more...

If you know precisely the way your television or final medium will scale up your final project, you can customize the safe zones. Under **Motion | Preferences** select the **Canvas** tab. Under **Zones**, as shown in the following screenshot, you can customize the color and size of your safe zones.

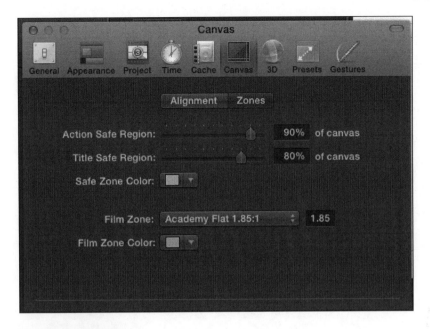

See also

► *Changing the text format* in *Chapter 5, Let's Make Text*
► The *Exporting to DVD* recipe of this chapter

Creating your own project presets

There are several instances where you may be presenting your final video on an LCD screen with unusual dimensions. If this is a common workflow for you, you can create your own project presets made available to you right from Motion's welcoming screen.

Getting ready

Launch Motion. Choose any project, frame rate, and duration you like. We won't be saving this project. Click on **Open**. Motion's interface launches. We'll go to Motion's preferences and set up our own project preset that will become available for us the next time we launch the application.

How to do it...

1. Go to the **Motion** menu and choose **Preferences**. Click on the **Presets** tab. You may recognize these presets. This is what's available to us whenever we set up a Motion project. Let's say all the projects we export for our main client need to be 900 by 700. These current presets are locked by default. To get around this, the **Medium** preset under **Presentation** is close to this, so we'll duplicate the setting to customize it.

2. Click on the **Duplicate** button at the bottom of the window. With the duplicate **Medium** selected under **Presentation**, click on **Edit**.

3. Name the preset anything you want. Make the **Width** and **Height** 900 by 700 as shown in the following screenshot. Depending on where you're exporting to, you may need to alter the **Pixel Aspect**, **Ratio**, **Field Order**, and **Frame Rate** values too.

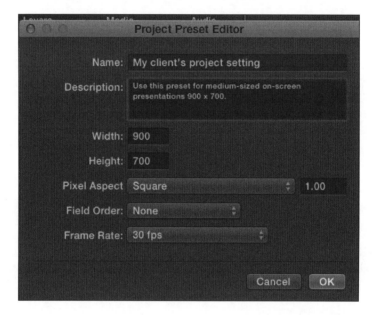

4. Enter a description for the preset and click on **OK**. Close out the **Preferences** window.

5. Motion needs to be closed in order for the preset to become available from the menu. Press *Command + Q* to close Motion. Launch Motion and choose **Motion project**. Look under **Presets** to see the setting you've just made available, as shown in the following screenshot:

Exporting a full-resolution copy of your project

The time has come to share your Motion project masterpieces with the world. If you've taken the time to set up your project properties for export, sharing your project will be extremely straightforward.

Getting ready

Locate a Motion project you've worked with in one of the previous exercises. Double-click to open it. Go through the project and make sure the play range is set to the beginning and end of your Timeline. If it's not, press *Option + X* to reset the play range.

How to do it...

1. From the **Share** menu, choose **Export Movie**.

2. A window opens with a series of options available to us. Look under the **Options** tab and you'll see there are a number of different codecs available to you such as **Apple Pro Res** and **h.264**. Keep the setting the same as source. Click on the **Render** tab at the top of the window.

3. The **Render** tab allows us to overwrite some of the options you've previously set. One thing to note is that Motion leaves the value of **Render Quality** in your projects set to **Normal**. To overwrite this, change the value of **Render Quality** to **Best** as shown in the following screenshot. Click on the **Summary** tab.

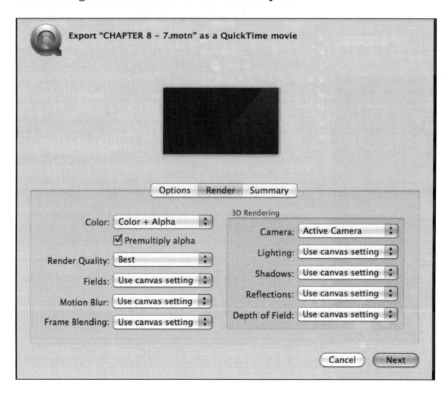

4. The **Summary** tab sums up your choices. It is the last step to check before you send it out. Click on **Next**.

5. Name the file, choose a location to save it too on your computer, and click on **OK**. Motion renders out your file. You will be unable to work while the file renders so, depending on the complexity of your project, this could be the appropriate time for a coffee break!

6. Once the process is done, the project opens up in QuickTime and starts to play automatically. If you need to play it again, press the Space bar after clicking on the player.

Exporting to DVD

As in FCP X, we can build a basic custom DVD right inside Motion and here's how to get it ready.

Getting ready

Make sure you have a DVD disc inside your computer. If the Finder comes up, choose **Ignore**. Open a Motion project you want to export by locating it on your hard drive and double-clicking on it. Check your project for anything you may want to change before exporting to DVD. If applicable, this may be a great opportunity to check whether your text lies within the safe zone boundaries.

How to do it...

1. From the **Share** menu, choose **DVD**.

2. Under the **Options** tab, there is a list of output devices. If you had an external DVD drive connected, it would be displayed here.

The **When disc loads** option is currently set to **Show Menu**, as displayed in the following screenshot. Set the value of **Disc template** to **White**, to change the color, and give the DVD an appropriate title. If you had a still image, you could add it as a background for the DVD too by clicking on the **Add** button and finding it on your system.

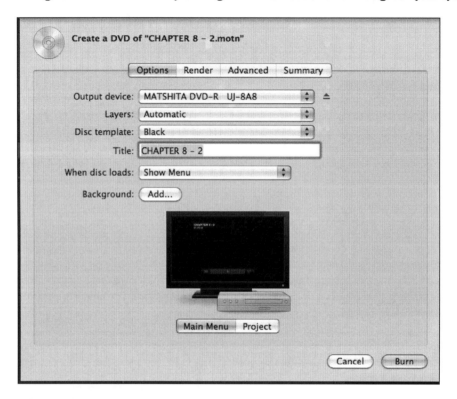

3. Click on the **Project** tab and hover your mouse over the TV screen to preview it and make sure it's in order.

4. Go through the remaining tabs at the top of the window to change any setting before export. Once you've double-checked it, click on **Burn**. Motion will first create two DVD files; one for audio and one for video. Once it finishes encoding the files, it will encode them to disc.

5. When Motion is finished, it will give you the option to burn another DVD. The great news is it doesn't need to encode the file again. All it needs to do is burn the file to disc.

See also

▶ The *Changing your background, color, and safe zones* recipe

▶ The *Exporting a full-resolution copy of your project* recipe

▶ The *Exporting a still image and image sequence* recipe

Exporting a still image and image sequence

Depending on your workflow, you may need to export your Motion project to another motion graphics, design, or VFX application. You could export an individual frame for your design team, to make sure your animations are on the right track, or export your project as a series of individual frames by creating an image sequence. Let's see both options in action.

Getting ready

Locate a Motion project you want to export as an image sequence and double-click on it to open it in Motion. Move your playhead to a frame you want to export prior to the image sequence.

How to do it...

1. From the **Share** menu, choose **Save Current Frame**. Select **PNG Image**. Click on the **Next** button. Save the file to your desktop and click on **OK**.

2. Navigate to the desktop and press the Space bar to preview it in the Finder.

3. Go back into Motion and navigate to **Share | Image Sequence**. From **Export** choose **DPX Image**. This is a format used in a lot of VFX applications. Click on the **Render** and **Summary** tab to customize your settings.

4. Click the **Next** button and navigate to a location of your choice, as shown in the following screenshot. Motion will automatically put the output in a folder for you based on the name you give your export. Click on the **Save** button.

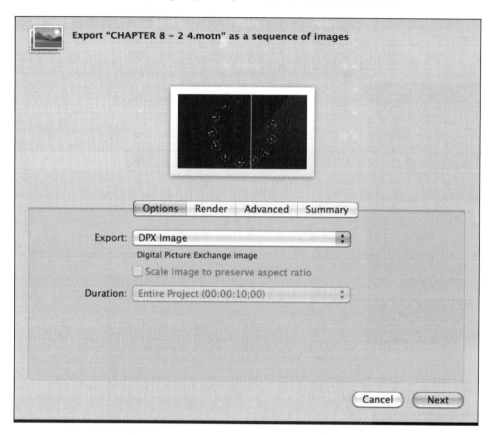

5. The **Share Monitor** window will open and render the image sequence in the background as shown in the following screenshot. Once complete, navigate to where you saved the image sequence. Close **Share Monitor** by selecting it from the Dock and press *Command + Q*.

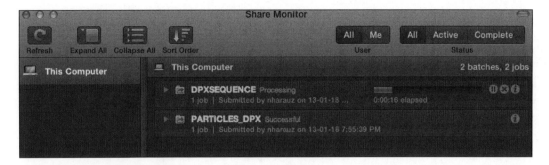

See also

▶ The *Changing your background, color, and safe zones* recipe

▶ The *Exporting a full-resolution copy of your project* recipe

▶ The *Exporting to DVD* recipe

Exporting an alpha channel and video separately

Just as with image sequences, some VFX applications can make use of the video and its alpha channel as separate files. Motion gives you the option to do just that in the **Render** menu under **Export** settings.

Getting ready

Locate a Motion project you've worked with in one of the previous exercises. Double-click to open it. Go through the project and make sure the play range is at the beginning and end of your Timeline. If it's not, click on *Option + X* to reset the play range.

How to do it...

1. From the **Share** menu, choose **Export Movie**.

2. Under the **Options** tab, customize your settings as you see fit. Click on the **Render** tab.

3. In the **Render** tab next to **Color**, choose **Alpha** as shown in the following screenshot. This will export out the alpha channel separately. You can also choose whether the alpha is pre-multiplied or not by clicking on the checkbox underneath.

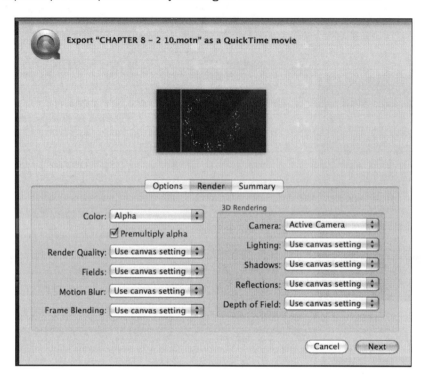

4. Click the **Next** button and find a place you want to save it to your system. Choose **Save**. The file renders out. Locate it on your system and preview it. Notice that everything that is opaque is white and everything transparent is black, as shown in the following screenshot. Gray represents values in between.

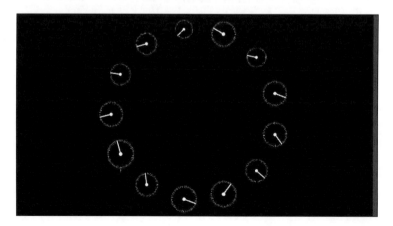

5. Repeat the process but this time, from the **Export** dialog box, choose **Color** to export out the color copy of your video. Choose **Next**. Navigate to where you saved your alpha file and choose **Save**. You've now created a separate video file and alpha channel movie.

See also

▶ The *Changing your background, color, and safe zones* recipe

▶ The *Exporting a full-resolution copy of your project* recipe

▶ The *Exporting a DVD* recipe

▶ The *Exporting a still image and image sequence* recipe

Exporting using Compressor

Compressor is a standalone application that is sold on the App Store. If you have Motion or FCP X, you should know that it opens up a ton of export options. Compressor allows you to export out several versions of your project at once while allowing you to continue working in Motion as it runs in the background.

Getting ready

Locate a Motion Project you've worked with in one of the previous exercises that's 1920 by 1080. Double-click to open it. Go through the project and make sure the play range is set to the beginning and end of your Timeline. If it's not, press *Option + X* to reset the play range to the length of your project.

How to do it...

1. From the **Share** menu, choose **Send To Compressor**.

2. Compressor launches. In order to send something out, you need at least one setting (which format?) and one destination (where will it go?). If you can't see the **Settings** and **Destination** tabs, navigate to **Window | Settings** and **Window | Destinations** to bring them up. The window is displayed in the following screenshot:

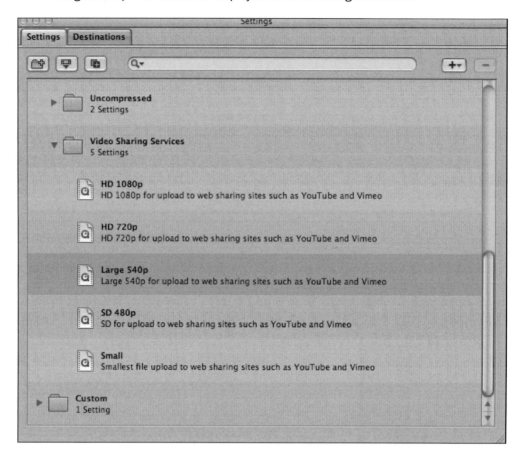

3. Under the **Settings** tab, click on the disclosure triangle next to **Video Sharing Services** to reveal the presets available. Drag the **Large 540p** setting to where it says **Drag Settings and Destinations Here** on the Motion project file as shown in the following screenshot:

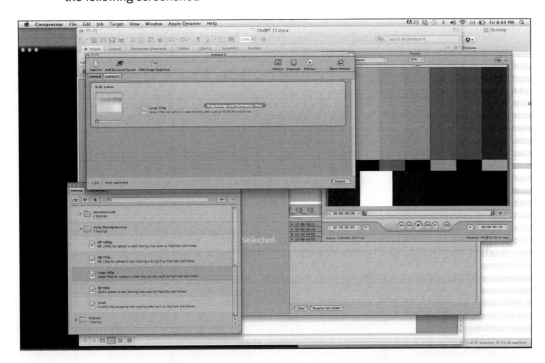

4. Go to the **Destinations** tab and under the Apple category, drag the word **Desktop** over the word **Source** on the **540p** setting you just added as shown in the following screenshot. The destinations may seem limited but we can create our own custom destinations as well as settings.

5. We could go back to the **Settings** tab and add another setting and destination if we wanted. For now, click on the **Submit** button at the bottom of the **Project** window.

6. Choose a name for this job and leave the other settings at their default. Click on **Submit**.

7. If you want to, you can see the process revealed in the **History** tab (**Window | History**). When the job is finished, it will read as successful.

How it works...

Compressor is a standalone application and there's a lot to it, so don't get overwhelmed if it was your first time here. Use the **Help** menu to read the documentation to see all the possibilities with Compressor, such as setting up a mini-rendering farm or creating droplets you can use to compress video on your desktop. Also, as long as you have Compressor on your system, you can export directly from Motion using Compressor settings. Go to the **Share** menu and choose **Export with Compressor** settings. Choose from one of the available presets.

See also

The following recipes of this chapter:

▶ The *Changing your background, color and safe zones* recipe

▶ The *Exporting a full-resolution copy of your project* recipe

▶ The *Exporting a DVD* recipe

▶ The *Exporting a still image and image sequence* recipe

▶ The *Export an alpha channel and video separately* recipe

Saving a template

In Motion, you can save a template for later use. It will be available in the **Template** section when you launch the application. This is a great way to automate your workflow where you have a show and are using drop zones to switch content on a consistent basis. This template can also be made available to FCP X by publishing it as a generator.

Getting ready

Locate a Motion project you've worked with in one of the previous exercises, preferably one you've applied drop zones to. Double-click to open it. Play back the project to make sure everything is set up the way you want it.

How to do it...

1. From the **File** menu, choose **Publish Template** as indicated in the following screenshot:

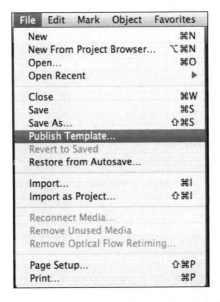

2. Name the template accordingly. If you have worked on some exercises in *Chapter 11, Publishing your Work to FCP X*, this window will look familiar to you. You can add the template to a category and theme you have previously created. If this is your first time creating a template, you'll have to create a new theme and category for it to go into.

3. Since we will not be publishing this template over to Final Cut, we'll leave the **Publish as Final Cut Generator** box unchecked. Click on **Publish**.

4. Close Motion by pressing *Command + Q*. Relaunch the application. Notice that, in the welcome screen on the left-hand side under **Compositions**, you should be able to see your template. Simply choose it and click on **Open**. It's ready to use!

See also

▸ *Publishing a Motion 5 generator and its parameters to FCP X* in Chapter 11, *Publishing your Work to FCP X*

▸ *Publishing parameters versus publishing rigs 101 – part 1* in Chapter 11, *Publishing your Work to FCP X*

▸ *Publishing parameters versus publishing rigs 101 – part 2* in Chapter 11, *Publishing your Work to FCP X*

▸ The *Changing your background, color, and safe zones* recipe

▸ The *Exporting a full-resolution copy of your project* recipe

▸ The *Exporting a DVD* recipe

▸ The *Exporting a still image and image sequence* recipe

Index

R

RAM Preview **178**
randomize behavior
  used, for creating random motion 104-108
random motion
  creating, randomize behavior used 104-108
randomness, particles
  adding, to parameters 236-238
real-time playback **84**
Record Keyframes button **146**
reflections
  about 330
  creating 331, 332
replicator
  3D options 271-273
  camera, adding to interact with 274-276
  creating 258, 259
  HUD parameters, changing 258, 259
  Inspector parameters, tweaking 261, 262
  parameters, keyframing 265, 267
  presets 268, 269, 271
rig **355-357**

S

safe zones **174**
Sample Color button **302**
Scrub Boxes tab **301**
sequence paint **207, 209, 210**
sequence replicator behavior **263-265**
sequence text **183-185**
shape masks
  using 213, 214
shapes
  and paint, relationship 210-213
  logo effect, creating with 226, 227
  outline, writing 122, 123
  style, changing over stroke 203-207
  used, for faking 3D extrusion 280-282
  width, changing over stroke 203, 205, 207
Shrink behavior
  applying, to still 80-83
slider
  combining 361-371
Snap Alignment to Motion behavior **89**
Special Characters library
  vector images, adding from 191-193

stabilize behavior
  adding, to clip 284, 286
still
  anchor point, moving 132-135
  Fade In behavior, applying 80, 82, 83
  Fade Out behavior, applying 80, 82, 83
  Grow behavior, applying 80, 82, 83
  in Timeline, sequencing 38-40
  Shrink behavior, applying 80, 82, 83
still image
  exporting 383
  position, changing 23-25
  scale, changing 23-25
  using, as stroke source 207

T

television screen
  video, adding 217, 219, 220
template
  customizing 28-33
  launching 28-33
  saving 390, 391
text
  about 169, 170
  animations, saving 189, 190
  behaviors 173
  creating, on path 179, 180
  filling, textures used 194, 195
  filling, videos used 194, 195
  format, changing 170-173
  format pane 170, 172
  from FCP X, changing 336-340
  from FCP X, opening 336-340
  play range, changing 178
  presets, saving 173
  RAM Preview 178
  render quality, changing for playback 177
  safe zones 174
  style, changing 174, 176
  styles, saving 189, 190
  textures, adding to face 177
  textures, adding to outline 177
  used, for faking 3D extrusion 280-282
text behavior
  adding 181-183
  intro, adding 118, 119

Thank you for buying
Apple Motion 5 Cookbook

About Packt Publishing

Packt, pronounced 'packed', published its first book "*Mastering phpMyAdmin for Effective MySQL Management*" in April 2004 and subsequently continued to specialize in publishing highly focused books on specific technologies and solutions.

Our books and publications share the experiences of your fellow IT professionals in adapting and customizing today's systems, applications, and frameworks. Our solution based books give you the knowledge and power to customize the software and technologies you're using to get the job done. Packt books are more specific and less general than the IT books you have seen in the past. Our unique business model allows us to bring you more focused information, giving you more of what you need to know, and less of what you don't.

Packt is a modern, yet unique publishing company, which focuses on producing quality, cutting-edge books for communities of developers, administrators, and newbies alike. For more information, please visit our website: www.packtpub.com.

Writing for Packt

We welcome all inquiries from people who are interested in authoring. Book proposals should be sent to author@packtpub.com. If your book idea is still at an early stage and you would like to discuss it first before writing a formal book proposal, contact us; one of our commissioning editors will get in touch with you.

We're not just looking for published authors; if you have strong technical skills but no writing experience, our experienced editors can help you develop a writing career, or simply get some additional reward for your expertise.

Sony Vegas Pro 11 Beginner's Guide

ISBN: 978-1-84969-170-3   Paperback: 264 pages

Edit videos with style and ease using Vegas Pro

1. Edit slick, professional videos of all kinds with Sony Vegas Pro

2. Learn audio and video editing from scratch

3. Speed up your editing workflow

4. A practical beginner's guide with a fast-paced but friendly and engaging approach towards video editing

Mastering Adobe Premiere Pro CS6 Hotshot

ISBN: 978-1-84969-478-0   Paperback: 284 pages

Take your video editing skills to new and exciting levels with eight fantastic projects

1. Discover new workflows and the exciting new features of Premiere Pro CS6

2. Take your video editing skills to exciting new levels with clear, concise instructions (and supplied footage)

3. Explore powerful time-saving features that other users don't even know about!

4. Work on actual real-world video editing projects such as short films, interviews, multi-cam, special effects, and the creation of video montages

Please check **www.PacktPub.com** for information on our titles

17175738R00230

Printed in Great Britain
by Amazon